# A Summary of Basic Beliefs

Rev. Msgr. John F. Barry, P.A.

**Sadlier**
A Division of William H. Sadlier, Inc.

**The Subcommittee on the Catechism, United States Conference of Catholic Bishops, has found the doctrinal content of this manual, copyright 2009, to be in conformity with the *Catechism of the Catholic Church*.**

## Acknowledgments

Scripture excerpts from the *New American Bible* with *Revised New Testament and Psalms*. Copyright ©1991, 1986, 1970. Confraternity of Christian Doctrine, Inc., Washington, D.C. Used with permission. All rights reserved. No portion of the *New American Bible* may be reprinted without permission in writing from the copyright holder.

Excerpts from the English translation of *Rite of Baptism for Children* ©1969, International Committee on English in the Liturgy, Inc. (ICEL); excerpts from the English translation of *The Roman Missal* ©1973, ICEL; excerpts from the English translation of *Rite of Penance* ©1974, ICEL; excerpts from the English translation of *Rite of Confirmation (Second Edition)* ©1975, ICEL; excerpts from the English translation of *A Book of Prayers* ©1982, ICEL; excerpts from the English translation of *Order of Christian Funerals* ©1985, ICEL; excerpts from the English translation of *Book of Blessings* ©1988, ICEL. All rights reserved.

Excerpts from *Catholic Household Blessings and Prayers* ©2007 United States Catholic Conference, Inc. Washington, D.C. Used with permission. All rights reserved.

Excerpts from *General Directory for Catechesis* copyright ©1997 Libreria Editrice Vaticana. Published in the United States in 1998 by the United States Catholic Conference of Catholic Bishops (USCCB), Washington, D.C. All rights reserved.

Excerpt from the *National Directory for Catechesis*, copyright ©2005, United States Conference of Catholic Bishops, Washington, D.C. All rights reserved.

Excerpt from Pope John Paul II, *Crossing the Threshold of Faith*, a Borzoi Book, published by Alfred A. Knopf, Inc. Copyright ©1994 by Arnoldo Mondadori Editore. Translation copyright ©1994 by Alfred A. Knopf, Inc.

---



Printed in the United States of America.

is a registered trademark of William H. Sadlier, Inc.

William H. Sadlier, Inc.
9 Pine Street
New York, NY 10005-1002

ISBN: 978-0-8215-1265-4
23456789/13 12 11 10 09

## Catechetical and Liturgical Consultants

Vilma Angulo
Director of Religious Education
All Saints Catholic Church
Sunrise, FL

John Benson
Catechist
All Saints Catholic Church
Sunrise, FL

Carol Craven
Director of Religious Education
St. Paul the Apostle Catholic Church
New Middletown, OH

Carole Eipers, D. Min.
Vice President, Executive Director of Catechetics
William H. Sadlier, Inc.

Mary Larsen
Director of Religious Education
St. Mary's Church
South Amboy, NJ

Deanna Ricciardi
Catechist
Immaculate Heart of Mary Catholic Church
Scarsdale, New York

Reverend Nicholas Shori
Pastor
St. Paul the Apostle Catholic Church
New Middletown, OH

## Official Theological Consultant

Most Reverend Edward K. Braxton, Ph.D., S.T.D.
Bishop of Belleville, IL

## Sadlier Consulting Team

Michaela Burke Barry
Ken Doran
Dulce M. Jiménez-Abreu
Saundra Kennedy, Ed.D.
William M. Ippolito
Ida Iris Miranda
Victor Venezuela

## Writing/Development Team

Rosemary K. Calicchio
Vice President, Publications

Blake Bergen
Editorial Director

Melissa D. Gibbons
Director of Research and Development

Mary Ann Trevaskiss
Supervising Editor

Maureen Gallo
Senior Editor

## Publishing Operations Team

Deborah Jones
Vice President, Publishing Operations

Vince Gallo
Creative Director

Francesca O'Malley
Associate Art Director

Jim Saylor
Photography Manager

**Production Staff**

Diane Ali
Cheryl Golding
Maria Jiménez
Maureen Morgan
Jovito Pagkalinawan

# Contents

## Before You Use *Our Catholic Faith*



## UNIT 1 Created and Saved



## UNIT 2 The Church, the People of God



## Living Our Faith

## UNIT 3 The Sacraments of Christian Initiation



## UNIT 4 Living as Jesus' Disciples

# Program Overview

**Our Catholic Faith** is an excellent summary of essential Catholic beliefs and practices. It is designed for middle-grade students and is an effective tool for those who are new to catechesis. It can be used as remote preparation for the sacraments.

## Each chapter incorporates teachings from the *Catechism of the Catholic Church.*

**UNIT 1 Created and Saved**

God Is the Creator
God Sends His Only Son
Jesus Christ Is Our Savior

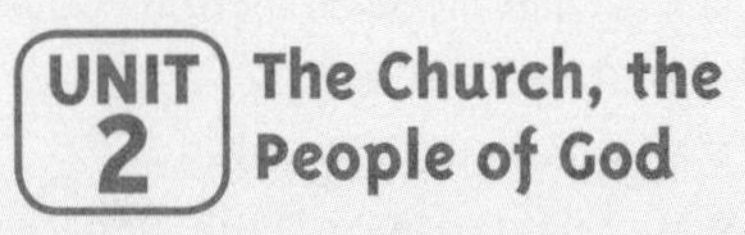

**UNIT 2 The Church, the People of God**

The Holy Spirit Is Sent
The Catholic Church
The Seven Sacraments

**UNIT 3 The Sacraments of Christian Initiation**

The Sacraments of Baptism and Confirmation
The Sacrament of the Eucharist
The Celebration of Mass

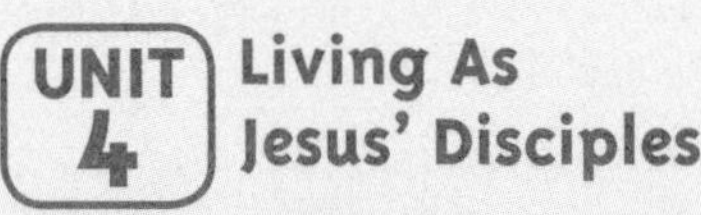

**UNIT 4 Living As Jesus' Disciples**

The Ten Commandments
The Beatitudes
The Sacrament of Penance and Reconciliation
Serving Others
The Communion of Saints
Mary, the Mother of God

## Text Features

Each chapter introduction engages the students' interest with a story or activity.

**14 core chapters of 6 pages each present three key doctrinal points; well organized and designed to foster faith development through the following:**

- Knowledge of basic Catholic beliefs, which are Trinitarian, Christocentric, and Ecclesial
- Identification with Jesus Christ and the Church
- Interaction with the Church community
- Personal reflection
- Prayer experiences

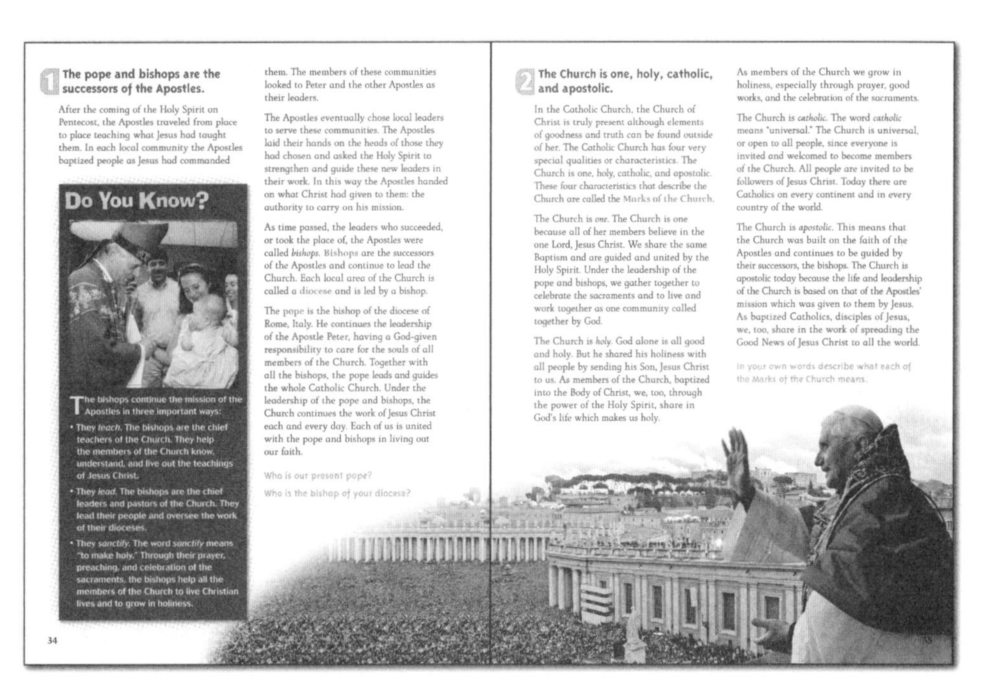

**1 The pope and bishops are the successors of the Apostles.**

After the coming of the Holy Spirit on Pentecost, the Apostles traveled from place to place teaching what Jesus had taught them. In each local community the Apostles baptized people as Jesus had commanded them. The members of these communities looked to Peter and the other Apostles as their leaders.

The Apostles eventually chose local leaders to serve these communities. The Apostles laid their hands on the heads of those they had chosen and asked the Holy Spirit to strengthen and guide these new leaders in their work. In this way the Apostles handed on what Christ had given to them: the authority to carry on his mission.

As time passed, the leaders who succeeded, or took the place of, the Apostles were called *bishops*. Bishops are the successors of the Apostles and continue to lead the Church. Each local area of the Church is called a diocese and is led by a bishop.

The pope is the bishop of the diocese of Rome, Italy. He continues the leadership of the Apostle Peter, having a God-given responsibility to care for the souls of all members of the Church. Together with all the bishops, the pope leads and guides the whole Catholic Church. Under the leadership of the pope and bishops, the Church continues the work of Jesus Christ each and every day. Each of us is united with the pope and bishops in living out our faith.

Who is our present pope?

Who is the bishop of your diocese?

**Do You Know?**

The bishops continue the mission of the Apostles in three important ways:

- They *teach*. The bishops are the chief teachers of the Church. They help the members of the Church know, understand, and live out the teachings of Jesus Christ.
- They *lead*. The bishops are the chief leaders and pastors of the Church. They lead their people and oversee the work of their dioceses.
- They *sanctify*. The word *sanctify* means "to make holy." Through their prayer, preaching, and celebration of the sacraments, the bishops help all the members of the Church to live Christian lives and to grow in holiness.

34

**2 The Church is one, holy, catholic, and apostolic.**

In the Catholic Church, the Church of Christ is truly present although elements of goodness and truth can be found outside of her. The Catholic Church has four very special qualities or characteristics. The Church is one, holy, catholic, and apostolic. These four characteristics that describe the Church are called the Marks of the Church.

The Church is *one*. The Church is one because all of her members believe in the one Lord, Jesus Christ. We share the same Baptism and are guided and united by the Holy Spirit. Under the leadership of the pope and bishops, we gather together to celebrate the sacraments and to live and work together as one community called together by God.

The Church is *holy*. God alone is all good and holy. But he shared his holiness with all people by sending his Son, Jesus Christ to us. As members of the Church, baptized into the Body of Christ, we, too, through the power of the Holy Spirit, share in God's life which makes us holy.

As members of the Church we grow in holiness, especially through prayer, good works, and the celebration of the sacraments.

The Church is *catholic*. The word *catholic* means "universal." The Church is universal, or open to all people, since everyone is invited and welcomed to become members of the Church. All people are invited to be followers of Jesus Christ. Today there are Catholics on every continent and in every country of the world.

The Church is *apostolic*. This means that the Church was built on the faith of the Apostles and continues to be guided by their successors, the bishops. The Church is apostolic today because the life and leadership of the Church is based on that of the Apostles' mission which was given to them by Jesus. As baptized Catholics, disciples of Jesus, we, too, share in the work of spreading the Good News of Jesus Christ to all the world.

In your own words describe what each of the Marks of the Church means.

**Review** includes questions to help students recall chapter content

**Chapters conclude with:**

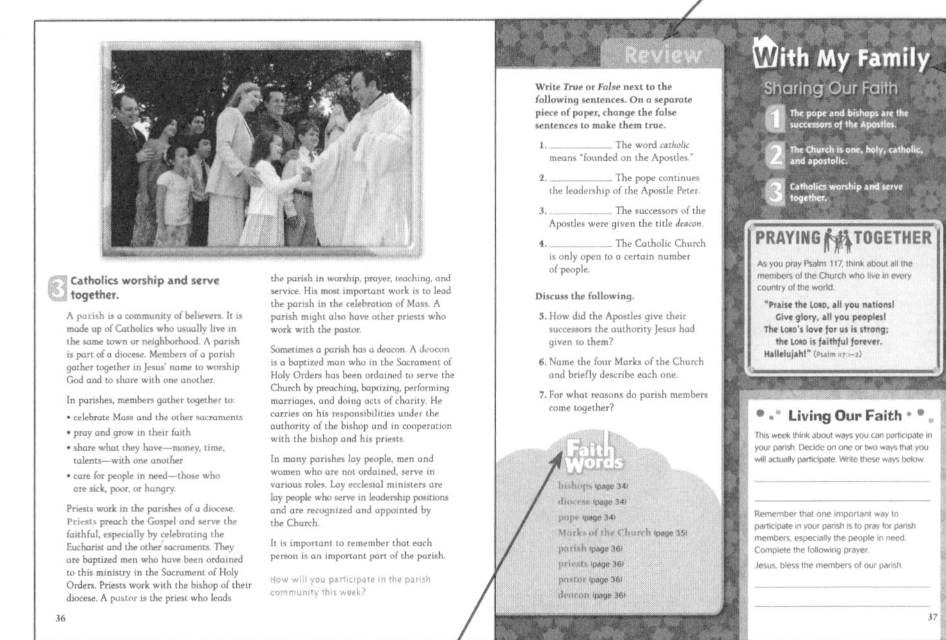

**3 Catholics worship and serve together.**

A parish is a community of believers. It is made up of Catholics who usually live in the same town or neighborhood. A parish is part of a diocese. Members of a parish gather together in Jesus' name to worship God and to share with one another.

In parishes, members gather together to:

- celebrate Mass and the other sacraments
- pray and grow in their faith
- share what they have—money, time, talents—with one another
- care for people in need—those who are sick, poor, or hungry.

Priests work in the parishes of a diocese. Priests preach the Gospel and serve the faithful, especially by celebrating the Eucharist and the other sacraments. They are baptized men who have been ordained to this ministry in the Sacrament of Holy Orders. Priests work with the bishop of their diocese. A pastor is the priest who leads the parish in worship, prayer, teaching, and service. His most important work is to lead the parish in the celebration of Mass. A parish might also have other priests who work with the pastor.

Sometimes a parish has a deacon. A deacon is a baptized man who in the Sacrament of Holy Orders has been ordained to serve the Church by preaching, baptizing, performing marriages, and doing acts of charity. He carries on his responsibilities under the authority of the bishop and in cooperation with the bishop and his priests.

In many parishes lay people, men and women who are not ordained, serve in various roles. Lay ecclesial ministers are lay people who serve in leadership positions and are recognized and appointed by the Church.

It is important to remember that each person is an important part of the parish.

How will you participate in the parish community this week?

36

**Review**

**Write *True* or *False* next to the following sentences. On a separate piece of paper, change the false sentences to make them true.**

1. ________ The word *catholic* means "founded on the Apostles."
2. ________ The pope continues the leadership of the Apostle Peter.
3. ________ The successors of the Apostles were given the title *deacon*.
4. ________ The Catholic Church is only open to a certain number of people.

**Discuss the following.**

5. How did the Apostles give their successors the authority Jesus had given to them?
6. Name the four Marks of the Church and briefly describe each one.
7. For what reasons do parish members come together?

**Faith Words**

bishops (page 34)
diocese (page 34)
pope (page 34)
Marks of the Church (page 35)
parish (page 36)
priests (page 36)
pastor (page 36)
deacon (page 36)

**With My Family**

Sharing Our Faith

1. The pope and bishops are the successors of the Apostles.
2. The Church is one, holy, catholic, and apostolic.
3. Catholics worship and serve together.

**PRAYING TOGETHER**

As you pray Psalm 117, think about all the members of the Church who live in every country of the world.

"Praise the LORD, all you nations!
Give glory, all you peoples!
The LORD's love for us is strong;
the LORD is faithful forever.
Hallelujah!" (Psalm 117:1–2)

**Living Our Faith**

This week think about ways you can participate in your parish. Decide on one or two ways that you will actually participate. Write these ways below.

________________

________________

Remember that one important way to participate in your parish is to pray for parish members, especially the people in need. Complete the following prayer.

Jesus, bless the members of our parish.

________________

________________

37

**With My Family *Sharing Our Faith*** emphasizes the key doctrinal points of the chapter and encourages each child to share faith at home

***Praying Together*** helps families deepen faith through prayer related to the lesson's theme

***Living Our Faith*** suggests a specific activity that family members can do together to live out their faith

**Faith Words** recalls the faith-based vocabulary introduced in the chapter

# At the end of each unit:

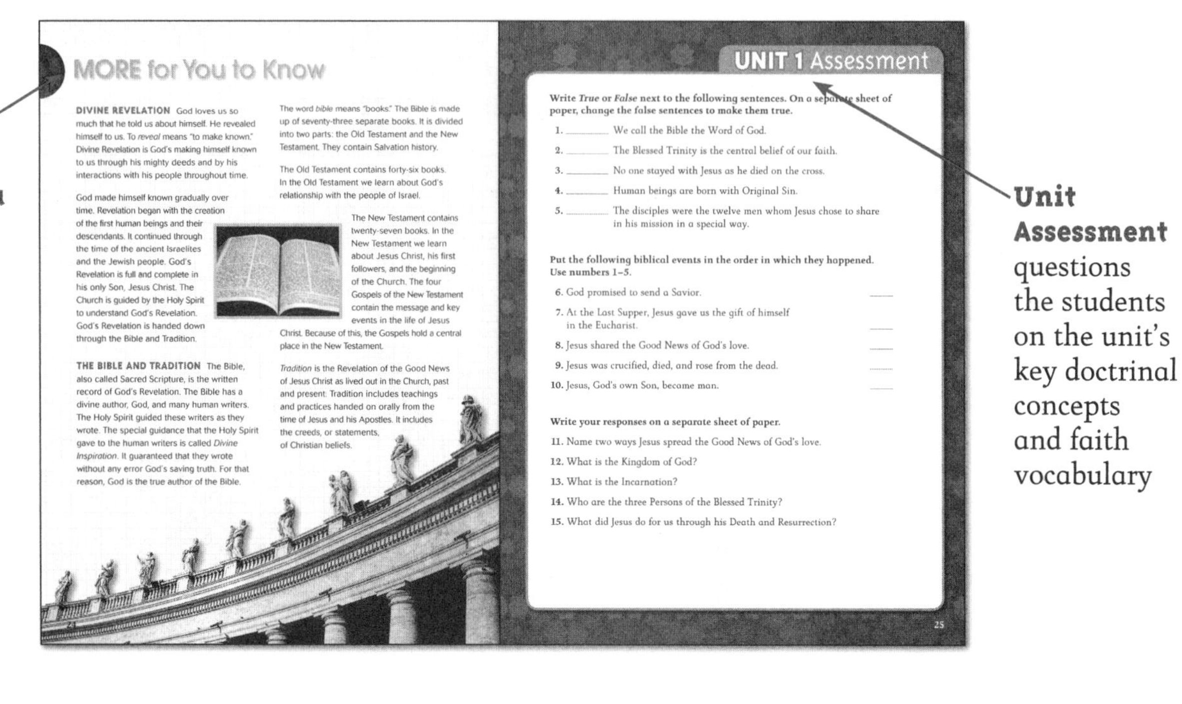

## MORE for You to Know

**DIVINE REVELATION** God loves us so much that he told us about himself. He revealed himself to us. To *reveal* means "to make known." Divine Revelation is God's making himself known to us through his mighty deeds and by his interactions with his people throughout time.

God made himself known gradually over time. Revelation began with the creation of the first human beings and their descendants. It continued through the time of the ancient Israelites and the Jewish people. God's Revelation is full and complete in his only Son, Jesus Christ. The Church is guided by the Holy Spirit to understand God's Revelation. God's Revelation is handed down through the Bible and Tradition.

**THE BIBLE AND TRADITION** The Bible, also called Sacred Scripture, is the written record of God's Revelation. The Bible has a divine author, God, and many human writers. The Holy Spirit guided these writers as they wrote. The special guidance that the Holy Spirit gave to the human writers is called *Divine Inspiration*. It guaranteed that they wrote without any error God's saving truth. For that reason, God is the true author of the Bible.

The word *bible* means "books." The Bible is made up of seventy-three separate books. It is divided into two parts: the Old Testament and the New Testament. They contain Salvation history.

The Old Testament contains forty-six books. In the Old Testament we learn about God's relationship with the people of Israel.

The New Testament contains twenty-seven books. In the New Testament we learn about Jesus Christ, his first followers, and the beginning of the Church. The four Gospels of the New Testament contain the message and key events in the life of Jesus Christ. Because of this, the Gospels hold a central place in the New Testament.

*Tradition* is the Revelation of the Good News of Jesus Christ as lived out in the Church, past and present. Tradition includes teachings and practices handed on orally from the time of Jesus and his Apostles. It includes the creeds, or statements, of Christian beliefs.

## UNIT 1 Assessment

**Write *True* or *False* next to the following sentences. On a separate sheet of paper, change the false sentences to make them true.**

1. ______ We call the Bible the Word of God.
2. ______ The Blessed Trinity is the central belief of our faith.
3. ______ No one stayed with Jesus as he died on the cross.
4. ______ Human beings are born with Original Sin.
5. ______ The disciples were the twelve men whom Jesus chose to share in his mission in a special way.

**Put the following biblical events in the order in which they happened. Use numbers 1–5.**

6. God promised to send a Savior. ____
7. At the Last Supper, Jesus gave us the gift of himself in the Eucharist. ____
8. Jesus shared the Good News of God's love. ____
9. Jesus was crucified, died, and rose from the dead. ____
10. Jesus, God's own Son, became man. ____

**Write your responses on a separate sheet of paper.**

11. Name two ways Jesus spread the Good News of God's love.
12. What is the Kingdom of God?
13. What is the Incarnation?
14. Who are the three Persons of the Blessed Trinity?
15. What did Jesus do for us through his Death and Resurrection?

25

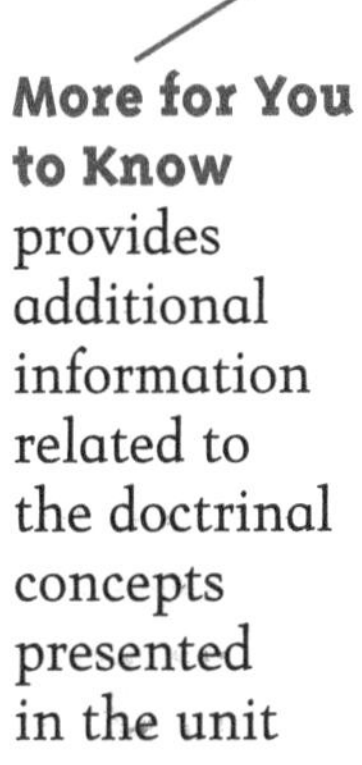

**More for You to Know** provides additional information related to the doctrinal concepts presented in the unit

**Unit Assessment** questions the students on the unit's key doctrinal concepts and faith vocabulary

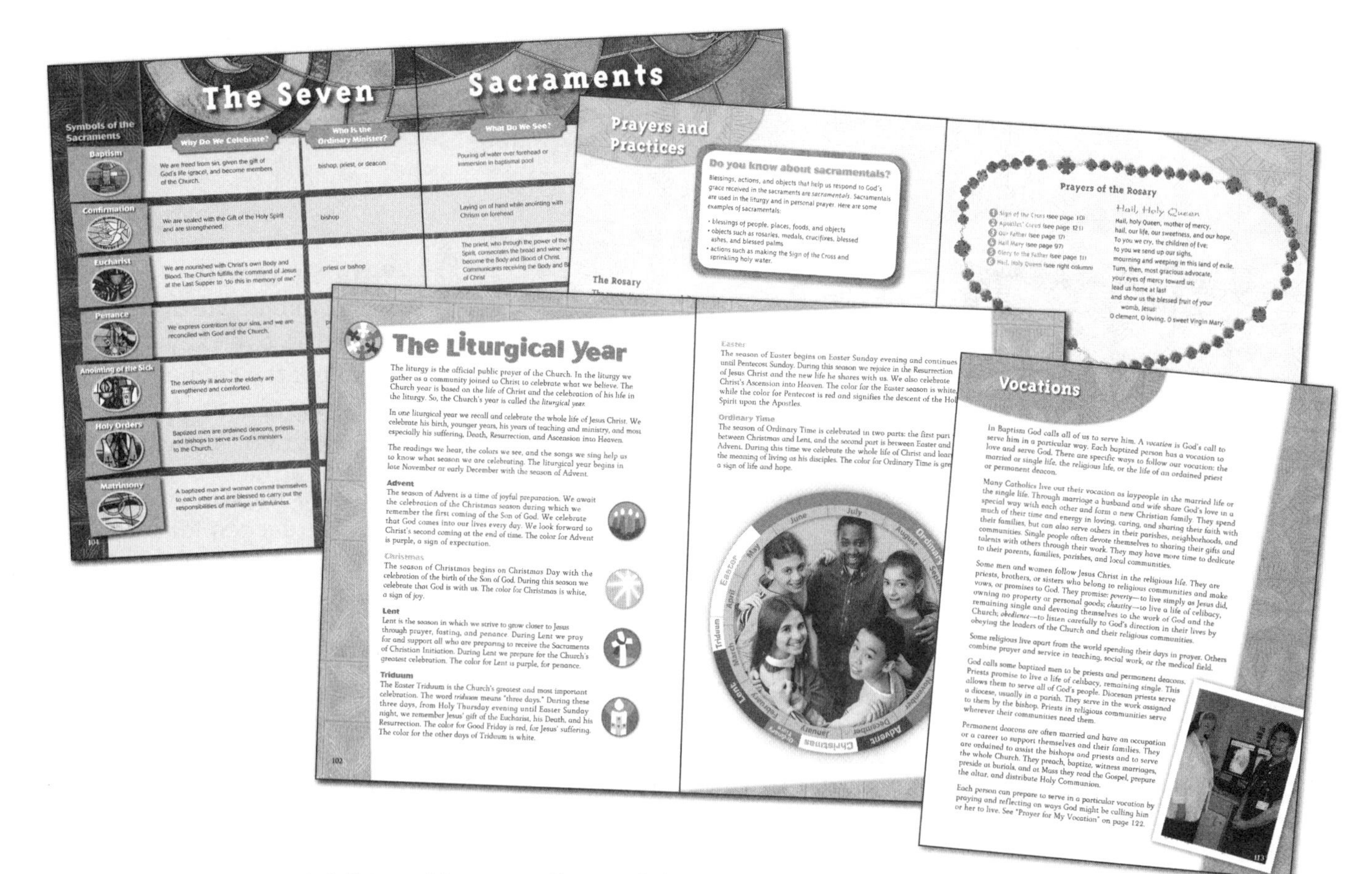


## Additional lessons for enrichment on:

- Liturgical Year
- Seven Sacraments
- Vocations
- Catholic Social Teaching
- Catholic Prayers and Practices

# Catechist Guide Features

The easy to use wrap around format provides preparation for the catechist as well as a three-step lesson plan—Introduction, Presentation, and Conclusion.

**Goals** provides direction for the catechist

**Getting Ready** alerts the catechist to the materials needed for each lesson

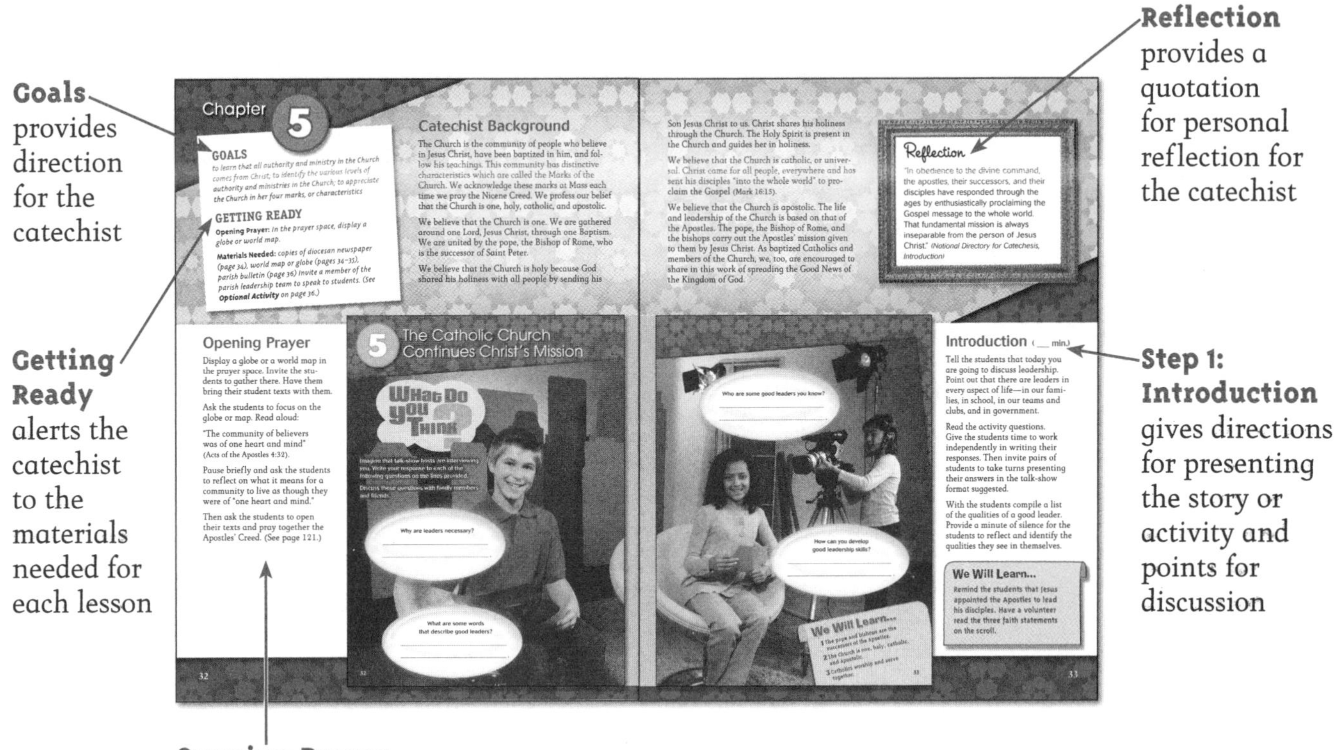


**Reflection** provides a quotation for personal reflection for the catechist

**Step 1: Introduction** gives directions for presenting the story or activity and points for discussion

**Opening Prayer** provides ideas for group prayer

**Step 2: Presentation** Provides instruction on the three key doctrinal points and gives suggestions for discussions and activities to foster faith development

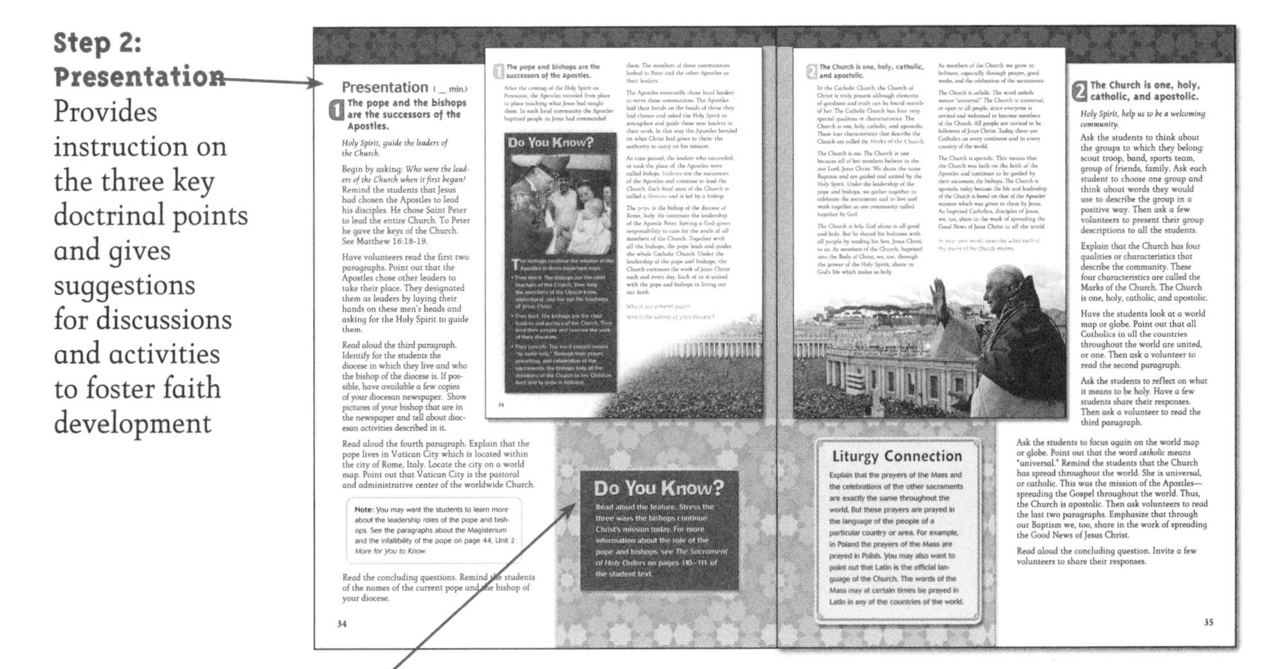


**Do You Know?** expands on the *Do You Know?* feature in the text

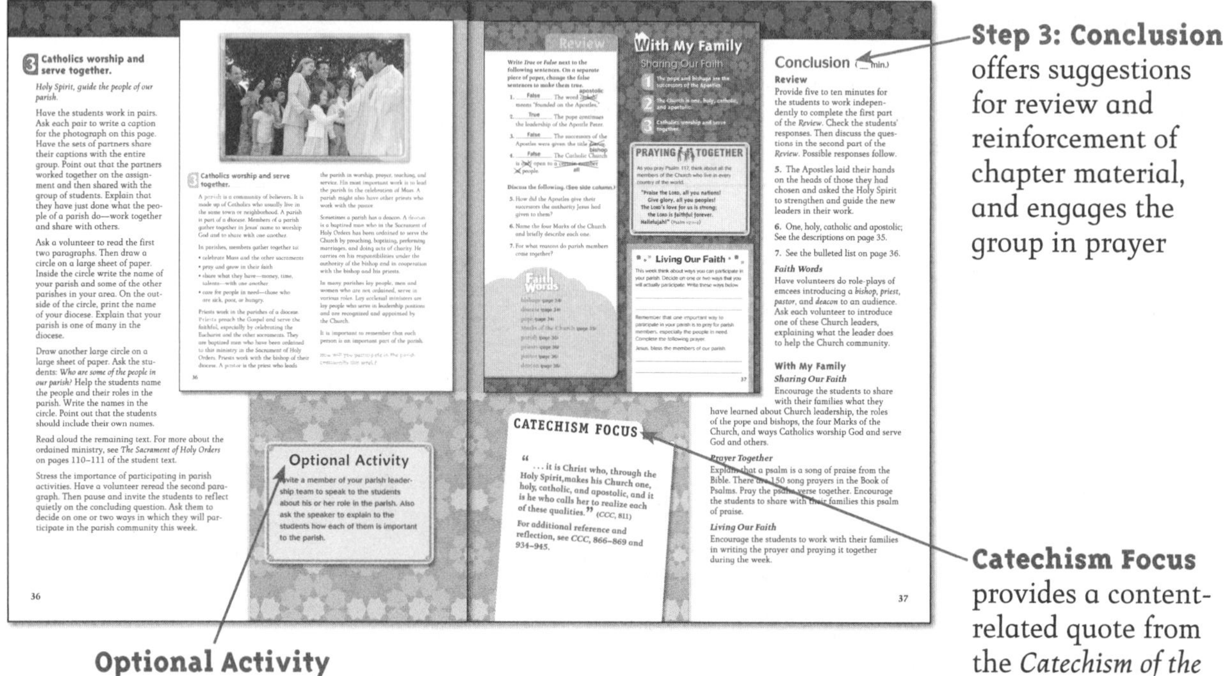

**3 Catholics worship and serve together.**

*Holy Spirit, guide the people of our parish.*

Have the students work in pairs. Ask each pair to write a caption for the photograph on this page. Have the sets of partners share their captions with the entire group. Point out that the partners worked together on the assignment and then shared with the group of students. Explain that they have just done what the people of a parish do—work together and share with others.

Ask a volunteer to read the first two paragraphs. Then draw a circle on a large sheet of paper. Inside the circle write the name of your parish and some of the other parishes in your area. On the outside of the circle, print the name of your diocese. Explain that your parish is one of many in the diocese.

Draw another large circle on a large sheet of paper. Ask the students: *Who are some of the people in our parish?* Help the students name the people and their roles in the parish. Write the names in the circle. Point out that the students should include their own names.

Read aloud the remaining text. For more about the ordained ministry, see *The Sacrament of Holy Orders* on pages 110–111 of the student text.

Stress the importance of participating in parish activities. Have a volunteer reread the second paragraph. Then pause and invite the students to reflect quietly on the concluding question. Ask them to decide on one or two ways in which they will participate in the parish community this week.

36

**Optional Activity**

Invite a member of your parish leadership team to speak to the students about his or her role in the parish. Also ask the speaker to explain to the students how each of them is important to the parish.

**CATECHISM FOCUS**

"... it is Christ who, through the Holy Spirit, makes his Church one, holy, catholic, and apostolic, and it is he who calls her to realize each of these qualities." (CCC, 811)

For additional reference and reflection, see CCC, 866–869 and 934–945.

**Conclusion** (__ min.)

**Review**

Provide five to ten minutes for the students to work independently to complete the first part of the *Review*. Check the students' responses. Then discuss the questions in the second part of the *Review*. Possible responses follow.

5. The Apostles laid their hands on the heads of those they had chosen and asked the Holy Spirit to strengthen and guide the new leaders in their work.

6. One, holy, catholic and apostolic; See the descriptions on page 35.

7. See the bulleted list on page 36.

***Faith Words***

Have volunteers do role-plays of emcees introducing a *bishop, priest, pastor,* and *deacon* to an audience. Ask each volunteer to introduce one of these Church leaders, explaining what the leader does to help the Church community.

**With My Family**

***Sharing Our Faith***

Encourage the students to share with their families what they have learned about Church leadership, the roles of the pope and bishops, the four Marks of the Church, and ways Catholics worship God and serve God and others.

***Prayer Together***

Explain that a psalm is a song of praise from the Bible. There are 150 song prayers in the Book of Psalms. Pray the psalm verse together. Encourage the students to share with their families this psalm of praise.

***Living Our Faith***

Encourage the students to work with their families in writing the prayer and praying it together during the week.

37

**Step 3: Conclusion** offers suggestions for review and reinforcement of chapter material, and engages the group in prayer

**Catechism Focus** provides a content-related quote from the *Catechism of the Catholic Church* and additional reference for the catechist

**Optional Activity** suggests ways to expand or extend the lesson

## Additional Resources

**We Believe & Pray: Prayers and Practices for Young Catholics (Grades 4–6)**

This prayer book includes traditional Church prayers and practices, including prayers in Latin, and others which specifically address young people's concerns such as "Prayer Before a Game."

Visit **www.sadlierreligion.com** for additional ideas and activities to use with the *Our Catholic Faith* program.

# Connecting with the Home

"Parents are the primary educators in the faith. Together with them, especially in certain cultures, all members of the family play an active part in the education of younger members. It is thus necessary to determine more concretely the sense in which the Christian family community is a locus of catechesis." (*General Directory for Catechesis,* 255)

The role of family—the domestic Church—in catechesis is very important. Developing a sensitivity to the various realities that impact family life can help teachers and catechists formulate different ways to improve communication and provide the support and resources that parents and other family members need.

Catechists and teachers can provide support in the following ways:

- **Let parents know who you are.** Make a point to personally contact each young person's parent or guardian. Be sensitive to language used in your communication with the families. Try to use a tone that is warm, open, and affirming of parents. Be aware of families whose first language is not English.

- **Let parents know the role of their children.** As evangelizers of their faith, the young people will spread the Good News of Jesus Christ in their home, parish, and the world.

- **Provide useful resources for the home.** At the end of each chapter, there is a page for review and sharing at home. Encourage the young people to share the prayers and the activities suggested on this page.

  Provide a copy of *Our Catholic Faith* text for use at home when the young person is unable to attend a session.

- **Encourage storytelling as a way to foster closeness within families.** Encourage the young people to discuss with their families specific topics related to faith, prayer, worship, and involvement with the parish community.

- **Encourage family participation in parish worship and other activities.** Send notices home about upcoming special events in the parish. Ask your parish leadership team to contact the families to invite them to participate in these events.

# Praying with Young People

"I firmly believe that, to this day, the greatest gift that we as catechists can share with the children is to develop a lifelong, personal relationship with God through the power of prayer." (John Stack, a former catechist in the Diocese of Pittsburgh, PA)

As a catechist, you are in a privileged situation to introduce and initiate formative experiences of prayer. Your own efforts to develop a prayerful attitude will help you communicate the importance of prayer to the young people in your care.

For each chapter of *Our Catholic Faith*, you will find an *Opening Prayer* suggestion in the Guide. You will also find an aspiration below each of the three faith statements in the Guide. At the end of each chapter in the student edition a prayer is given in the *Responding in Prayer* section. Use these various prayers with your group as you work through each chapter.

## Prayer Space

Designate an easily accessible area of your meeting place as the group's prayer space. In the space set up a small table or bench as a prayer table. Cover the table with a cloth. (If possible use a cloth representing the color for the current liturgical season, see page 103 in the student text). This space will be the focal point for *Opening Prayers* and other prayer celebrations. Sadlier has a prayer kit, *We Gather in Prayer*, that you may want to use. See www.customerservice@sadlier.com.

Have available a Bible, a cross or crucifix, and a battery-operated candle to place on the prayer table. These may be placed on the table before gathering for prayer or carried in procession as the students gather in the prayer space.

## Introducing the Five Forms of Prayer

**Blessing** To bless is to dedicate someone or something to God or to make something holy in God's name. Grace before and after meals is an example of blessing prayers. (See page 122.) Have the young people pray these prayers and reflect on the meaning of the words.

**Thanksgiving** Each day is filled with potential to open us up to the goodness of God. Use symbols from the Bible, nature, and liturgy (water, oil, fire, light, incense), and invite young people to think about these symbols as they pray in thanksgiving for God's gifts.

**Praise** When we praise God, we give him glory. Take time to praise God together in word, song, and prayerful gestures. Pray together psalms of praise, particularly Psalm 147 through Psalm 150.

**Petition** Jesus invited us to take all our needs to God in prayer. In prayers of petition we acknowledge our relationship with God. Through our prayer we ask for forgiveness of our sins, turning our minds and hearts back to God. The Act of Contrition is a prayer of petition.

**Intercession** A prayer of intercession is a type of a prayer of petition. In a prayer of intercession, we are asking for something on behalf of another person or a group of people. This can be through short, one-line intercessions in a spontaneous fashion. Use news headlines or current events to help young people expand their prayers beyond their immediate needs to the people in the world who are poor, suffering, or in need of consolation.

## Determining Readiness for the Sacraments of Penance and Eucharist

There is a possibility that a few of the young people in your group may not have celebrated the Sacraments of Penance and/or Eucharist. *Our Catholic Faith* is not intended to be a sacramental preparation program. However, it does include an in-depth presentation of the meaning, purpose, and celebration of the Sacraments of Penance (Chapter 12) and Eucharist (Chapters 8–9).

Sacramental readiness is discerned in a number of ways. It requires observance and attentiveness by parents, clergy, catechists, and others involved in the faith formation of the young people. As young people grow in faith and understanding, their readiness and receptivity for the sacraments will become more evident.

Because of readiness needs of individuals or time factors, it may not be feasible to involve the young people in regular sacramental programs and classes. Do include them, however, in prayers, blessings, and rituals for candidates who are preparing for First Penance and First Eucharist.

Consider and consult with all those involved with the young people in the sacramental process, especially the parents or guardians and other family members, as well as the Director of Religious Education, the pastor, the pastoral associates, the RCIA director, and coordinators of other parish ministries. Consider using pages XV and XVI to help the catechists, parents, director of religious education, and pastor discern the young people's readiness to celebrate the Sacraments of Penance and Eucharist.

## Catechesis for First Penance

The following points are essential to a basic understanding of the Sacrament of Penance. These are based on the guidelines for First Penance as outlined in the *National Directory for Catechesis* and developed throughout the *Our Catholic Faith* text.

**1.** God loves us unconditionally, and Jesus shows us how to love God, others, and ourselves. The Sacrament of Penance restores us to loving relationships with God and the faith community. It celebrates God's mercy and forgiveness.

- Stress the unconditional love of God when presenting Chapters 1, and 10–12.
- Emphasize how Jesus is the model for love, compassion, and faith when teaching Chapters 2–3 and 12.
- Throughout the teaching of *Our Catholic Faith*, encourage the young people to consider the loving choices they can make within their daily lives.

**2.** There is both good and evil in the world. When we sin, we freely choose to do what we know is wrong and against God's will. When we realize that we have chosen to sin, we turn to Christ and the Church for sacramental forgiveness and reconciliation.

- Emphasize these points when teaching Chapter 12.
- Whenever talking about sin, make clear the distinction between sinful choices and mistakes.

**3.** Our conscience is the most basic awareness in us of what is right or wrong. It is very important that we form our conscience by studying the teachings of Jesus Christ and the Church. Examining our conscience each day helps us to grow closer to God, to seek his forgiveness, and to make loving choices. The Holy Spirit guides us in developing an informed conscience.

- Emphasize these points when presenting Chapter 12.
- Acknowledge how difficult it is to make good choices, especially when among peers. Encourage the young people to pray often to the Holy Spirit for guidance, grace, and courage.

**4.** Praying an Act of Contrition involves two parts: expressing sorrow for our sin and resolving not to sin again.

- Emphasize this point when teaching Chapter 12.
- Encourage the young people to pray often for forgiveness and for the ability to forgive others. Incorporate this type of prayer into the lessons throughout the year.

**5.** Two ways that the Church celebrates the Sacrament of Penance are individually or celebrating with a group (with individual confession and absolution). See page 108.

- Invite the group to visit the parish church. Show the young people the reconciliation room and/or a confessional. Ask a priest to talk with the group about the sacramental action, symbols, and prayers.

**6.** Peace means being in harmonious relationships with God, with those around us, and with ourselves. Sharing the peace of Christ with others is an important and ongoing part of the Sacrament of Penance.

- Emphasize this point when teaching Chapter 12.
- Invite young people to reflect on what type of peace they long for, what the world needs, and how it can be brought about.

These points are drawn out in a handout on page XV. Copy the page, and give it to the young people in your group who are preparing for First Penance. Invite the young people to write their responses to questions 1–6. You can use the discussion questions as part of an interview, group discussion, or at-home sharing with parents and other family members

## Catechesis for First Eucharist

The following points are essential to a basic understanding of the Eucharist. These are developed in *Our Catholic Faith*.

**1.** In the Eucharist the Catholic community comes together to celebrate its faith in Christ as the Son of God. This community lives out its faith in Christ through the way its members show love and compassion toward others.

- Emphasize this point when teaching Chapters 8 and 9.
- Use the liturgical-year chart on page 103 to emphasize that the Catholic community expresses its faith in Jesus through the celebration of seasons and feasts.

**2.** As a community of believers, we are nourished and guided by the Word of God. In the Mass Catholics hear God's Word through the readings from the Old and New Testaments.

- Emphasize this point when teaching Chapter 9.
- Help your group become familiar with the Lectionary which contains the cycle of readings used at Mass throughout the liturgical year.
- Show the young people the *Book of the Gospels* which a deacon or priest uses to proclaim the Gospel at Mass.

**3.** The Eucharist commemorates the life, Death, Resurrection, and Ascension of Jesus. When we celebrate the Eucharist, we give thanks for the love given and the sacrifice offered for us by Jesus for the Salvation of all.

- Emphasize this point when presenting Chapters 8 and 9.
- Nurture a spirit of thanksgiving among the young people, emphasizing that this is what the word *Eucharist* means.

**4.** In the Eucharist, the sacrifice of Jesus on the cross is made present. Jesus' words and actions from the Last Supper are repeated: talking, blessing, breaking, eating. When we share the Eucharist we do so in remembrance of Jesus Christ, who is really present under the appearances of bread and wine.

- Emphasize this point when teaching Chapters 8 and 9.
- Stress the Real Presence of Christ in the Eucharist and refer often to the actions mentioned above.

**5.** When we pray the Our Father, we pray the prayer that Jesus taught us. Our Amen prayed before we receive Holy Communion affirms our belief in the Real Presence of Jesus in the Eucharist.

- Emphasize this point when teaching Chapter 9.
- Pray the Our Father often with the young people and encourage them to reflect upon the words.
- Demonstrate the two ways we can receive the Communion Host—in the hand or on the tongue. Encourage the young people to do this with reverence.

**6.** When we receive Holy Communion, we are nourished by Jesus himself. We are strengthened by the Holy Spirit so that we might share the life of Christ with others.

- Throughout the *Our Catholic Faith* program, encourage the young people to name specific ways they can be witnesses to their faith in their homes, schools, and neighborhoods.

These points are drawn out in a handout on page XVI. Copy the page, and give it to the young people in your group who are preparing for First Eucharist. Invite the young people to write their responses to the questions 1–6. You can use the discussion questions as part of an interview, group discussion, or at-home sharing with parents and other family members.

# Preparing for the Sacrament of Penance and Reconciliation

**Write your responses to the following questions.**

1. Use your own words to tell about the Sacrament of Penance and Reconciliation. How does it restore us to loving relationships with God and other people?

_______________________________________________

_______________________________________________

2. What is sin? What is the difference between committing a sin and making a mistake?

_______________________________________________

_______________________________________________

3. Explain what it means to make an examination of conscience.

_______________________________________________

_______________________________________________

4. What prayer of forgiveness do we use in the Sacrament of Penance and Reconciliation? What do we express in this prayer?

_______________________________________________

_______________________________________________

5. Name two ways of celebrating the Sacrament of Penance and Reconciliation.

_______________________________________________

_______________________________________________

6. How does the Sacrament of Penance and Reconciliation restore peace in our lives?

_______________________________________________

_______________________________________________

**Discuss.**

- How does Jesus teach us to show love towards God and other people? What can draw us away from this love?
- Why is it sometimes hard to make choices that show love for God, others, and for ourselves?
- Why is it important to think each day about the good and bad choices we make? When and how might we do this?
- When we pray to forgive others, what help might we ask of God? When we pray for others to forgive us, what might we ask God to help us to do?
- What questions do you have about celebrating the Sacrament of Penance and Reconciliation for the first time?
- Name one way young people can bring the peace of Christ to others each day.

## Preparing for the Sacrament of Eucharist

**Write your responses to the following questions.**

1. Why does the parish community come together to celebrate on Sundays?

2. Where do the readings at Mass come from?

3. During the celebration of Mass, what do we remember about the sacrifice that Jesus made for us?

4. What did Jesus share with his disciples at the Last Supper? What did he ask us to do "in remembrance" of him?

5. How is Jesus present to us in the Eucharist?

6. How does the Eucharist nourish us and help us to show the love of Christ to others?

**Discuss.**

- What are some ways for young people to participate in the life of the parish?
- Name one of your favorite stories about Jesus.
- What do we give thanks for when we celebrate the Mass? What gifts of God are you thankful for?
- What questions do you have about receiving Holy Communion for the first time?
- How is Jesus present to us each day?
- What are some ways that young people can share the love of Christ with others?

# Teaching Strategies

"The Church, in transmitting the faith,
does not have a particular method nor any single method."
(*General Directory for Catechesis,* 148)

The use of varied techniques better serves the different ways in which people learn. Here are some of those appropriate for use with the young people.

## Guest Speakers

Young people can be helped to grow in their faith by meeting, listening to, and conversing with Catholics whose faith values are central to their personal and professional lives. Consider inviting members of your parish leadership team to speak with the students.

## Group Discussion

Group discussion blends both spontaneity and structure. The catechist helps the group to focus on a topic, to respect the contributions of each member, to make sure that all participants have a chance to speak, and to conclude when the discussion has run its course. Consider setting a five-to-ten minute time limit for students in this age group.

## Brainstorming

Brainstorming is a way to elicit as many ideas and solutions as possible on a particular topic. While eliciting responses, avoid criticism or negative comments about any response. After the ideas and suggestions have been listed on the chalkboard or on a large sheet of paper, ask the students to reflect on the list. Guide a discussion after the reflection. Take time with the students to edit the list together. Consider saving the list to refer to later in the lesson as a way to review.

## Role-Playing

Role-playing offers the young people an opportunity to act out situations that may or may not be part of one's personal experience. Role-playing helps students to observe how they and others respond to different situations and to develop ways of living their faith.

## Visuals

The photographs and illustrations in the text can serve as visual statements of the content, as links to the lesson, or as catalysts for exploring initial thoughts and emotions.

When presenting the doctrinal content, use the visuals in the text as a starting point or a concluding point for the key concepts.

## Multimedia

Videos and music are effective tools for communicating religious truths. Consider using the resources that can be found in your parish media center, or in that of a neighboring parish, or in a diocesan media center. Preview all materials in preparation for the lesson and check to make sure the equipment is available and in good working order.

## Study Guides

Help the students review the major concepts presented in *Our Catholic Faith* by using the three Study Guide pages that follow, pages XVIII–XX. Copy and distribute the three pages at the end of the course.

Read and discuss the questions and answers on the Study Guide sheets. Help the students identify which concepts need clarification. Then refer the students to the specific page in the unit and chapter referenced after each question and answer.

# Study Guide

1. **What is the Bible?**
The Bible is the book about God's love for us and about our call to live as God's people. God is the author of the Bible since he guided the writers to record the things he wanted to share with us. We call the Bible the Word of God. (Unit 1, Chapter 1, page 8)

2. **What is Original Sin?**
Original Sin is the first sin committed by the first human beings, Adam and Eve. This sin weakened human nature and brought ignorance, suffering, and death into the world. And from then on all human beings have been born with Original Sin. (Unit 1, Chapter 1, page 9)

3. **What is the Blessed Trinity?**
The Blessed Trinity is the three Persons in one God: God the Father, God the Son, and God the Holy Spirit. (Unit 1, Chapter 1, page 10)

4. **What is the Incarnation?**
The Incarnation is the truth that God the Son, the second Person of the Blessed Trinity, became man. (Unit 1, Chapter 2, page 14)

5. **Who are the Apostles?**
The Apostles are the twelve men Jesus chose to share in his mission in a special way. (Unit 1, Chapter 2, page 15 )

6. **What is the Kingdom of God?**
The Kingdom of God is the power of God's love active in our lives and in the world. (Unit 1, Chapter 2, page 16)

7. **What did Jesus do for us on the night before he died?**
At the Last Supper on the night before Jesus died, he gave himself to the disciples in the bread and wine which became his Body and Blood in the Sacrament of the Eucharist. (Unit 1, Chapter 3, page 20)

8. **Who is our Savior?**
Our Savior is Jesus Christ who died and rose from the dead to save us. (Unit 1, Chapter 3, page 22)

9. **Why did Jesus Christ suffer, die, and rise to new life?**
Jesus Christ suffered, died, and rose to new life to save us from the power of sin and death. (Unit 1, Chapter 3, page 22)

10. **What happened on Pentecost?**
On Pentecost the Holy Spirit came upon Jesus' disciples. It was on this day that the Church began. (Unit 2, Chapter 4, page 29)

11. **What is the Church?**
The Church is the community of people who are baptized and follow Jesus Christ and his teachings. (Unit 2, Chapter 4, page 29)

12. **Who is the pope?**
The pope is the Bishop of Rome who is the successor of Saint Peter and who,with the bishops, leads the Catholic Church. (Unit 2, Chapter 5, page 34)

**13. Who are the bishops of the Church?**
The bishops are men who have received the fullness of the Sacrament of Holy Orders and continue the Apostles' mission of leadership and service. (Unit 2, Chapter 5, page 43)

**14. What are the Marks of the Church?**
The Marks of the Church are the four characteristics of the Church: one, holy, catholic, and apostolic. (Unit 2, Chapter 5, page 35)

**15. What is a parish?**
A parish is a community of believers who worship God together and work together in serving God and others. (Unit 2, Chapter 5, page 36)

**16. What is a sacrament?**
A sacrament is an effective sign given to us by Jesus Christ through which we share in God's life. (Unit 2, Chapter 6, page 41)

**17. What is grace?**
Grace is our share in God's life. (Unit 2, Chapter 6, page 41)

**18. What are the Sacraments of Christian Initiation?**
Baptism, Confirmation, and Eucharist are the three Sacraments of Christian Initiation. Through these sacraments we are born into the Church, strengthened, and nourished. (Unit 2, Chapter 6, page 42)

**19. What is the Sacrament of Baptism?**
Baptism is the sacrament in which we are freed from sin, become children of God, and are welcomed into the Church. (Unit 3, Chapter 7, page 50)

**20. What is the Sacrament of Confirmation?**
Confirmation is the sacrament in which we receive the Gift of the Holy Spirit in a special way. (Unit 3, Chapter 7, page 52)

**21. What is the Sacrament of the Eucharist?**
Eucharist is the sacrament of the Body and Blood of Christ. Through the power of the Holy Spirit and the words and actions of the priest, Jesus truly becomes present to us in the Sacrament of the Eucharist. He is truly present to us under the appearances of bread and wine. We receive Jesus Christ himself in Holy Communion. (Unit 3, Chapter 8, page 56)

**22. What is the Mass?**
The Mass is the celebration of the Eucharist. This celebration is the center of the Church's life. (Unit 3, Chapter 8, page 56)

**23. What are the four parts of the Mass?**
The four parts of the Mass are: the Introductory Rites, the Liturgy of the Word, the Liturgy of the Eucharist, and the Concluding Rites. (Unit 3, Chapter 9, page 62)

**24. What are the Ten Commandments?**
The Ten Commandments are the laws of God's covenant given to Moses on Mount Sinai. (Unit 4, Chapter 10, page 70)

**25. How do Catholics keep the Lord's Day holy?**
For Catholics Sunday is the Lord's Day. Participating in the Mass is the most important way of keeping the Lord's Day holy because we participate in the celebration of the Eucharist, the center of the Christian life. Also on Sundays we must rest from work and take time to relax and do things with our families. (Unit 4, Chapter 10, page 72)

**26. What are the Beatitudes?**
The Beatitudes are Jesus' teaching that describe the way to live as his disciples. (Unit 4, Chapter 11, page 77)

**27. What is a virtue?**
A virtue is a good habit that helps us to act according to God's love for us. (Unit 4, Chapter 11, page 78)

**28. What are the theological virtues?**
The theological virtues are gifts given to us directly by God. There are three theological virtues: faith, hope, and charity. (Unit 4, Chapter 11, page 78)

**29. What is sin?**
Sin is a thought, word, deed, or omission against God's law. (Unit 4, Chapter 12, page 83)

**30. What is our conscience?**
Our conscience is our ability to know the difference between good and evil, right and wrong. (Unit 4, Chapter 12, page 83)

**31. What is the Sacrament of Penance and Reconciliation?**
Penance and Reconciliation is the sacrament in which we receive God's forgiveness of our sins. (Unit 4, Chapter 12, pages 82–83)

**32. What are the four main parts of the Sacrament of Penance?**
The four main parts of the Sacrament of Penance are contrition, confession, penance, and absolution. (Unit 4, Chapter 12, page 83)

**33. What are the Works of Mercy?**
The Works of Mercy are the loving acts that we do to care for the needs of others. By doing the Corporal Works, we take care of people's physical, material needs. By doing the Spiritual Works, we care for the needs of people's minds, hearts, and souls. (Unit 4, Chapter 13, pages 89–90)

**34. Who is Mary?**
Mary is Jesus' Mother, his first disciple, and the greatest saint of the Church. She is the Mother of God and Mother of the Church. (Unit 4, Chapter 14, pages 95–96)

**35. What is the Communion of Saints?**
The Communion of Saints is the union of the baptized members of the Church on earth with those who are in Heaven, and those who are in Purgatory. (Unit 4, Chapter 14, page 94)

# Time Allotment Charts

Three charts are offered to show how each chapter might be treated in alternative ways according to a five-day, a three-day, or a once-a-week program.

## Five-Day Program

| Opener | Section One | Section Two | Section Three | Review |
|---|---|---|---|---|
| Introduction | Presentation | Presentation | Presentation | Conclusion |

## Three-Day Program

| Section One | Section Two | Section Three |
|---|---|---|
| Introduction<br>Presentation | Presentation | Presentation<br>Conclusion |

## Once-a-Week Program

Although there are time constraints in a once-a-week program, the catechist needs to emphasize key doctrinal points and, subsequently, use the results from the *Our Catholic Faith* program survey to determine what points still require clarification for the young people.

After doing so, the catechist would:

- Discuss the content of the three doctrinal points found in the Presentation.
- Use the Conclusion to pray and plan ways for the students to live their faith.

# Chapter 1

## GOALS

*to realize that God created the world; to learn that the Blessed Trinity is the central belief of our faith; to appreciate God's promise to send a Savior*

## GETTING READY

**Opening Prayer:** *Place a small table in a space set aside for a prayer gathering. On the table place an open Bible, a cross, and a battery-operated candle.*

**Materials Needed:** *markers for introductory activity (pages 6–7), Bible(s), highlighters or colored pencils, writing paper and a decorated gift bag or box for* ***Optional Activity*** *(page 10)*

## Catechist Background

What do you expect from those whom you love? Do you expect trust, care, forgiveness, faithfulness, and respect?

God is our loving Father. His love for us is everlasting. In the two accounts of Creation in the Book of Genesis, we learn that our life is a gift that God has given us out of love. Because of his great love for us, God has entrusted us with so many wonderful gifts in Creation. He expects us to use these gifts carefully and to take care of them as we work in partnership with him.

One of God's greatest gifts to us is the gift of free will, the ability to choose to do good or evil. As we learn in the third chapter of Genesis, Adam and Eve chose to turn away from God's love. They committed the first sin, Original Sin. Despite their

## Opening Prayer

Invite the students to gather in a place that you have prepared as a prayer space. (See guide page XII.)

As each student approaches the space, give him or her a copy of the *Our Catholic Faith* text. Have the students hold the texts as you pray together the following psalm verse.

*"Make known to me your ways,*
*Lord;*
*teach me your paths."*
(Psalm 25:4)

Introduce yourself and then have each student in the group introduce himself or herself. After the introductions point out that you are all on a journey of faith together. Emphasize that each person has something to contribute to and something to learn from the group.

Then pray again the psalm verse, substituting the pronoun *me* with *us*.

## 1 God Is the Creator

### A Wonderful World

God has filled our world with so many wonderful gifts.

6

choice, God never stopped loving Adam and Eve. God promised that he would not turn away from them and his people. He would send someone to save them from sin. Through the power of the Holy Spirit, God would send his only Son to save all people from sin.

Through the mystery of the Blessed Trinity we are privileged to live in relationship with God. The Trinity is God's Revelation of himself as one God in three distinct Persons: Father, Son, and Holy Spirit. The Blessed Trinity is central to our faith.

Throughout our lives we come to know that the three Persons of the Trinity are joined together in unfathomable love. And because we are made in God's image, we, too, are meant to be in loving relationship with God and others.

## Reflection

"People travel to wonder at the height of the mountains, at the huge waves of the seas, at the long course of the rivers, at the vast compass of the ocean, at the circular motion of the stars, and yet they pass by themselves without wondering."

*Saint Augustine of Hippo*

Which of God's wonderful gifts are your favorites?

Describe these gifts in words or through art.

**We Will Learn...**

1 God created the universe.
2 God promised to send a Savior.
3 There are three Persons in one God.

7

## Introduction ( __ min.)

Ask students to open their texts to pages 6 and 7 and look at the photographs of some of God's gifts of Creation. Invite volunteers to identify their favorite gifts.

Then ask the students to write about or draw their favorite gift (favorite animal, flower, body of water, land form) in the space provided. Invite the students to share their work with the others.

### We Will Learn...

**Explain that God created us because he loves us. Thus, learning the important truths of our faith is learning about God's love for us. Ask a volunteer to read the three doctrinal, or faith, statements listed on the scroll.**

## Presentation ( __ min.)

### 1 God created the universe.

*O God, how wonderful are your works.*

Explain to the students that we can read about God's gifts to us in the Bible. Show a Bible to the students. Then invite a volunteer to read the first paragraph on text page 8. Stress that God is the author of the Bible and that the Bible is the Word of God. Explain that there are many books in the Bible, and that all of them are about God's love for us.

For a more in-depth presentation about the Bible, use the material that is found on page 24 of the student's text, Unit I: *More for You to Know*.

Ask the students if they know what the first book of the Bible is about. Then invite a volunteer to read the second paragraph. Have the students highlight or underline the third sentence. Stress how wonderful it is that God made each person in his image and likeness.

Invite a volunteer to read the third and fourth paragraphs. You may want to read aloud Genesis 1:1—2:4. Point out that each day represents a long period of time.

Ask: *What can we do to thank God for his gifts of Creation?* Then invite a volunteer to read the last paragraph.

Read aloud the two concluding questions. Pause briefly to allow the students to reflect quietly. Then invite volunteers to share their responses.

### 1 God created the universe.

The Bible is the book about God's love for us and about our call to live as God's people. God is the author of the Bible since he guided the writers to record the things he wanted to share with us. We call the Bible the Word of God.

As we read the first book of the Bible, Genesis, we learn that everything in the universe was created by God. In the story of Creation, we read that after God created the sky, the bodies of water, the land, and the animals, God created human beings. God loved human beings so much he created us in his image and likeness. "God created man in his image; . . . /male and female he created them." (Genesis 1:27)

God gave the first human beings, whom we call Adam and Eve, the ability to love, to think and wonder, to ask questions and look for answers, and to make choices. God's plan for human beings was that they be happy with him forever.

God gave the first humans the whole of Creation to enjoy and protect. God wanted people to love and to be happy and to share in his goodness and beauty. We can read the whole story of Creation in Genesis 1:1—2:4 and Genesis 2:4–25.

When we see the beauty of Creation, we realize a loving God has given us everything. We should take time to thank him. We can do this by respecting each person because she or he is made in the image and likeness of God. We can also do this by taking care of the world—God's gift to us—so that we can share its goodness with all people.

In what ways can you show respect for others this week?

In what ways can you care for God's gifts of Creation?

**Do You Know?**

God alone created the world. He created each person in his image and likeness. Each person is a unity of body and soul. The soul is the invisible and the spiritual reality that makes each of us human. The soul is immortal, which means it will never die. At death the soul is separated from the body. But the soul will be reunited with the body when Christ comes in glory at the end of time.

8

**Do You Know?**

Before you present this feature, you may want to refer to the Church's teaching about the unity of a person's body and soul. See paragraphs 362–368 of the *Catechism of the Catholic Church*.

Ask a volunteer to read *Do You Know?* You may want to point out to the students that this teaching is part of the Tradition of the Church. See more about the Bible and Tradition on page 24, Unit 1: *More for You to Know*.

## 2 God promised to send a Savior.

One of God's greatest gifts to humans is the gift of free will. The first humans were free to choose either to do good or evil. God would not force them to do anything. God trusted them to act out of love for him rather than selfishness. In God's plan, humans would live in peace and harmony. They would never be sick or die.

But in Genesis, we learn how evil entered the world. We read that tempted by the devil, Adam and Eve chose not to use their freedom wisely. They chose to act selfishly and to turn away from the loving God who had created them. When they chose to turn away from God, they committed the first sin, called **Original Sin**. This sin weakened human nature and brought ignorance, suffering, and death into the world.

From then on all human beings have been born with Original Sin.

Even though the first humans sinned, God still loved them. He promised that he would not turn away from his people. God promised that he would send a Savior—someone who would save them from sin. In God's plan, through the power of the Holy Spirit, God the Father would send his only Son to save all people from sin.

Why do you think free will is one of God's greatest gifts?

9

## 2 God promised to send a Savior.

*God, your love for us is beyond measure.*

Explain that in the beginning life was ideal for Adam and Eve. They did not have anything to fear. They did not have to work. Food was provided for them.

Then have volunteers read the first and second paragraphs. Point out that we, too, have the gift of free will. Ask the students to highlight or underline the first two sentences of the first paragraph. Also explain that we are born with Original Sin, but this sin is washed away when we are baptized.

**Note:** See Chapter 7 for more information about Baptism and Original Sin.

Stress that God's love for Adam and Eve was so great that he did not abandon them after they sinned. Ask a volunteer to read the third paragraph. Emphasize how loving and wonderful it was that God promised to send a Savior to save people from sin. Tell the students that, in the next chapter, they will learn about God keeping his promise.

Read the concluding question about free will. Point out that when we love someone, we trust that person. Through God's gift of free will, we are able to choose to love him and others. We are free to choose to be unselfish or selfish. Yet God gives us free will in order that we may choose what is true and good.

### A Saint's Example

You may want to share the following information about Saint Francis of Assisi with the students.

Saint Francis of Assisi loved God very much and is known for his respect and care for God's gifts of Creation. The Church celebrates the saint's feast on October 4 every year. On this day in some parishes, the priest or deacon blesses pets and other animals.

## There are three Persons in one God.

*May everything we do be done in the name of the Father, the Son, and the Holy Spirit.*

On the board or on chart paper draw a triangle that has three equal sides. Point out that there is one triangle having three sides. Also draw a shamrock. Point out that there is one plant having three leaves.

Read aloud the first paragraph about the mystery of the Blessed Trinity. Explain that by *mystery* we mean a religious truth that we could not have known had it not been revealed by God himself. It is a reality that we cannot fully understand. Emphasize that the Blessed Trinity is God the Father, God the Son, and God the Holy Spirit: three Persons in one God, joined together in love.

Ask the students to read the words of the prayer in the upper right corner of page 10. Then direct attention to the student shown as she makes the Sign of the Cross. Explain that we should use our right hand when praying this prayer, and we should be respectful in praying the words and making the prayer gestures.

Invite the students to stand and pray together the Sign of the Cross. Explain to the students that we pray these words at the beginning of the Mass and at other times when we are praying.

Read the concluding question and ask volunteers to share their responses. Possible responses include: as we begin to say our morning and nighttime prayers, when we begin to pray together in church or in another setting, at the beginning of Mass. You may want to point out that some people pray the Sign of the Cross when they pass in front of a church.

### 3 There are three Persons in one God.

God the Father, God the Son, and God the Holy Spirit are three Persons in one God. We call the three Persons in one God: God the Father, God the Son, and God the Holy Spirit, the **Blessed Trinity**. The Blessed Trinity is a mystery of faith. It is a belief that we will not fully understand until we are sharing life forever with God in Heaven. The Blessed Trinity is the central belief of our faith and of our life of faith.

One way to show our belief in the Blessed Trinity is to pray the Sign of the Cross.

When will you pray the Sign of the Cross this week?

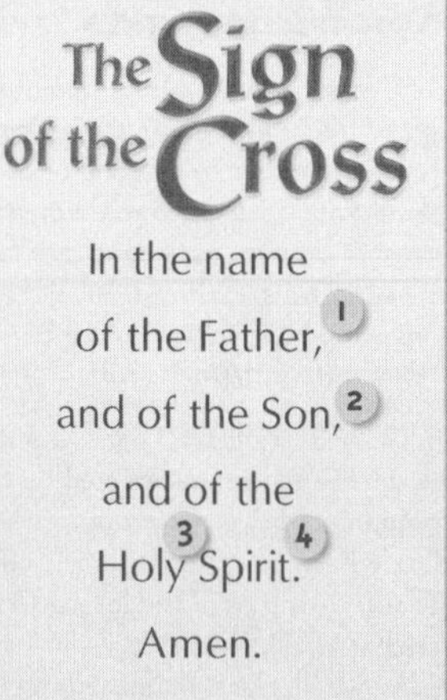

10

## Optional Activity

**Invite the students to write a thank-you note to God for his gifts of Creation, especially for the gifts and talents that God has given to each of them. Ask the students to express in their notes how they can use their talents and abilities to care for, conserve, and share the earth's resources. When the students are finished writing, have them fold the notes and put them in a specially decorated gift bag or box. Place this bag or box in the prayer space.**

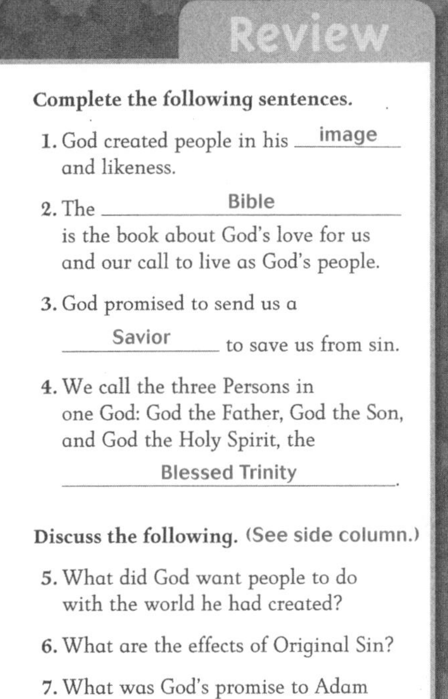

## Review

**Complete the following sentences.**

1. God created people in his image and likeness.
2. The Bible is the book about God's love for us and our call to live as God's people.
3. God promised to send us a Savior to save us from sin.
4. We call the three Persons in one God: God the Father, God the Son, and God the Holy Spirit, the Blessed Trinity.

**Discuss the following.** (See side column.)

5. What did God want people to do with the world he had created?
6. What are the effects of Original Sin?
7. What was God's promise to Adam and Eve after they sinned?

**Faith Words**

Bible (page 8)
Original Sin (page 9)
Blessed Trinity (page 10)

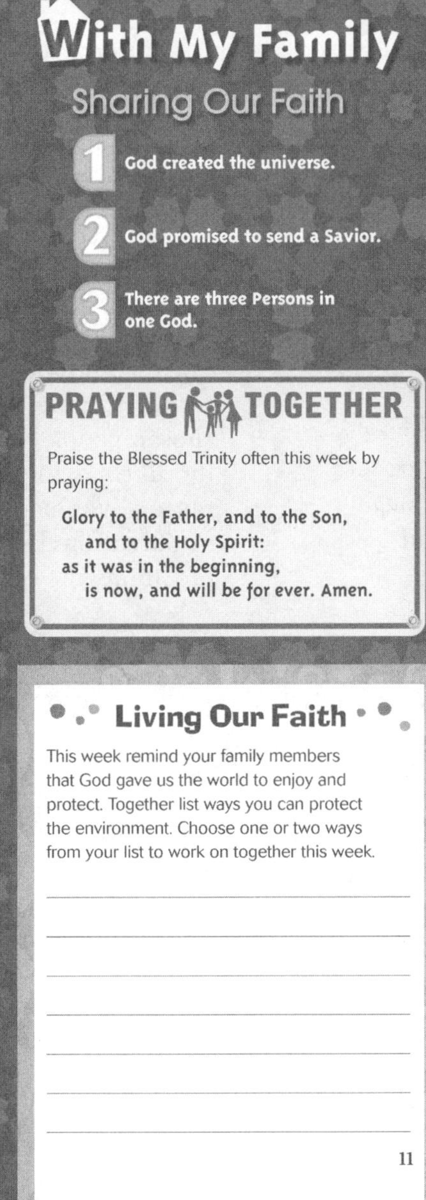

## With My Family

### Sharing Our Faith

1. God created the universe.
2. God promised to send a Savior.
3. There are three Persons in one God.

**PRAYING TOGETHER**

Praise the Blessed Trinity often this week by praying:

Glory to the Father, and to the Son,
and to the Holy Spirit:
as it was in the beginning,
is now, and will be for ever. Amen.

**Living Our Faith**

This week remind your family members that God gave us the world to enjoy and protect. Together list ways you can protect the environment. Choose one or two ways from your list to work on together this week.

11

continued... (11/14/10)

## Conclusion (__ min.)

### Review

Provide five to ten minutes for the students to work independently to complete the first part of the *Review*. Check the students' answers. Then discuss the questions in the second part of the *Review*. Possible responses follow.

**5.** God gave Adam and Eve the whole of Creation to enjoy and protect. He wanted people to appreciate his gifts and to be happy in the beautiful world he had made.

**6.** Original Sin weakened human nature. It brought ignorance, suffering, and death into the world.

**7.** God promised Adam and Eve that he would send a Savior, someone who would save them from sin.

### *Faith Words*

On a large sheet of paper, draw three circles. Write a Faith Word in the center of each circle. Have the students think of other words associated with each Faith Word. Then write these words in the appropriate circle.

## CATECHISM FOCUS

"The mystery of the Most Holy Trinity is the central mystery of the Christian faith and of Christian life. God alone can make it known to us by revealing himself as Father, Son, and Holy Spirit."
(CCC, 261)

For additional reference and reflection, see *CCC*, paragraphs 262–267.

### With My Family

#### *Sharing Our Faith*

Encourage the students to share with their families what they have learned about God the Creator and the Blessed Trinity.

#### *Praying Together*

Read the prayer together. Pray each verse of the prayer and ask students to repeat the verse. Encourage the students to share with their families this prayer of praise.

#### *Living Our Faith*

Have a volunteer read the paragraph. Encourage the students to discuss with their families specific ways they can protect the environment. Suggest that each student write the family plan on the lines provided.

# Chapter 2

## GOALS

*to learn that Jesus Christ is true God and true man; to understand that Jesus taught people to know and love God; to respond to the invitation to become followers of Jesus*

## GETTING READY

**Opening Prayer:** *On the prayer table, place a Bible opened to the beginning of the Gospel of Luke.*

**Materials Needed:** *markers and pens for introductory activity (pages 12–13), globe or world map (page 14), costumes and props for* ***Optional Activity*** *(page 15)*

## Catechist Background

For thousands of years after Adam and Eve sinned, God's people waited to hear good news. They waited to hear the Good News of the coming of the Messiah—the Savior whom God had promised to send. In the fullness of time, God kept his promise. He sent his only Son, Jesus Christ, to live among his people and share their humanity.

The coming into the world of Jesus Christ was and is the ultimate "Good News"— not only for God's chosen people, but for all people everywhere, and for all time. In the Person of Jesus Christ, God reveals who he is, shows us how to live, and offers us Salvation. In his Person and in his teaching, Jesus proclaims the coming of God's Kingdom among us.

## Opening Prayer

Ask the students to remain seated. Read the following script, and invite the students to visualize themselves in the scene: *It is late at night. Darkness fills the sky. You are in a field tending sheep. Suddenly you look up. You see a bright light and an angel of the Lord.*

*The angel says to you and the other shepherds: "Do not be afraid; for behold, I proclaim to you good news of great joy that will be for all the people. For today in the city of David a savior has been born for you who is Messiah and Lord. And this will be a sign for you: you will find an infant wrapped in swaddling clothes and lying in a manger."* (Luke 2:10–12)

*You and the other shepherds go to visit the infant. As soon as you see him in the manger, you realize this child is no ordinary child. You go to tell others about what you have seen and heard.*

Allow time for the students to reflect on what they would tell others.

# 2 God Sends His Only Son

## A Day for Good News

Last Tuesday Mr. Diaz picked up Victor and Rosa after school. They ran to the car. They could not wait to share their great news.

Victor told his dad, "Our principal announced the prize winners of the school read-a-thon. Guess what! Mrs. Fielding announced my name as the second prize winner. I was so surprised!"

Mr. Diaz said, "I'm so proud of you, Victor. What is your prize?"

Victor answered,

"______________________________

______________________________

______________________________."

(fill in your answer)

Then Rosa said, "I have good news, too. My friend Emily's cat had kittens last Sunday. Emily brought in some pictures. The kittens are so cute! Emily's mom said that I could have one of the kittens. I told Emily that I would have to talk to you and Mom first. If you say yes, I'm going to name the kitten

______________________________."

(fill in your answer)

By healing the sick, forgiving sinners, befriending the poor, feeding the hungry, and calling all people to live just and peaceful lives, Jesus Christ reveals what the Kingdom of God is like.

By sending out the Apostles, Jesus gathered other followers to continue the work of proclaiming and working for the Kingdom of God. This gathering of Jesus' disciples is the Church. All members of the Church are called to work for, envision, and pray for the fulfillment of God's Kingdom.

## Reflection

"At daybreak, Jesus left and went to a deserted place. The crowds went looking for him, and when they came to him, they tried to prevent him from leaving them. But he said to them, 'To the other towns also I must proclaim the good news of the kingdom of God, because for this purpose I have been sent.'"

*(Luke 4:42–43)*

Mr. Diaz said, "Now I have good news to tell you. Grandpa sent me a text message today. He and Grandma are coming to visit. They are going to drive from their new home in South Carolina. They'll be here in time for the family picnic next Saturday."

Victor and Rosa cheered. Then Victor said, "We have a lot to tell Mom when she comes home tonight."

Mr. Diaz said, "You're right, Victor. I think we should celebrate."

He continued, "Let's go out for dinner. On the way to the restaurant we can take turns telling Mom our good news."

Rosa said, "And maybe Mom will have good news to tell us, too!"

• • •

**What good news have you heard recently?**

**Who shared the good news with you?**

**With whom did you share the news?**

### We Will Learn...

**1** Jesus Christ is true God and true man.

**2** Jesus shares the Good News of God's love.

**3** Jesus teaches about the Kingdom of God.



## Introduction ( ___ min.)

Have volunteers read the story "A Day for Good News." As you come to each fill-in-the-blank, pause briefly to allow students to write their responses. Then discuss with the students why they think Victor, Rosa, and Mr. Diaz were eager to share their good news.

Invite volunteers to share their responses to the questions that follow the story. Discuss why people like to share good news.

If time permits, have the students suggest a few "good news" headlines. Print the headlines and display them in the prayer space.

### We Will Learn...

Remind the students that before Jesus was born, God's people were waiting to hear that the Savior had come to save them from sin. Ask a volunteer to read the three faith statements on the scroll.

# Presentation ( __ min.)

## 1 Jesus Christ is true God and true man.

*God, our loving Father, thank you for keeping your promise to your people.*

Display a globe or world map. Point out the country of Israel. Explain to the students that this is the land where Jesus lived. Most of the people who lived there at that time were Jewish. They believed and worshiped the one true God.

On the board or on chart paper, write the word *Incarnation*. Tell the students that today they will learn about this mystery of our faith.

Read the first three paragraphs on page 14. You may want to read aloud the Scripture account, Luke 1:26–38.

Read aloud the fourth paragraph. Explain that Jesus being both human and divine is a mystery of our faith.

Point out that Jesus was born in Bethlehem, but he grew up in the small town of Nazareth. He lived there with Mary and Joseph and other relatives. Also explain that as Jesus was growing up, he studied and obeyed God's laws. With his family he prayed every day. Each week Jesus, Mary, and Joseph joined other Jewish families to worship God.

Read the last paragraph. Stress that Jesus is divine; he is Lord.

**Note:** In Old Testament times the transcendent God was referred to as Lord. Using the title Lord was a sign of respect. In the time of Jesus, people who believed that he was the Son of God called Jesus *Lord*. In fact the earliest expression of Christian faith was "Jesus is Lord" (Philippians 2:11).

Ask the students to respond to the concluding question.

### 1 Jesus Christ is true God and true man.

The truth that God the Son, the second Person of the Blessed Trinity, became man is called the **Incarnation**. We learn about this mystery of our faith in the Bible.

In the Gospel of Luke, we read that one day the angel Gabriel gave a message to a young Jewish woman named Mary. Gabriel told Mary that God wanted her to be the mother of his Son. The angel also told Mary that she was to name the child *Jesus*, which means "God saves."

Mary told the angel that she did not fully understand how this would happen. The angel answered, "The holy Spirit will come upon you, and the power of the Most High will overshadow you. Therefore the child to be born will be called holy, the Son of God" (Luke 1:35).

Mary agreed to be the Mother of God's Son. She gave birth to a son and called him Jesus. Jesus Christ is truly the Son of God and Mary's Son. Jesus Christ is both divine and human. **Divine** is a word we use to describe God.

Jesus Christ is divine; he is Lord. He did things only God can do. He is also human; he is like us in all things, except he is without sin.

What do we mean by the Incarnation?

#### Do You Know?

Angels are creatures created by God as pure spirits. They do not have physical bodies. Angels serve God as his messengers. They serve God in his saving plan for us and constantly give him praise.

#### Do You Know?

Have a volunteer read the feature. The Church's teaching about angels may be found in paragraphs 328–336 of the *Catechism of the Catholic Church*. After a volunteer reads the paragraph, you may want to share the following words of Saint Basil as quoted in *CCC*, 336: "Beside each believer stands an angel as protector and shepherd leading him to life."

## 2 Jesus shares the Good News of God's love.

When Jesus was about thirty years old, he began his work among the people. Jesus was to share the love of God with all people and to save all people from sin. So Jesus' mission was to spread the Good News of God's love.

And all of Jesus' words and actions—from his miracles and prayers to his Crucifixion and Resurrection—were carried out through the guidance of the Holy Spirit. Jesus' whole life was a continual teaching.

Through his words and actions Jesus taught people to know and love God. He

- fed the hungry
- cured the sick
- forgave sinners
- was a friend to those who were sick or in need
- showed people how to love God
- taught people to love others as God loves them.

Jesus told the people that God loves, forgives, and cares for all of us. No one is left out. He called people to follow him and share his mission. Many people accepted Jesus' invitation. Those who followed him were his **disciples**.

Jesus chose twelve of his disciples to lead the community of his followers. These twelve men whom Jesus chose to share in his mission in a special way are the **Apostles**.

This week how can you show that you want to follow Jesus as his disciple?

15

## 2 Jesus shares the Good News of God's love.

*Jesus Christ, we want to tell others about you.*

Have the students focus on the illustration of Jesus on pages 14 and 15. Invite them to imagine that they are in the crowd. Ask: *If someone introduced you to Jesus, what would you say to him?* Pause briefly. Then invite volunteers to share their responses.

Read aloud the following: "Jesus returned to Galilee in the power of the Spirit, and news of him spread throughout the whole region"(Luke 4:14). Then ask a volunteer to read aloud the first paragraph.

Invite volunteers to read aloud the second and third paragraphs. If time permits, read one of the accounts of Jesus' miracles of healing: Jesus cures Peter's mother-in-law (Luke 4:38–39); the healing of someone who was paralyzed (Matthew 9:1–8).

Read the fourth paragraph. Explain that Jesus invited many people to follow him. These people were known as Jesus' disciples. Point out that Peter, Andrew, Martha, and Mary were some of the first disciples of Jesus. They learned from Jesus how to love and to help one another. They followed Jesus' example of caring for people who were sick and poor. They tried to be kind and fair to all people.

Explain that from his disciples Jesus chose twelve men to be the leaders of the group. These men are Jesus' Apostles. Then ask a volunteer to read the last paragraph.

Pause briefly. Invite the students to reflect quietly about ways they can show that they are disciples of Jesus. Then ask volunteers to share their responses. Suggest that each student choose one or two ways that are "do-able" for him or her this week.

## Optional Activity

**Invite the students to imagine that, in Jesus' time, there were TV news programs. Have them work in small groups to present a segment about Jesus' words and deeds for a particular day or week. Allow the students time to prepare the segment. Then invite the groups to share their program segments with the other groups.**

## Jesus teaches about the Kingdom of God.

*Jesus, you are our Teacher.*

Ask the students to think about the people who have taught them important lessons about daily living. Point out that these people probably taught by the words they said and the example they gave.

Explain to the students that Jesus was the "Teacher of teachers." Then have a volunteer read the first two paragraphs on page 16.

Explain that Jesus taught people about God's love by talking about things people were familiar with in their everyday lives and activities: shepherds and sheep, farming, birds and flowers, light and darkness. Then read aloud the third paragraph. Also read aloud the parable of the treasure (Matthew 13:44) and the parable of the mustard seed (Matthew 13:31–32).

Stress that every person is invited to be a part of God's Kingdom; no one is excluded. Then read aloud the last two paragraphs.

Discuss with the students how we live for God's Kingdom. Some specific and practical ways include: listening to parents and teachers, helping out at home, not excluding people from groups we belong to, reading the Bible, and studying our faith.

**Note:** More about Jesus' teachings about the Kingdom of God is presented in Chapter 11: *Jesus Teaches About True Happiness.*

### 3 Jesus teaches about the Kingdom of God.

Crowds of people followed Jesus everywhere he went. They wanted to hear him teach. Jesus often spoke about the Kingdom of God. He told them, "The kingdom of God is at hand" (Mark 1:15).

The Kingdom of God is not a place you can find on a map. The **Kingdom of God** is the power of God's love active in our lives and in our world. The Kingdom of God was made present through Jesus' words and actions.

Jesus taught us about God's Kingdom in special stories called parables. In one parable Jesus said that the Kingdom of God was like a great treasure that people would want above all things. (See Matthew 13:44.)

In another parable Jesus said that the Kingdom of God was like a mustard seed, a tiny seed that grows into a very large plant. (See Matthew 13:31–32.)

Jesus taught that the way to live for God's Kingdom is by turning away from sin and doing what God asks us to do. All people are invited to become a part of the Kingdom and to spread God's love in the world. All people are invited to become faithful followers of Jesus.

The Kingdom of God will not be complete until Jesus returns in glory at the end of time. So each day we work and live for God's Kingdom as we look forward to being with God forever in Heaven.

How do we live for the Kingdom of God?

16

## Liturgy Connection

Pray the Lord's Prayer with the students. It is on page 17. Explain that each Sunday at Mass we pray this prayer together before we receive Holy Communion. The prayer ends with the words "For the kingdom, the power and the glory are yours, now and for ever."

More information about the Lord's Prayer may be found on page 44, Unit 2: *More for You to Know* and on page 116 in the *About Prayer* section.

## Review

**Write the letter of the answer that best defines each term.**

1. d Apostles
2. c parable
3. b divine
4. a disciples

a. those who followed Jesus

b. a word used to describe God

c. a special story Jesus told

d. the twelve men whom Jesus chose to share in his mission in a special way

**Discuss the following.** (See side column.)

5. What is the Incarnation?
6. What is the Kingdom of God?

### Faith Words


Incarnation (page 14)
divine (page 14)
disciples (page 15)
Apostles (page 15)
Kingdom of God (page 16)

## With My Family

### Sharing Our Faith

1. Jesus Christ is true God and true man.
2. Jesus shares the Good News of God's love.
3. Jesus teaches about the Kingdom of God.

### PRAYING TOGETHER

In the Lord's Prayer we pray for the fulfillment of God's Kingdom.

**Our Father, who art in heaven,**
**hallowed be thy name;**
**thy kingdom come;**
**thy will be done on earth**
**as it is in heaven.**
**Give us this day our daily bread;**
**and forgive us our trespasses**
**as we forgive those who trespass against us;**
**and lead us not into temptation,**
**but deliver us from evil. Amen.**

### Living Our Faith

This week with your family, read and discuss one or two of Jesus' parables about the Kingdom of God. (See Matthew 13.) Decide which parable is most meaningful for you. Then write about or draw a picture of one or two ways you can help spread the Kingdom of God.

17

## Conclusion ( __ min.)

### Review

Provide five to ten minutes for the students to work independently to complete the first part of the *Review*. Check the students' answers. Then discuss the questions in the second part of the *Review*. Possible responses follow.

**5.** The Incarnation is the truth that God the Son, the second Person of the Blessed Trinity, became man. Jesus Christ is true God and true man. He is both divine and human.

**6.** The Kingdom of God is the power of God's love active in our lives and in our world. Jesus made the Kingdom present by his words and actions, but it will not be complete until Jesus comes in glory at the end of time.

### *Faith Words*

On a large sheet of paper print each Faith Word without including the vowels (__ p __ stl __ s for Apostles). Provide a clue for the word, and then ask a volunteer to fill in the missing vowels.

## CATECHISM FOCUS

**"Jesus' invitation to enter his kingdom comes in the form of parables, a characteristic feature of his teaching. Through his parables he invites people to the feast of the kingdom, but he also asks for a radical choice: to gain the kingdom, one must give everything. Words are not enough; deeds are required"** *(CCC, 546)*

### With My Family

#### *Sharing Our Faith*

Encourage the students to share with their families what they have learned about the Incarnation of Jesus, the Good News Jesus shared by his words and deeds, and Jesus' teaching about the Kingdom of God.

#### *Praying Together*

Invite the students to pray the Lord's Prayer. Point out that this prayer is also known as the Our Father. Encourage the students to discuss with their family the meaning of the words of this prayer. Refer the students to page 116.

#### *Living Our Faith*

Have a volunteer read the paragraph. Encourage the students to work on the activity with their families.

# Chapter 3

## GOALS

*to learn that, by Jesus' Death and Resurrection, he freed us from sin and opened for us the way to new life; to appreciate all that Jesus has done for us*

## GETTING READY

**Opening Prayer:** *On the prayer table, place a crucifix or cross.*

**Materials Needed:** *crucifix (page 21), highlighters or colored pencils, poster board, strips cut from yellow construction paper, paste or glue for* ***Optional Activity*** *(page 22)*

## Catechist Background

What do you think is the most crucial turning point in history? The discovery of fire, the invention of electricity, and the arrival of the technological age have brought about radical changes in the world. However, no discovery, invention, or event is as crucial a turning point as Jesus Christ's journey from death to new life.

Jesus knew that he was going to make this journey. He prepared his disciples, especially on the night before he died. It was then at the Last Supper that Jesus gave his followers his own Body and Blood to nourish us and sustain us on our own faith journey. "On the eve of his Passion while still free, Jesus transformed this Last Supper with the apostles into

## Opening Prayer

Invite the students to gather in the prayer space. Ask them to visualize Jesus talking to a group of his followers. Then read the following:

*"I came so that they might have life and have it more abundantly."*
(John 10:10)

Then invite the students to respond "have mercy on us" after you read each of the following titles of Jesus from the Litany of the Holy Name of Jesus:

- *Jesus, Son of the living God*
- *Jesus, model of obedience*
- *Jesus, model of goodness*
- *Jesus, Good Shepherd*
- *Jesus the true light*
- *Jesus, our way and our life.*

Then conclude by praying:
*Lord, may we who honor the holy name of Jesus enjoy his friendship in this life and be filled with eternal joy in the kingdom where he lives and reigns for ever and ever. Amen.*

# 3 Jesus Christ Is Our Savior

Last month Alexa Federov's home was partly destroyed by a storm. So she and her parents went to stay at her Aunt Anna's house. Every day Alexa's parents traveled back to their home, and worked to clean up and repair the house.

One morning when Alexa woke up, she heard noises outside. She got up and went to see what was happening. It was Aunt Anna carefully hammering broken dishes on a table in the driveway. Alexa was confused and asked, "What are you doing, Aunt Anna?"

Aunt Anna explained, "Your mom and dad brought back a box of these broken dishes. Your mom treasured these dishes because the set was a wedding gift from your grandparents. Your mom was upset when she saw the dishes broken and scattered. She couldn't bring herself to throw away the pieces."

Alexa asked, "Then why are you breaking the dishes into smaller pieces?"

"I'm going to use the pieces to make a special gift for your mom. I'm going to make a mosaic cross. Would you like to help me, Alexa?" Aunt Anna asked.

the memorial of voluntary offering to the Father for the salvation of men." (*CCC*, 610).

On the next day—the day we now call Good Friday—Jesus suffered, died, and was buried. However, Jesus' journey did not end after his burial. Early on the third day, Sunday morning, Jesus rose to new life. His journey has made all the difference in our lives of faith: ". . . . by his death, Christ liberates us from sin; by his Resurrection, he opens for us the way to a new life" (*CCC*, 654).

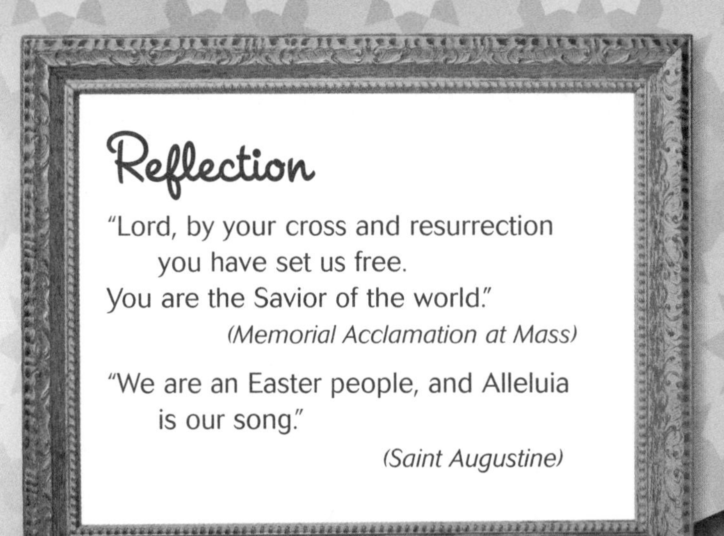

## Reflection

"Lord, by your cross and resurrection
you have set us free.
You are the Savior of the world."

*(Memorial Acclamation at Mass)*

"We are an Easter people, and Alleluia
is our song."

*(Saint Augustine)*

Alexa wanted to help, so she and Aunt Anna worked on the mosaic all morning. While they were working, Alexa asked, "Why are we making a cross?"

Aunt Anna said, "For me a cross is a sign of hope. I think about Jesus' love for us. I remember that he died on the cross and rose from the dead for us. I also remember that he promised to be with us always. When your house is repaired, your parents can hang the cross where all of you will see it often. As you look at it, you can think about Jesus' love. You can remember that Jesus is with you in happy, peaceful times as well as in troubled, stormy times."

• • •

**What do you think Alexa's parents will say when they see the cross?**

**What do you think about when you see a cross?**

### We Will Learn...

1 Jesus gave us the Eucharist at the Last Supper.

2 Jesus died on the cross to save us from sin.

3 Jesus rose from the dead and brought us new life.



## Introduction ( __ min.)

Before reading the story, explain that a mosaic is a work of art that is made by laying small pieces of colored material (tiles, paper) on a surface to make a picture. Then ask volunteers to read "Sign of Hope and Love."

Discuss the questions that follow the story. Possible responses to the second question include Jesus giving his life for us and our faith in Jesus. If time permits, you may want to have the students role-play Aunt Anna and Alexa giving the cross to Alexa's parents.

### We Will Learn...

**Have a volunteer read the three faith statements. Explain to the students that, in this chapter, they will be learning about the final days of Jesus and his rising from death to new life.**

# Presentation ( _ min.)

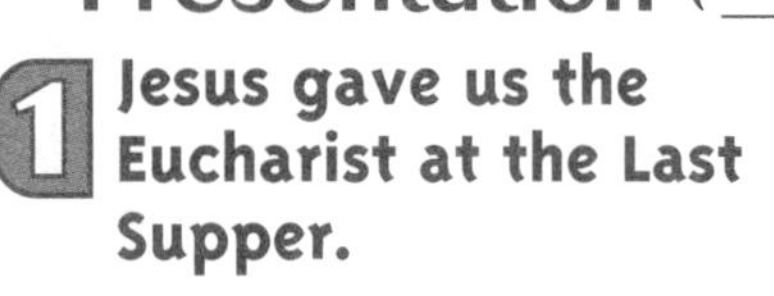

## 1 Jesus gave us the Eucharist at the Last Supper.

*Jesus, we thank you for giving us the gift of yourself in the Eucharist.*

You may want to begin by asking: *How can the people we love stay present with us when we are separated from them by distance or death?* Possible responses include: by treasuring tokens of their love or friendship; by continuing a favorite shared tradition; by remembering and celebrating time spent with them.

Point out that Jesus was Jewish. The Jewish people praised and worshiped the one true God. On special feasts they remembered and celebrated God's presence with them and what he did for them. Then ask a volunteer to read the first two paragraphs on page 20.

Explain that Jesus knew that one day he would not be with his disciples in the same way he was before his Death, but he wanted to be present to them always. Have the students focus on the illustration on page 20. Then read aloud the third and fourth paragraphs.

Emphasize that Jesus gave us the gift of himself on the night before he died. The bread and wine became his Body and Blood. Have a volunteer read the last two paragraphs. Ask the students to highlight or underline the last three sentences in the last paragraph. Tell the students that they will learn more about the Sacrament of the Eucharist in Chapter 8.

You may want to read the Scripture account of the preparations for the Passover and the meal Jesus shared (Luke 22: 1–20). Point out that Jesus asked us to celebrate the gift of himself in the Eucharist when he said "do this in memory of me" (Luke 22:19). Invite volunteers to respond to the concluding question.

### 1 Jesus gave us the Eucharist at the Last Supper.

Every year Jewish people gather to celebrate the Feast of Passover. In the time of Jesus, many gathered in Jerusalem for the feast. They praised and worshiped God in the Temple there.

Jesus and his disciples went to Jerusalem on the Sunday before Jesus died. They stayed in the city all week, and Jesus taught outside the Temple every day.

On the night before Jesus died, he and his disciples gathered to celebrate the Passover meal. At the meal Jesus gave the disciples a special way to remember him and to be with him. Here is what Jesus said and did at the meal. "While they were eating, he took bread, said the blessing, broke it, and gave it to them, and said, 'Take it; this is my body.'

Then he took a cup, gave thanks, and gave it to them, and they all drank from it. He said to them, 'This is my blood.'" (Mark 14:22–24)

Since this was the last meal Jesus shared with his disciples before he died, we call this meal the **Last Supper**. At the Last Supper Jesus gave himself to the disciples in the bread and wine which became his Body and Blood.

At the Last Supper Jesus gave us the gift of the Eucharist. The Eucharist is the sacrament of the Body and Blood of Jesus Christ. Jesus is really present under the appearances of bread and wine. This true presence of Jesus Christ in the Eucharist is called the **Real Presence**.

On the night before Jesus died, what did he do for his disciples?

20

## Liturgy Connection

The Church celebrates Christ's passing from death to new life when we celebrate the Triduum. The Triduum begins with Evening Mass of the Lord's Supper on Holy Thursday Evening. It continues through Good Friday, the Easter Vigil Mass on Holy Saturday Evening, and Easter Sunday. For more information see pages 102–103.

## 2 Jesus died on the cross to save us from sin.

Some powerful leaders did not believe that Jesus was the Son of God. They plotted against him. After the Last Supper, Jesus went to pray in a garden with some of the Apostles. While they were there, the leaders had Jesus arrested.

The next morning Jesus was sentenced to die. The soldiers forced Jesus to carry a heavy cross to Calvary, a hill outside Jerusalem. There Jesus was crucified—that is, nailed to a cross. Yet, even as he was dying, Jesus forgave those who had crucified him. He prayed: "Father, forgive them, they know not what they do" (Luke 23:34).

### Do You Know?

On the Feast of Passover the Jewish people remember and celebrate the wondrous way that God saved their ancestors from slavery and death in Egypt. God "passed over" the houses of his people, protecting them from the suffering that came to the Egyptians—the death of every first-born son. God then saved Moses and the Israelites by helping them to cross the Red Sea and flee Egypt. God made a covenant, an agreement, with Moses as he had made an everlasting covenant with Noah and all living beings after the flood and as he had with Abraham and his descendants. By the covenant God made with Moses and the Israelites, God would be their God, protecting and providing for them, and they would be his people.

Through Jesus Christ's Death and Resurrection, a new covenant was made between God and his people. Through this new covenant we are saved. We can share in God's life again.

Jesus' mother Mary, other women disciples, and the Apostle John stayed by Jesus as he suffered and died on the cross. Many of Jesus' disciples hid because they were afraid that they, too, would be arrested.

*Christ of Saint John of the Cross*, Salvador Dali, 1951

After Jesus died, his body was taken down from the cross and laid in a tomb. A great stone was rolled in front of it. Then, filled with sadness, the disciples left to return to the places where they were staying.

Why was Jesus sentenced to die?

21

## 2 Jesus died on the cross to save us from sin.

*Jesus, you are our Savior.*

Ask: *Where did Jesus go after the Last Supper?* Read the first paragraph on page 21. You may want to read the Scripture account of Jesus' arrest. (See Luke 22:47–53.)

Then ask volunteers to read the next three paragraphs. Explain that Jesus forgave those who caused his suffering: from the cross Jesus said, "Father, forgive them, they know not what they do" (Luke 23:34).

Emphasize that Jesus' mother Mary, other women disciples, and the Apostle John stayed with Jesus as he suffered and died on the cross. Point out how brave they were in staying with Jesus. You may want to read the account of the Crucifixion of Jesus, in John 19:17–30 and the account of his burial in John 19:38–42.

Ask the concluding question. Remind the students that some powerful leaders did not believe Jesus was the Son of God.

If possible, show the students a crucifix. Explain that a cross with the figure of Jesus on it is called a crucifix. Point out that we remember Jesus' suffering and Death every time we see a crucifix or cross.

### Do You Know?

Before presenting *Do You Know?* you may want to read about the Passover in Chapters 12–14 of the Book of Exodus and about the covenant God made with his people in Chapters 19–24. The word *covenant* will be defined in Chapter 10. Remind the students that on the night before he died, Jesus invited his disciples to celebrate the special meal for the Passover. Then read aloud the paragraphs.

## 3 Jesus rose from the dead and brought us new life.

*Alleluia! Alleluia! Alleluia!*

Explain to the students that the Jewish Sabbath starts on Friday evening at sundown. It is the custom for the Jewish people to be in their homes for the Sabbath meal at sundown.

Then explain that it was close to sundown when Jesus was placed in the tomb. The women disciples did not have time to anoint Jesus' body with oil. They were going to do this early on Sunday morning.

Read aloud the first two paragraphs on page 22. Then read the Scripture account: Luke 24:1–12. If time permits, have the students act out the scenes.

Explain that we celebrate Jesus' rising from the dead on Easter Sunday. It is a very joyful celebration because Jesus' rising to new life affects all people. Read aloud the remaining paragraphs.

Ask the students to highlight or underline the definitions for the words *Resurrection* and *Savior*.

Pause for a minute of quiet reflection. Invite the students to put themselves in the place of Jesus' disciples. Ask: *How did you feel when you heard that Jesus had risen from the dead?* Have a few volunteers share their responses.

**Note:** You may want to tell the students that the photograph on page 22 was taken in Israel, the Holy Land.

### 3 Jesus rose from the dead and brought us new life.

Early on the Sunday morning after Jesus died, some women disciples went to the tomb to anoint Jesus' body. As the women neared the tomb, they saw that the stone in front of it had been rolled back. The women thought someone had stolen Jesus' body.

But then the women saw two men in dazzling garments. The men said, "Why do you seek the living one among the dead? He is not here, but he has been raised" (Luke 24:5–6).

The women ran to tell the Apostles that Jesus had risen from the dead just as he had told them he would do. The mystery of Jesus Christ rising from the dead is the **Resurrection.**

Through his Death and Resurrection, Jesus Christ saved us from the power of sin and death. Jesus is our Savior. **Savior** is a title given to Jesus because he died and rose from the dead to save us. Jesus promised that his faithful followers would also share in his Resurrection and have eternal life. Through Jesus Christ, our risen Savior, we have new life—we share in God's own life now and have the hope of living with God forever.

Each year we celebrate the Feast of the Resurrection of Jesus Christ on Easter Sunday.

How do you think Jesus' disciples felt when they heard that he had risen from the dead?

22

## Optional Activity

Make a poster. On a large sheet of paper, draw a picture of Jesus' empty tomb. Have the students suggest different words or phrases to describe what Jesus' Death and Resurrection meant for the world. Write these words or phrases on strips of yellow paper cut to resemble beams of light. Then paste or glue the beams of light emanating from the tomb. Display the poster in the prayer space.

## Review

**Write *True* or *False* next to the following sentences. On a separate piece of paper, change the false sentences to make them true.**

1. False Jesus and his disciples went to ~~Egypt~~ Jerusalem to celebrate the Feast of Passover.
2. True Jesus gave himself to us in the Eucharist on the night before he died.
3. False ~~Most~~ Only a few of Jesus' disciples stayed with Jesus as he died on the cross.
4. True The women disciples shared the news about Jesus rising.

**Discuss the following.** (See side column.)

5. Why were Jesus and his disciples in Jerusalem during the week before he died?
6. Why did some powerful leaders have Jesus arrested and sentenced to death?
7. What did Jesus do for us through his Death and Resurrection?

Last Supper (page 20)
Real Presence (page 20)
Resurrection (page 22)
Savior (page 22)

## With My Family

### Sharing Our Faith

**Jesus gave us the Eucharist at the Last Supper.**

**Jesus died on the cross to save us from sin.**

**3 Jesus rose from the dead and brought us new life.**

### PRAYING TOGETHER

At Mass after the bread and wine are changed into the Body and Blood of Christ, the priest invites us to proclaim our faith. Here are two of the acclamations we pray:

**Lord, by your cross and resurrection**
**you have set us free.**
**You are the Savior of the world.**

**Dying you destroyed our death,**
**Rising you restored our life.**
**Lord Jesus, come in glory.**

Pray these acclamations often during the week. Remember all that Jesus has done for us by his Death on the cross and his Resurrection.

### Living Our Faith

In this chapter you learned that as Jesus was dying on the cross, he forgave those who crucified him. With your family talk about the importance of forgiveness. If there are people who have hurt you or treated you unfairly, forgive them by talking with them or by forgiving them in your heart. Ask forgiveness of any person whom you have hurt.

23

# Conclusion (__ min.)

### Review

Provide five to ten minutes for the students to work independently to complete the first part of the *Review*. Check the students' answers. Then discuss the questions in the second part of the *Review*. Possible responses follow.

**5.** Jesus and his disciples were in Jerusalem to celebrate the Passover. This is the feast in which the Jewish people remember and celebrate God's delivering their ancestors from slavery and death in Egypt.

**6.** They did not believe Jesus was the Son of God.

**7.** Through Jesus' Death and Resurrection he saved us from the power of sin and death. We have new life now and have the hope of living with God forever.

***Faith Words***

Have the students look up each word in the Glossary in the back of the text. Then ask volunteers to use each word in a sentence.

***More for You to Know***

The articles on page 24, Unit 1: *More for You to Know*, provide additional or supplemental information related to concepts presented in Chapters 1–3: Divine Revelation, the Bible, and Tradition.

### With My Family

***Sharing Our Faith***

Encourage the students to share with their families what they have learned in this chapter.

***Praying Together***

Read the two acclamations and ask students to pray these words often.

***Living Our Faith***

Encourage the students to discuss with their families ways of forgiving and asking for forgiveness.

## CATECHISM FOCUS

"The Resurrection of Jesus is the crowning truth of our faith in Christ, a faith believed and lived as the central truth by the first Christian community; handed on as fundamental by Tradition; established by the documents of the New Testament; and preached as an essential part of the Paschal mystery along with the cross." *(CCC, 638)*

# MORE for You to Know

**DIVINE REVELATION** God loves us so much that he told us about himself. He revealed himself to us. To *reveal* means "to make known." Divine Revelation is God's making himself known to us through his mighty deeds and by his interactions with his people throughout time.

God made himself known gradually over time. Revelation began with the creation of the first human beings and their descendants. It continued through the time of the ancient Israelites and the Jewish people. God's Revelation is full and complete in his only Son, Jesus Christ. The Church is guided by the Holy Spirit to understand God's Revelation. God's Revelation is handed down through the Bible and Tradition.

**THE BIBLE AND TRADITION** The Bible, also called Sacred Scripture, is the written record of God's Revelation. The Bible has a divine author, God, and many human writers. The Holy Spirit guided these writers as they wrote. The special guidance that the Holy Spirit gave to the human writers is called *Divine Inspiration*. It guaranteed that they wrote without any error God's saving truth. For that reason, God is the true author of the Bible.

The word *bible* means "books." The Bible is made up of seventy-three separate books. It is divided into two parts: the Old Testament and the New Testament. They contain Salvation history.

The Old Testament contains forty-six books. In the Old Testament we learn about God's relationship with the people of Israel.

The New Testament contains twenty-seven books. In the New Testament we learn about Jesus Christ, his first followers, and the beginning of the Church. The four Gospels of the New Testament contain the message and key events in the life of Jesus Christ. Because of this, the Gospels hold a central place in the New Testament.

*Tradition* is the Revelation of the Good News of Jesus Christ as lived out in the Church, past and present. Tradition includes teachings and practices handed on orally from the time of Jesus and his Apostles. It includes the creeds, or statements, of Christian beliefs.

# UNIT 1 Assessment

**Write *True* or *False* next to the following sentences. On a separate sheet of paper, change the false sentences to make them true.**

1. True We call the Bible the Word of God.
2. True The Blessed Trinity is the central belief of our faith.
3. False ~~No one~~ Mary, John, and a few women disciples stayed with Jesus as he died on the cross.
4. True Human beings are born with Original Sin.
5. False The ~~disciples~~ Apostles were the twelve men whom Jesus chose to share in his mission in a special way.

**Put the following biblical events in the order in which they happened. Use numbers 1–5.**

6. God promised to send a Savior. 1
7. At the Last Supper, Jesus gave us the gift of himself in the Eucharist. 4
8. Jesus shared the Good News of God's love. 3
9. Jesus was crucified, died, and rose from the dead. 5
10. Jesus, God's own Son, became man. 2

**Write your responses on a separate sheet of paper.**

11. Name two ways Jesus spread the Good News of God's love. See page 15 of Chapter 2.
12. What is the Kingdom of God? the power of God's love active in our lives and in the world
13. What is the Incarnation? the truth that God the Son, the second Person of the Blessed Trinity, became man
14. Who are the three Persons of the Blessed Trinity? God the Father, God the Son, and God the Holy Spirit
15. What did Jesus do for us through his Death and Resurrection? Through his Death and Resurrection, Jesus Christ saved us from the power of sin and death.

# Chapter 4

## GOALS

*to understand that the Holy Spirit came to guide Jesus' disciples in continuing his mission; to appreciate that the Holy Spirit is with the Church always*

## GETTING READY

**Opening Prayer:** *Have index cards available.*

**Materials Needed:** *highlighters or colored pencils, poster board, magazines and newspapers, markers, paste or glue for* ***Optional Activity*** *(page 29)*

## Catechist Background

How does the Holy Spirit strengthen you to follow Jesus?

Jesus knew that, after he returned to his Father in Heaven, his Apostles and disciples would need the gifts of patience, guidance, and courage to continue his mission. On the night before he died, Jesus promised to send the Holy Spirit to help them and guide them. He told his followers, "The Advocate, the holy Spirit that the Father will send in my name— he will teach you everything and remind you of all that [I] told you" (John 14:26).

## Opening Prayer

Invite the students to gather in the prayer space. Ask them to think about the people who help and guide them in living as Jesus' disciples. Offer the following prayer, having the students pray the response "Lord, we thank you" after each of the following petitions:

- *For the people who show us your love and care*
- *For the people who teach us the truths of our faith*
- *For the people who guide us in following Jesus' example.*

Then invite volunteers to add their own petitions.

Have index cards available. Give one to each student. Invite the students to write on the cards the names of those who help them. Collect the cards and place them on the table in the prayer space.

# 4 The Holy Spirit Is Sent to Help Us

### A Family Helper

After dinner Brian was doing his homework. His older brother Kevin walked into the family room. He asked, "Brian, what do you have for homework tonight?"

Brian answered, "Right now I'm completing a writing assignment. I'm writing about a person I admire, and I'm giving a few reasons for my choice."

Kevin asked, "Who are you writing about?"

"Surprise, Kevin! I'm writing about you," Brian answered.

Kevin pointed to himself and said, "Me? Why are you writing about me?"

Brian explained, "You do a lot for me, Kevin. You really came to the rescue when Dad told us we were moving to Springfield. Do you remember how upset I was? I ran outside and sat on the back steps. You were upset, too, but you came outside and talked to me. You helped calm me down, especially when you told me to think about moving as an adventure. You told me we'd have new places to explore and new friends to meet."

"That wasn't a big deal," Kevin said.

"It was a big deal to me," Brian answered. "Then after we moved you watched out for me. That first week of school was the hardest for me, but you waited for me every day after school.

At Pentecost the disciples experienced the transforming power of the Holy Spirit. He strengthened them to proclaim the Good News of Jesus. The Church, founded by Jesus Christ, continued to grow. Many were baptized and received the Gift of the Holy Spirit.

The Holy Spirit continues to set in motion the mission of the Church to proclaim the Good News of Jesus Christ. This year you have accepted the challenge and responsibility to respond to the prompting of the Holy Spirit by teaching young people about the truths of our faith. Be assured that the Holy Spirit is with you as your source of wisdom, patience, and guidance.

## Reflection

"For this reason I kneel before the Father, from whom every family in heaven and on earth is named, that he may grant you in accord with the riches of his glory to be strengthened with power through his Spirit in the inner self, and that Christ may dwell in your hearts through faith. . . ."

*(Ephesians 3:14–17)*

You stayed with me at the first Nature Scout meeting we went to, and you introduced me to some of the scouts you knew from school."

Kevin said, "I only did what I thought an older brother should do. Now let's see what you think about your older brother when I win a game of chess. Whoever loses helps with the dishes every night this week!"

How did Kevin help Brian?

Who are your family helpers?

How do they help your family?

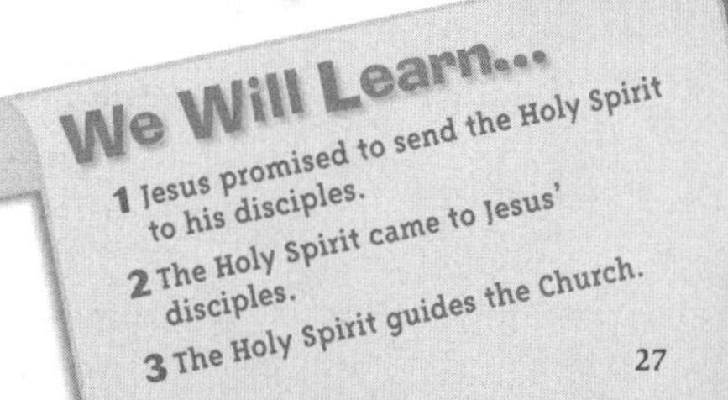




## Introduction ( ___ min.)

Ask the students to think about the last time they needed help and who helped them. Then invite volunteers to read the story "A Family Helper."

Have the students identify the ways that Kevin helped Brian. Then discuss with the students who their family helpers are. Ask each student to think about the last time he or she helped out a family member. Also discuss why it is important for members of families to help and guide each other.

### We Will Learn...

**Remind the students that the Holy Spirit is the third Person of the Blessed Trinity. Then point out that when it was time for the risen Jesus to return to his Father in Heaven, he promised to send the Holy Spirit to guide his disciples. Ask a volunteer to read the three faith statements on the scroll.**

# Presentation ( __ min.)

## 1 Jesus promised to send the Holy Spirit to his disciples.

*Jesus, thank you for being with us always.*

You may want to begin by reading one of the following Scripture accounts of the risen Christ's appearances to his disciples:

- the disciples on the road to Emmaus (Luke 24:13–35)
- the appearance to the disciples in Jerusalem (Luke 24: 36–49 and/or John 20:19–29)
- or Jesus on the beach (John 21:1–19).

After reading, point out that Jesus wanted the disciples to be confident in continuing to spread the Good News of God's love.

Have volunteers read aloud the first two paragraphs. Stress Jesus' promise to be with us always.

Explain to the students what we mean by Jesus' Ascension. Then tell the students that after the Ascension the disciples returned to Jerusalem to await the coming of the Holy Spirit.

### 1 Jesus promised to send the Holy Spirit to his disciples.

Jesus knew that after his work on earth was complete his disciples would need help in living as he had asked them to live. Jesus promised that the Holy Spirit would come to them and strengthen them. The Holy Spirit would help the disciples to remember all that Jesus had taught them.

After Jesus' Death and Resurrection, he appeared to his disciples several times. Then forty days after he rose from the dead, Jesus called his Apostles to a mountain in Galilee. He told them that he wanted them to continue his mission to bring the Good News of God's love to the world. Jesus said, "Go, therefore, and make disciples of all nations, baptizing them in the name of the Father, and of the Son, and of the holy Spirit, teaching them to observe all that I have commanded you. And behold, I am with you always, until the end of the age" (Matthew 28:19–20).

After Jesus gave this mission to the Apostles, he returned to his Father in Heaven. Jesus' return in all his glory to his Father in Heaven is called the Ascension.

After Jesus' Ascension, the Apostles returned to Jerusalem. There with the other disciples they prayed as they waited for the Holy Spirit to come to them.

Why did Jesus promise his disciples that the Holy Spirit would come to them?

What was the mission Jesus gave to his Apostles?

28

Read aloud the concluding questions. Pause briefly to allow time for students to reflect on the question. Then invite volunteers to share their responses. For the first question possible responses include: the Holy Spirit would help them to follow Jesus' example; the Holy Spirit would give them strength and courage in continuing Jesus' mission. For the second question, have the students highlight or underline the words from Scripture in the second paragraph.

## Liturgy Connection

Every year the Church celebrates Jesus' Ascension forty days after Easter Sunday. In some dioceses the feast is celebrated on the Sunday before Pentecost Sunday. On the feast of the Ascension we gather with our parish community for Mass. See *The Liturgical Year* on page 99. Talk with your students about other ways they and their families can observe this holy day.

## 2 The Holy Spirit came to Jesus' disciples.

Early on Sunday morning, fifty days after Jesus rose from the dead, Jesus' disciples were together in Jerusalem. They were praying and waiting for the Holy Spirit. As they prayed, something amazing happened. "And suddenly there came from the sky a noise like a strong driving wind, and it filled the entire house in which they were. Then there appeared to them tongues as of fire, which parted and came to rest on each one of them. And they were all filled with the holy Spirit and began to speak in different tongues, as the Spirit enabled them to proclaim." (Acts of the Apostles 2:2–4)

On this day Peter and the disciples were no longer afraid to speak about Jesus and his teachings. They left the house and went out into the streets. Crowds of people were in Jerusalem to celebrate a great Jewish feast. Peter spoke to these people, telling them to be baptized and thus to receive the Gift of the Holy Spirit. "Those who accepted his message were baptized, and about three thousand persons were added that day." (Acts of the Apostles 2:41)

The day the Holy Spirit came upon Jesus' disciples is called **Pentecost**. It was on this day that the Church began. The **Church** is the community of people who are baptized and follow Jesus Christ. On Pentecost and throughout the whole year we remember that the Holy Spirit is with the Church always.

How did the Holy Spirit help Peter and the disciples on Pentecost?



## 2 The Holy Spirit came to Jesus' disciples.

*Holy Spirit, fill us with courage and love.*

Invite the students to focus on the Scripture art. Ask: *What do you think is happening in the picture?* Have volunteers share their responses.

Have the students remain focused on the art as you read aloud the first two paragraphs. Point out that Mary, the mother of Jesus, was with the disciples when the Holy Spirit came to them. Explain that when the disciples began to speak to the crowds, they spoke in different languages.

This symbolized that from her very beginning the Church's mission is worldwide. If time permits, have the students act out the actions of the disciples after they received the Holy Spirit.

Point out that about three thousand people were baptized that day. Explain that the day on which the Holy Spirit came to the disciples is called Pentecost. Emphasize that it was on this day that the Church began. Have the students highlight or underline the definition of *Church*. Ask the students to point to themselves and say: *We are baptized. We are followers of Jesus Christ. We are the Church.*

Read the concluding question. Ask volunteers to share their responses. Possible responses include: the Holy Spirit helped them to be brave enough to speak to all the people gathered in the streets of Jerusalem; the Holy Spirit helped the disciples remember all that Jesus had taught them.

### Optional Activity

Have the students work in small groups to make prayer to the Holy Spirit collages. Provide each group with poster board, magazines, and newspapers. Instruct each group to print the prayer on the poster and illustrate it with magazine or newspaper photos. Display the completed posters in the prayer space.

## The Holy Spirit guides the Church.

*Holy Spirit, help us to live in unity and love.*

You may want to introduce the material on this page by reading about the early Christians as described in Acts of the Apostles 2:42–47.

Ask a volunteer to read the first two paragraphs. Have the students highlight or underline Saint Peter's description of the Church.

Explain to the students that Saint Peter and the other Apostles traveled to distant places spreading the Good News of God's love to all. If a world map or globe is available, point out some of the places where the Apostles traveled to—where the countries of Greece, Turkey, and Italy are today.

Ask a volunteer to read the third and fourth paragraphs. Stress that the Holy Spirit continues to help and guide the Church today.

For additional information about Scripture and Tradition, refer to Unit 1: *More for You to Know* on page 24.

### 3 The Holy Spirit guides the Church.

Jesus had chosen the Apostle Peter as the head of the Church. On Pentecost, the Holy Spirit filled Peter and the other disciples of Jesus with courage and love. With the help of the Holy Spirit, they began to share the Good News of Jesus Christ with everyone they met. They showed others how to live according to the teachings of Jesus by:

- sharing what they had with the poor
- taking care of those who were sick or disabled
- gathering together to pray
- celebrating the Eucharist in Jesus' memory
- celebrating the presence of the risen Christ among them.

More and more people asked to be baptized. They wanted to follow Jesus and to be part of his community—to be members of the Church. The Apostle Peter described the Church as "God's people" (1 Peter 2:10) —the people baptized as God's children, brothers and sisters of Jesus.

With the guidance of the Holy Spirit, the Church spread throughout the world. The Holy Spirit helped the Church, the People of God, to love God and one another.

The Holy Spirit helped the members of the Church to share the Good News of Jesus Christ with everyone in the world. And the Holy Spirit continues to help and guide the Church today in the interpretation of Sacred Scripture and in the official teachings of the Church, which we call Tradition. Through Tradition the Holy Spirit teaches us to pray.

How did the Holy Spirit help the early Christians?

#### Do You Know?

The early Christians needed to understand the special relationship Jesus Christ had with his community, the Church. Saint Paul, an early Christian who traveled to different countries sharing the Good News of Jesus Christ, explained that the Church is the Body of Christ (1 Corinthians 12:27). Christ is the Head (Colossians 1:18), but everyone in the Church is an important part of the Body of Christ.

Each member of the Church receives the Holy Spirit at Baptism. Saint Paul also taught that the Church is the Temple of the Holy Spirit (1 Corinthians 3:16). So the Holy Spirit is at the heart of the Church's life and growth, uniting us through our love for and belief in Jesus Christ.

30

Invite volunteers to respond to the concluding question. Possible responses include that the Holy Spirit strengthened and guided the early Christians to do all the things that are listed in the first paragraph.

### Do You Know?

Before you present *Do You Know?* you may want to tell the students the story of Saint Paul's conversion (Acts of the Apostles 9:1–19). Then read aloud the *Do You Know?* Stress that the Church is the Body of Christ and the Temple of the Holy Spirit.

## Review

Complete the following sentences.

1–2. The Ascension is
Jesus' return in all his glory
to his Father in Heaven.

3–4. The Church is
the community of people
who are baptized and follow
Jesus Christ.

Discuss the following. (See side column.)

5. Before he returned to Heaven, what did Jesus ask his disciples to do?
6. Describe briefly what happened on Pentecost.
7. How did the early Christians share their love for God and one another?

Ascension (page 28)
Pentecost (page 29)
Church (page 29)

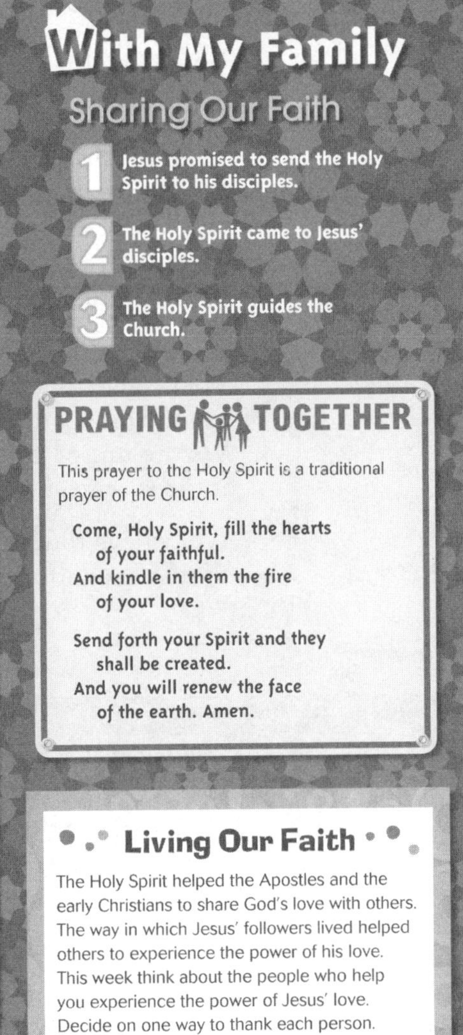

## With My Family

### Sharing Our Faith

1. Jesus promised to send the Holy Spirit to his disciples.
2. The Holy Spirit came to Jesus' disciples.
3. The Holy Spirit guides the Church.

### PRAYING TOGETHER

This prayer to the Holy Spirit is a traditional prayer of the Church.

**Come, Holy Spirit, fill the hearts**
**of your faithful.**
**And kindle in them the fire**
**of your love.**

**Send forth your Spirit and they**
**shall be created.**
**And you will renew the face**
**of the earth. Amen.**

### Living Our Faith

The Holy Spirit helped the Apostles and the early Christians to share God's love with others. The way in which Jesus' followers lived helped others to experience the power of his love. This week think about the people who help you experience the power of Jesus' love. Decide on one way to thank each person.

| Name | Way of Thanks |
|---|---|
| | |
| | |



# Conclusion (__ min.)

### Review

Provide five to ten minutes for the students to work independently to complete the first part of the *Review*. Check the student's answers. Discuss the questions in the second part of the *Review*. Possible responses follow.

**5.** Jesus asked his disciples to continue his mission, which was to bring the Good News of God's love to the world.

**6.** The disciples were praying as they waited for the Holy Spirit to come to them. Suddenly they heard a sound like the wind, and tongues of fire appeared above their heads. The disciples were filled with the Holy Spirit.

**7.** See page 30 for the bulleted list of possible responses.

***Faith Words***

Ask the students to write a sentence for each Faith Word.

### With My Family

***Sharing Our Faith***

Encourage the students to share with their families what they have learned about Jesus' Ascension, the coming of the Holy Spirit on Pentecost, and the beginning of the Church.

***Praying Together***

Read the prayer together. Discuss the meaning of the verses. Then encourage the students to share with their families this traditional prayer of the Church. Also ask them to discuss with their families what the words of the prayer mean to them.

***Living Our Faith***

Have a volunteer read the activity directions. Encourage the students to work with their families in identifying people who help them experience the power of God's love. Also encourage the students to thank the people in the ways that have been suggested.

## CATECHISM FOCUS

**"The mission of Christ and the Holy Spirit is brought to completion in the Church, which is the Body of Christ and the Temple of the Holy Spirit. This joint mission henceforth brings Christ's faithful to share in his communion with the Father in the Holy Spirit." (*CCC*, 737)**

**For additional reference and reflection, see *CCC*, 731–736.**

# Chapter 5

## GOALS

*to learn that all authority and ministry in the Church comes from Christ; to identify the various levels of authority and ministries in the Church; to appreciate the Church in her four marks, or characteristics*

## GETTING READY

**Opening Prayer:** *In the prayer space, display a globe or world map.*

**Materials Needed:** *copies of diocesan newspaper (page 34), world map or globe (pages 34–35), parish bulletin (page 36) Invite a member of the parish leadership team to speak to students. (See **Optional Activity** on page 36.)*

## Catechist Background

The Church is the community of people who believe in Jesus Christ, have been baptized in him, and follow his teachings. This community has distinctive characteristics which are called the Marks of the Church. We acknowledge these marks at Mass each time we pray the Nicene Creed. We profess our belief that the Church is one, holy, catholic, and apostolic.

We believe that the Church is one. We are gathered around one Lord, Jesus Christ, through one Baptism. We are united by the pope, the Bishop of Rome, who is the successor of Saint Peter.

We believe that the Church is holy because God shared his holiness with all people by sending his

## Opening Prayer

Display a globe or a world map in the prayer space. Invite the students to gather there. Have them bring their student texts with them.

Ask the students to focus on the globe or map. Read aloud:

"The community of believers was of one heart and mind"
(Acts of the Apostles 4:32).

Pause briefly and ask the students to reflect on what it means for a community to live as though they were of "one heart and mind."

Then ask the students to open their texts and pray together the Apostles' Creed. (See page 121.)

# 5 The Catholic Church Continues Christ's Mission

## What Do You Think?

Imagine that talk-show hosts are interviewing you. Write your response to each of the following questions on the lines provided.

Discuss these questions with family members and friends.

Why are leaders necessary?

______________________________

______________________________.

What are some words that describe good leaders?

______________________________

______________________________.

Son Jesus Christ to us. Christ shares his holiness through the Church. The Holy Spirit is present in the Church and guides her in holiness.

We believe that the Church is catholic, or universal. Christ came for all people, everywhere and has sent his disciples "into the whole world" to proclaim the Gospel (Mark 16:15).

We believe that the Church is apostolic. The life and leadership of the Church is based on that of the Apostles. The pope, the Bishop of Rome, and the bishops carry out the Apostles' mission given to them by Jesus Christ. As baptized Catholics and members of the Church, we, too, are encouraged to share in this work of spreading the Good News of the Kingdom of God.

## Reflection

"In obedience to the divine command, the apostles, their successors, and their disciples have responded through the ages by enthusiastically proclaiming the Gospel message to the whole world. That fundamental mission is always inseparable from the person of Jesus Christ." *(National Directory for Catechesis, Introduction)*

Who are some good leaders you know?

______________________________

______________________________.

How can you develop good leadership skills?

______________________________

______________________________.

**We Will Learn...**

1 The pope and bishops are the successors of the Apostles.

2 The Church is one, holy, catholic, and apostolic.

3 Catholics worship and serve together.

33

## Introduction ( ___ min.)

Tell the students that today you are going to discuss leadership. Point out that there are leaders in every aspect of life—in our families, in school, in our teams and clubs, and in government.

Read the activity questions. Give the students time to work independently in writing their responses. Then invite pairs of students to take turns presenting their answers in the talk-show format suggested.

With the students compile a list of the qualities of a good leader. Provide a minute of silence for the students to reflect and identify the qualities they see in themselves.

### We Will Learn...

Remind the students that Jesus appointed the Apostles to lead his disciples. Have a volunteer read the three faith statements on the scroll.

# Presentation ( __ min.)

## 1 The pope and the bishops are the successors of the Apostles.

*Holy Spirit, guide the leaders of the Church.*

Begin by asking: *Who were the leaders of the Church when it first began?* Remind the students that Jesus had chosen the Apostles to lead his disciples. He chose Saint Peter to lead the entire Church. To Peter he gave the keys of the Church. See Matthew 16:18-19.

Have volunteers read the first two paragraphs. Point out that the Apostles chose other leaders to take their place. They designated them as leaders by laying their hands on these men's heads and asking for the Holy Spirit to guide them.

Read aloud the third paragraph. Identify for the students the diocese in which they live and who the bishop of the diocese is. If possible, have available a few copies of your diocesan newspaper. Show pictures of your bishop that are in the newspaper and tell about diocesan activities described in it.

Read aloud the fourth paragraph. Explain that the pope lives in Vatican City which is located within the city of Rome, Italy. Locate the city on a world map. Point out that Vatican City is the pastoral and administrative center of the worldwide Church.

**Note:** You may want the students to learn more about the leadership roles of the pope and bishops. See the paragraphs about the Magisterium and the infallibility of the pope on page 44, Unit 2: *More for You to Know.*

Read the concluding questions. Remind the students of the names of the current pope and the bishop of your diocese.

### 1 The pope and bishops are the successors of the Apostles.

After the coming of the Holy Spirit on Pentecost, the Apostles traveled from place to place teaching what Jesus had taught them. In each local community the Apostles baptized people as Jesus had commanded them. The members of these communities looked to Peter and the other Apostles as their leaders.

The Apostles eventually chose local leaders to serve these communities. The Apostles laid their hands on the heads of those they had chosen and asked the Holy Spirit to strengthen and guide these new leaders in their work. In this way the Apostles handed on what Christ had given to them: the authority to carry on his mission.

As time passed, the leaders who succeeded, or took the place of, the Apostles were called *bishops*. **Bishops** are the successors of the Apostles and continue to lead the Church. Each local area of the Church is called a **diocese** and is led by a bishop.

The **pope** is the bishop of the diocese of Rome, Italy. He continues the leadership of the Apostle Peter, having a God-given responsibility to care for the souls of all members of the Church. Together with all the bishops, the pope leads and guides the whole Catholic Church. Under the leadership of the pope and bishops, the Church continues the work of Jesus Christ each and every day. Each of us is united with the pope and bishops in living out our faith.

Who is our present pope?

Who is the bishop of your diocese?

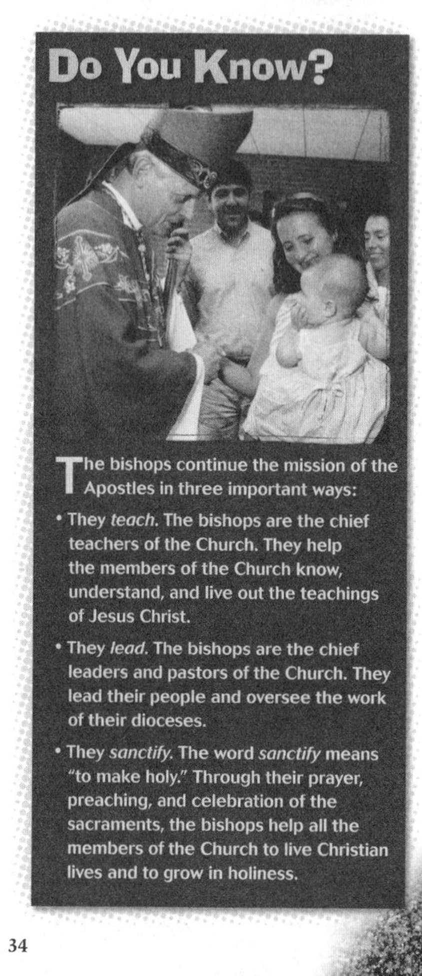

**Do You Know?**

The bishops continue the mission of the Apostles in three important ways:

- They *teach.* The bishops are the chief teachers of the Church. They help the members of the Church know, understand, and live out the teachings of Jesus Christ.
- They *lead.* The bishops are the chief leaders and pastors of the Church. They lead their people and oversee the work of their dioceses.
- They *sanctify.* The word *sanctify* means "to make holy." Through their prayer, preaching, and celebration of the sacraments, the bishops help all the members of the Church to live Christian lives and to grow in holiness.

34

## Do You Know?

Read aloud the feature. Stress the three ways the bishops continue Christ's mission today. For more information about the role of the pope and bishops, see *The Sacrament of Holy Orders* on pages 110–111 of the student text.

## 2 The Church is one, holy, catholic, and apostolic.

In the Catholic Church, the Church of Christ is truly present although elements of goodness and truth can be found outside of her. The Catholic Church has four very special qualities or characteristics. The Church is one, holy, catholic, and apostolic. These four characteristics that describe the Church are called the **Marks of the Church**.

The Church is *one*. The Church is one because all of her members believe in the one Lord, Jesus Christ. We share the same Baptism and are guided and united by the Holy Spirit. Under the leadership of the pope and bishops, we gather together to celebrate the sacraments and to live and work together as one community called together by God.

The Church is *holy*. God alone is all good and holy. But he shared his holiness with all people by sending his Son, Jesus Christ to us. As members of the Church, baptized into the Body of Christ, we, too, through the power of the Holy Spirit, share in God's life which makes us holy.

As members of the Church we grow in holiness, especially through prayer, good works, and the celebration of the sacraments.

The Church is *catholic*. The word *catholic* means "universal." The Church is universal, or open to all people, since everyone is invited and welcomed to become members of the Church. All people are invited to be followers of Jesus Christ. Today there are Catholics on every continent and in every country of the world.

The Church is *apostolic*. This means that the Church was built on the faith of the Apostles and continues to be guided by their successors, the bishops. The Church is apostolic today because the life and leadership of the Church is based on that of the Apostles' mission which was given to them by Jesus. As baptized Catholics, disciples of Jesus, we, too, share in the work of spreading the Good News of Jesus Christ to all the world.

In your own words describe what each of the Marks of the Church means.

35

## 2 The Church is one, holy, catholic, and apostolic.

*Holy Spirit, help us to be a welcoming community.*

Ask the students to think about the groups to which they belong: scout troop, band, sports team, group of friends, family. Ask each student to choose one group and think about words they would use to describe the group in a positive way. Then ask a few volunteers to present their group descriptions to all the students.

Explain that the Church has four qualities or characteristics that describe the community. These four characteristics are called the Marks of the Church. The Church is one, holy, catholic, and apostolic.

Have the students look at a world map or globe. Point out that all Catholics in all the countries throughout the world are united, or one. Then ask a volunteer to read the second paragraph.

Ask the students to reflect on what it means to be holy. Have a few students share their responses. Then ask a volunteer to read the third paragraph.

Ask the students to focus again on the world map or globe. Point out that the word *catholic* means "universal." Remind the students that the Church has spread throughout the world. She is universal, or catholic. This was the mission of the Apostles—spreading the Gospel throughout the world. Thus, the Church is apostolic. Then ask volunteers to read the last two paragraphs. Emphasize that through our Baptism we, too, share in the work of spreading the Good News of Jesus Christ.

Read aloud the concluding question. Invite a few volunteers to share their responses.

### Liturgy Connection

**Explain that the prayers of the Mass and the celebrations of the other sacraments are exactly the same throughout the world. But these prayers are prayed in the language of the people of a particular country or area. For example, in Poland the prayers of the Mass are prayed in Polish. You may also want to point out that Latin is the official language of the Church. The words of the Mass may at certain times be prayed in Latin in any of the countries of the world.**

## 3 Catholics worship and serve together.

*Holy Spirit, guide the people of our parish.*

Have the students work in pairs. Ask each pair to write a caption for the photograph on this page. Have the sets of partners share their captions with the entire group. Point out that the partners worked together on the assignment and then shared with the group of students. Explain that they have just done what the people of a parish do—work together and share with others.

Ask a volunteer to read the first two paragraphs. Then draw a circle on a large sheet of paper. Inside the circle write the name of your parish and some of the other parishes in your area. On the outside of the circle, print the name of your diocese. Explain that your parish is one of many in the diocese.

Draw another large circle on a large sheet of paper. Ask the students: *Who are some of the people in our parish?* Help the students name the people and their roles in the parish. Write the names in the circle. Point out that the students should include their own names.

Read aloud the remaining text. For more about the ordained ministry, see *The Sacrament of Holy Orders* on pages 110–111 of the student text.

Stress the importance of participating in parish activities. Have a volunteer reread the second paragraph. Then pause and invite the students to reflect quietly on the concluding question. Ask them to decide on one or two ways in which they will participate in the parish community this week.

### 3 Catholics worship and serve together.

A **parish** is a community of believers. It is made up of Catholics who usually live in the same town or neighborhood. A parish is part of a diocese. Members of a parish gather together in Jesus' name to worship God and to share with one another.

In parishes, members gather together to:

- celebrate Mass and the other sacraments
- pray and grow in their faith
- share what they have—money, time, talents—with one another
- care for people in need—those who are sick, poor, or hungry.

Priests work in the parishes of a diocese. **Priests** preach the Gospel and serve the faithful, especially by celebrating the Eucharist and the other sacraments. They are baptized men who have been ordained to this ministry in the Sacrament of Holy Orders. Priests work with the bishop of their diocese. A **pastor** is the priest who leads the parish in worship, prayer, teaching, and service. His most important work is to lead the parish in the celebration of Mass. A parish might also have other priests who work with the pastor.

Sometimes a parish has a deacon. A **deacon** is a baptized man who in the Sacrament of Holy Orders has been ordained to serve the Church by preaching, baptizing, performing marriages, and doing acts of charity. He carries on his responsibilities under the authority of the bishop and in cooperation with the bishop and his priests.

In many parishes lay people, men and women who are not ordained, serve in various roles. Lay ecclesial ministers are lay people who serve in leadership positions and are recognized and appointed by the Church.

It is important to remember that each person is an important part of the parish.

How will you participate in the parish community this week?

36

## Optional Activity

**Invite a member of your parish leadership team to speak to the students about his or her role in the parish. Also ask the speaker to explain to the students how each of them is important to the parish.**

## Review

**Write *True* or *False* next to the following sentences. On a separate piece of paper, change the false sentences to make them true.**

1. False The word ~~catholic~~ apostolic means "founded on the Apostles."
2. True The pope continues the leadership of the Apostle Peter.
3. False The successors of the Apostles were given the title ~~deacon~~ bishop.
4. False The Catholic Church is ~~only~~ open to ~~a certain number of~~ all people.

**Discuss the following.** (See side column.)

5. How did the Apostles give their successors the authority Jesus had given to them?
6. Name the four Marks of the Church and briefly describe each one.
7. For what reasons do parish members come together?

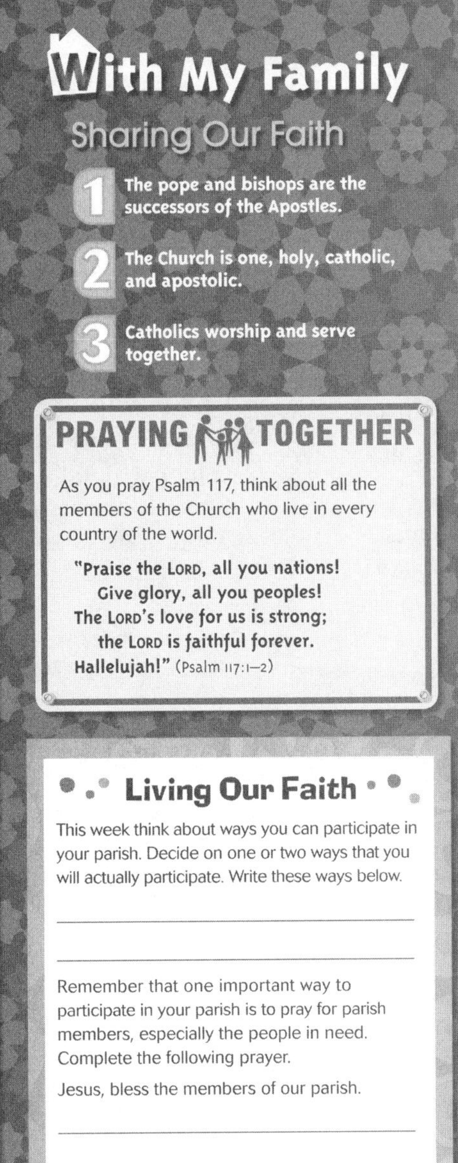

## With My Family

### Sharing Our Faith

1. The pope and bishops are the successors of the Apostles.
2. The Church is one, holy, catholic, and apostolic.
3. Catholics worship and serve together.

### PRAYING TOGETHER

As you pray Psalm 117, think about all the members of the Church who live in every country of the world.

**"Praise the LORD, all you nations!**
**Give glory, all you peoples!**
**The LORD's love for us is strong;**
**the LORD is faithful forever.**
**Hallelujah!"** (Psalm 117:1–2)

### Living Our Faith

This week think about ways you can participate in your parish. Decide on one or two ways that you will actually participate. Write these ways below.

________________________________

________________________________

Remember that one important way to participate in your parish is to pray for parish members, especially the people in need. Complete the following prayer.

Jesus, bless the members of our parish.

________________________________

________________________________

37

# Conclusion ( __ min.)

### Review

Provide five to ten minutes for the students to work independently to complete the first part of the *Review*. Check the students' responses. Then discuss the questions in the second part of the *Review*. Possible responses follow.

**5.** The Apostles laid their hands on the heads of those they had chosen and asked the Holy Spirit to strengthen and guide the new leaders in their work.

**6.** One, holy, catholic and apostolic; See the descriptions on page 35.

**7.** See the bulleted list on page 36.

***Faith Words***

Have volunteers do role-plays of emcees introducing a *bishop*, *priest*, *pastor*, and *deacon* to an audience. Ask each volunteer to introduce one of these Church leaders, explaining what the leader does to help the Church community.

### With My Family

***Sharing Our Faith***

Encourage the students to share with their families what they have learned about Church leadership, the roles of the pope and bishops, the four Marks of the Church, and ways Catholics worship God and serve God and others.

***Prayer Together***

Explain that a psalm is a song of praise from the Bible. There are 150 song prayers in the Book of Psalms. Pray the psalm verse together. Encourage the students to share with their families this psalm of praise.

***Living Our Faith***

Encourage the students to work with their families in writing the prayer and praying it together during the week.

## CATECHISM FOCUS

**"... it is Christ who, through the Holy Spirit,makes his Church one, holy, catholic, and apostolic, and it is he who calls her to realize each of these qualities."** (*CCC*, 811)

**For additional reference and reflection, see *CCC*, 866–869 and 934–945.**

# Chapter 6

## GOALS

*to learn that God shares his life and love with us through the sacraments; to recognize and appreciate Jesus' gift of the sacraments and their importance to us as members of the Church*

## GETTING READY

**Opening Prayer:** *On the prayer table, place a Bible, a cross or crucifix, a battery-operated candle, and a bowl of holy water.*

**Materials Needed:** *a large sheet of paper (pages 38–39), highlighters or colored pencils, a large sheet of paper for* ***Optional Activity*** *(page 42)*

## Catechist Background

Jesus is the ultimate sign of God's love. Throughout the Gospels we read that Jesus' physical actions had a spiritual effect.

When the risen Christ returned to his Father in Heaven, he left his followers empowered by the Holy Spirit to form the Church. Thus the Church became the sacrament, or outward sign, of the risen Christ. Baptized in the name of the Father, the Son, and the Holy Spirit, the first Christians gathered to celebrate God's love in the Eucharist. Gradually, the Church discerned that there are specifically Seven Sacraments instituted by Christ.

## Opening Prayer

Explain to the young people that today you will begin by celebrating God's great love. Ask the students to process to the prayer space as you pray aloud Psalm 100:1–2, 5. Have the students repeat each verse.

*"Shout joyfully to the Lord, all*
*you lands;*
*worship the Lord with cries*
*of gladness;*
*Give thanks to God, bless his name;*
*good indeed is the Lord,*
*Whose love endures forever,*
*whose faithfulness lasts*
*through every age."*

Then read aloud: *"For where two or three are gathered together in my name, there am I in the midst of them"* (Matthew 18:20).

Ask the students to pray: *Jesus, thank you for being with us always.*

# 6 The Church Celebrates Seven Sacraments

### DIFFERENT SIGNS

A sign stands for or tells us about something. A sign can be something that we see, such as a stop sign. A sign can be something that we do, such as shaking hands as a sign of friendship. An event or a person can also be a sign. For example, a police officer in a uniform can be a sign of authority, and a parade can be a sign of a holiday.

Choose one of the following words or phrases to complete the caption for each picture.

**strength** **achievement** **spring** **danger ahead** **a celebration** **guidance** **love**

A blaring whistle can be a sign of ______________________

A light from a lighthouse can be a sign of ______________________

A piñata can be a sign of

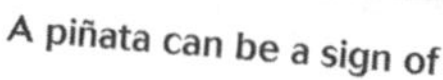

These Seven Sacraments which had long been in practice by the Church became defined as a matter of faith at the Council of Trent in 1547. The Seven Sacraments include three Sacraments of Christian Initiation (Baptism, Confirmation, and Eucharist); two Sacraments of Healing (Penance and Anointing of the Sick); and two Sacraments at the Service of Communion (Holy Orders and Matrimony).

The sacraments are effective signs in that they bring about what they represent. Through them we are healed, nourished, and made holy. The sacraments are the work of the Trinity, and they are acts of the Church. They help us to build up the Body of Christ, and they help us respond individually to our call to holiness. In the sacraments we receive the gift of sanctifying grace, God's life within us.

## Reflection

"The seven sacraments touch all the stages and all the important moments of Christian life: they give birth and increase, healing and mission to the Christian's life of faith. There is thus a certain resemblance between the stages of natural life and the stages of the spiritual life."

*(CCC, 1210)*

## Introduction ( __ min.)

Ask a volunteer to read the explanation about signs and the activity directions. Have the students work independently to complete the captions. Then discuss their responses: piñata/a celebration; light/guidance; whistle/danger ahead; rock/strength; flowers/spring; first-prize ribbon/achievement; a hug/love.

Ask the students to think of signs for friendship, happiness, and healing. List the responses on a sheet of paper. Place the paper in the prayer space.

### We Will Learn...

Point out to the students that in this chapter they will learn about seven special signs that Jesus gave to the Church. These signs, the sacraments, are signs of God's love. Ask a volunteer to read the three faith statements on the scroll.

## Presentation (__ min.)

### 1 Jesus is the greatest sign of God's love.

*Jesus, we believe that you are with us always.*

Ask the students to think about what it must have been like for Jesus' disciples to witness his many acts of kindness, his healing, and his forgiveness. Invite volunteers to share their responses.

Read aloud the first paragraph and the list of Jesus' loving ways. Then share some of the Gospel stories that illustrate Jesus' loving actions:

- the blessing of the children (Matthew 19:13–15)
- the healing of two blind men (Matthew 9:27–31)
- the feeding of four thousand people (Matthew 15: 32–39)
- Jesus and Zacchaeus (Luke 19:1–10).

Have the students highlight or underline the statement: "Jesus is the greatest sign of God's love."

Read the concluding paragraph. Stress that Jesus promised his disciples that he would be with us always. He is with us through the power of the Holy Spirit. Ask volunteers to respond to the concluding question.

### 1 Jesus is the greatest sign of God's love.

Jesus Christ is the Son of God. Everything that Jesus said or did pointed to God's love for us. So all of Jesus' words and actions are signs of God's love. In the Gospels we read about these words and actions. We read about:

- ways that Jesus opened his arms and welcomed all
- ways that Jesus spent time with people whom others disliked or neglected
- ways that Jesus fed those who were hungry
- ways that Jesus touched people and healed them both physically and spiritually
- ways that Jesus comforted sinners and forgave their sins
- the way that Jesus gave his life to save us all from sin.

For all of these reasons Jesus is the greatest sign of his Father's love.

Jesus knew that his disciples needed him to be present with them. Yet he would have to leave them and return to his Father in Heaven. So Jesus promised them that he would always be with them through the power of the Holy Spirit.

In what ways did Jesus show people God's love for them?

40

## Optional Activity

Have the students work in small groups. Ask each group to prepare a role-play for one of the Gospel stories about Jesus showing God's love to others. Then have the groups take turns presenting their role-plays.

## 2 The Church celebrates seven special signs, the sacraments.

Over time, the Catholic Church recognized certain symbolic actions as signs of the risen Christ made present in the community through the power of the Holy Spirit. Eventually the Church named seven of these actions or signs it had received from Jesus Christ as the Seven Sacraments. These Seven Sacraments are Baptism, Confirmation, Eucharist, Penance and Reconciliation, Anointing of the Sick, Holy Orders, and Matrimony.

All Seven Sacraments are signs of God's presence in our lives. But sacraments are different from all other signs. They are effective signs which means that they truly bring about what they represent. For example, in Baptism we not only celebrate being children of God, we actually become children of God. In Penance and Reconciliation we not only celebrate that God forgives, we actually receive God's forgiveness.

This is why we say that a sacrament is an effective sign given to us by Jesus Christ through which we share in God's life. This gift of God's life in us is grace. Through the Holy Spirit we receive grace in each sacrament. This grace, called *sanctifying grace*, heals us of sin and helps us to grow in holiness. As God's goodness and holiness grows within us, we become more like Jesus. Grace strengthens us to live as Jesus called us to live.

How does the grace we receive in the sacraments help us?

CONFIRMATION

BAPTISM

EUCHARIST

### Do You Know?

God freely offers his grace to us in the sacraments. Through the grace we receive in the sacraments, we respond to the presence of God in our lives. We show that we are open to this grace by fully participating in the celebration of each sacrament and by making a commitment to live as disciples of Jesus.

41

## 2 The Church celebrates seven special signs, the sacraments.

*Jesus, thank you for the gift of the sacraments.*

On the board or a large sheet of paper, write the word *sacrament*. Explain that it comes from the Latin word *sacrare* which means "to consecrate or make holy."

Emphasize that the Catholic Church celebrates Seven Sacraments. Ask the students to name the sacraments they know about. Then ask a volunteer to read aloud the first paragraph.

Ask: *What does it mean to be effective?* Have a few volunteers share their responses. Possible responses include: to get things done, to make an impact, or to influence. Then explain that sacraments are effective signs. Read aloud the second paragraph.

Stress that, through each of the sacraments, we share in God's life and that God's life within us is the gift of grace. Stress with the students that the grace we receive in the sacraments is called sanctifying grace. Ask the students to highlight or underline the first two sentences in the last paragraph. Then have a volunteer finish reading the paragraph.

Read the concluding question. Invite a few volunteers to share their responses. Possible responses include: we grow in holiness; we become more like Jesus; we are strengthened to live as Jesus wants us to live.

### Do You Know?

Have a volunteer read the feature. Ask: *How do you think we can fully participate in the celebration of each sacrament?* Possible responses include: we can listen to the prayers being said by the priest, bishop, or deacon; we can pray the responses carefully and respectfully; we can join in singing the hymns.

## 3 The sacraments unite us as the Body of Christ.

*God, help us to be open to your grace.*

Remind the students that the Church is the Body of Christ. Christ is the Head, and we are its members. Then read aloud the first paragraph. Stress that the sacraments join Catholics all over the world with Jesus and with one another.

Read the paragraphs about the three groups of sacraments. Ask the students to look at the photos of the sacramental celebrations on pages 41 and 42.

Then have the students turn to pages 104–105 in their texts. Help the students read the *Seven Sacraments* chart. Tell the students that they will be learning more about the sacraments in the following chapters. For more about the Sacraments at the Service of Communion, see *The Sacrament of Holy Orders* on pages 110–111 and *The Sacrament of Matrimony* on page 112.

Read the last paragraph aloud. Stress that sanctifying grace enables each of us to respond to God's presence in our life.

Have each of the students identify the sacraments that he or she has received.

### 3 The sacraments unite us as the Body of Christ.

During the celebration of the sacraments, Christ is joined in a special way with the Church. The Church, the whole Body of Christ, celebrates each sacrament. The priest and other members of the Church who participate in the sacraments represent the whole Church. The sacraments unite Catholics all over the world with Jesus and with one another.

There are three groups of sacraments: Sacraments of Christian Initiation, Sacraments of Healing, and Sacraments at the Service of Communion.

- The Sacraments of Christian Initiation are Baptism, Confirmation, and the Eucharist. Through these sacraments we are born into the Church, strengthened, and nourished.
- The Sacraments of Healing are Penance and Reconciliation, and Anointing of the Sick. Through them we experience God's forgiveness, peace, and healing.
- The Sacraments at the Service of Communion are Holy Orders and Matrimony. In Holy Orders a baptized man is consecrated and in Matrimony a man and woman are blessed to serve God and the Church through a particular vocation.

It is through the grace that we receive in the sacraments that we are able to respond to the presence of God in our lives.

Which sacraments have you received?

PENANCE

MATRIMONY

ANOINTING of the SICK

HOLY ORDERS

42

## Optional Activity

Consider doing the following activity to help the students learn the names of the sacraments. On a large sheet of paper, print the name of each sacrament, but leave a blank space for the vowels (example: B__PT__SM). If time permits, switch the activity by printing the vowels and leaving blank spaces for students to write in the consonants (example:__A__ __ I __ __).

## Review

Choose a phrase to complete each sentence.

| Christian Initiation | effective signs |
|---|---|
| God's life | the Holy Spirit |

1. The sacraments are **effective signs** given to us by Jesus Christ through which we share in God's life.
2. Through the Sacraments of **Christian Initiation** we are born into the Church, strengthened, and nourished.
3. Grace is our share in **God's life**.
4. Jesus' presence continued in the disciples' lives through the power of **the Holy Spirit**.

Discuss the following. (See side column.)

5. Why is Jesus the greatest sign of God's love?
6. How are the Seven Sacraments different from all other signs?
7. What are the three groups of sacraments?

sacrament (page 41)

grace (page 41)

## With My Family

### Sharing Our Faith

1. Jesus is the greatest sign of God's love.
2. The Church celebrates seven special signs, the sacraments.
3. The sacraments unite us as the Body of Christ.

### PRAYING TOGETHER

Pray the following prayer for the people in your parish who are preparing to receive the sacraments.

**God our Father, you gave us your only Son**
**who is the greatest sign of your love.**
**Be with the people in our parish**
**who are preparing to receive the sacraments.**
**Jesus, help them to remember that you are present with them**
**as they celebrate these sacraments.**
**Holy Spirit, help each person be open to the grace**
**he or she will receive in the sacrament.**
**We ask this through Christ our Lord. Amen.**

### Living Our Faith

In this chapter you have learned about the Seven Sacraments. This week talk with your family about the sacraments each of you has received. As you discuss, list the celebrations here.

_______________

_______________

43

# Conclusion ( _ min.)

### Review

Provide five to ten minutes for the students to work independently to complete the first part of the *Review*. Check the students' answers. Clarify any misconceptions. Then discuss the questions in the second part of the *Review*. Possible responses follow.

**5.** Everything that Jesus said and did pointed to God's love for us.

**6.** The Seven Sacraments are effective signs. They truly bring about what they represent.

**7.** The three groups of sacraments are the Sacraments of Christian Initiation, the Sacraments of Healing, and the Sacraments at the Service of Communion.

***Faith Words***

Have students write one sentence that includes both words.

***More for You to Know***

On page 44 you will find *More for You to Know* for Unit 2. The articles on this page provide additional or supplemental information related to the concepts presented in Chapters 4–6. The topics of these articles are: the Deposit of Faith, the infallibility of the pope, and the Lord's Prayer.

### With My Family

***Sharing Our Faith***

Encourage the students to share with their families what they have learned about the Seven Sacraments.

***Praying Together***

With the students read the prayer. Encourage the students to pray the prayer with their families this week.

***Living Our Faith***

Encourage the students to work with their families to complete the chart.

## CATECHISM FOCUS

"Grace is a participation in the life of God. It introduces us into the intimacy of the Trinitarian life: by Baptism the Christian participates in the grace of Christ, the Head of his Body. As an 'adopted son' he can henceforth call God 'Father,' in union with the only Son. He receives the life of the Spirit who breathes charity into him and who forms the Church." (*CCC*, 1997)

See also *CCC*, paragraphs 1996, 1999, and 2000.

# MORE for You to Know

**DEPOSIT OF FAITH** The Deposit of Faith is all the truth contained in Scripture and Tradition. Jesus Christ revealed and entrusted this truth to the Apostles. They, in turn, entrusted this truth to their successors, the bishops, and the entire Church.

It is within the Church, the community of faith, that we discover the truth. The Magisterium, the living teaching office of the Church, guides us in understanding the truth. The Magisterium consists of the pope and bishops. They teach us the correct understanding of the message of Scripture and Tradition and ways to live out this message.

In each generation, the whole Church continues to share and build upon the faith of the Apostles. With the guidance of the Holy Spirit, the Church hands on all the truths she has received through God's Revelation. The Church's faith is always developing, and God's Revelation is living and active in the Church.

**INFALLIBILITY** Infallibility is the gift of the Holy Spirit that keeps the Church free from error—in her beliefs and teachings—in matters concerning Divine Revelation and the Deposit of Faith. The pope also has the gift of infallibilty when he defines a truth pertaining to faith and morals.

**THE LORD'S PRAYER** During the Sermon on the Mount, Jesus taught his followers the Lord's Prayer, a prayer to God the Father. This prayer is an essential prayer of the Church—integrated into her liturgical prayer and sacraments.

In the first part of the Lord's Prayer, we give glory to God, we pray for the coming of God's Kingdom, and we pray to God for the ability to do his will.

In the second part of the Lord's Prayer, we ask God for everything we need for ourselves and for the world. We ask God to heal us of our sin. We pray that God will protect us from all that could draw us away from his love. We ask God to guide us in choosing good in our lives, and we ask him for the strength to follow his law.

# UNIT 2 Assessment

**Circle the correct answer.**

1. The Church celebrates (**three**/**seven**/**four**) Sacraments of Christian Initiation.
2. There are (**nine**/**seven**/**four**) Marks of the Church.
3. On Pentecost, Peter spoke to the crowd and (**only a few**/**only twelve**/**about three thousand**) people were baptized.
4. The Church is catholic, open to (**all**/**some**/**many**) people.
5. (**Each person**, **Only the pastor**, **Only the deacon**) is important to the parish.

**Complete the following statements.**

6. The ____pope____ and the bishops continue the leadership of the Apostle Peter and the other Apostles.
7. The Catholic Church has four Marks: one, ____holy____, catholic, and apostolic.
8. A ____sacrament____ is an effective sign given to us by Jesus Christ through which we share in God's life.
9. The ____Church____, the whole Body of Christ, celebrates each sacrament.
10. Through the Sacraments of ____Christian Initiation____ we are born into the Church, strengthened, and nourished.

**Write your responses on a separate sheet of paper.**

11. Write one reason why Jesus sent the Holy Spirit to his disciples. See page 28 of Chapter 4.
12. Choose one of the four Marks of the Church and explain its meaning. See page 35 of Chapter 5.
13. Identify ways Jesus showed his disciples that he is the greatest sign of God's love.
14. What is the Church? The Church is the community of people who are baptized and follow Jesus Christ.
15. Name two ways in which you can participate in your parish. See page 36 of Chapter 5.

# Semester 1 Assessment

**Circle the letter of the correct answer.**

1. The truth that God the Son became man is _____.
   a. the Resurrection
   b. the Ascension
   c. Pentecost
   (d.) the Incarnation

2. One of the Sacraments of Christian Initiation is _____.
   a. Matrimony
   (b.) Confirmation
   c. Anointing of the Sick
   d. Holy Orders

3. The people who serve in a parish are _____.
   a. deacons
   b. lay people
   c. priests
   (d.) all of the above

4. Jesus' return in all his glory to his Father in Heaven is called _____.
   a. the Resurrection
   (b.) the Ascension
   c. Pentecost
   d. the Incarnation

5. The Church is _____. This means that the Church is universal, open to all people.
   a. one
   b. holy
   (c.) catholic
   d. apostolic

**Complete the following.**

6. The greatest sign of God's love is ___Jesus Christ___
   _____________________.

7. God's plan for human beings was that ___they will be happy with him forever.___
   _____________________.

8. The Apostles are the twelve men whom Jesus chose to share in his mission in a special way.

9. Jesus told his followers that the Kingdom of God is like a great treasure that people would want above all things or a mustard seed that would grow into a large plant.

10. Through the grace we receive in each sacrament, God's goodness and holiness grows within us, and we become more like Jesus.

**Circle the correct answer.**

11. The Sacrament of Penance and Reconciliation is a Sacrament of (**Healing**, **Christian Initiation**).

12. Each local area of the Church is called a (**deacon**, **diocese**).

13. A (**diocese**, **sacrament**) is an effective sign because it truly brings about what it represents.

14. The day the Holy Spirit came upon Jesus' disciples is called (**Easter Sunday**, **Pentecost**). It was on this day that the Church began.

15. Jesus Christ is (**only divine**, **divine and human**).

**Write your responses.**

16. What did Jesus do for his disciples at the Last Supper?
Jesus gave himself to the disciples in the bread and wine which became his Body and Blood.

17. What is the role of the pope and bishops?
The pope and the bishops are the leaders of the Church.

18. Name the Marks of the Church. Choose one and describe what it means.
The Church is one, holy, catholic, and apostolic. See page 35 of Chapter 5

19. What is the Kingdom of God?
The Kingdom of God is the power of God's love active in our lives and in our world.

20. Write two ways you can participate in your parish community.
See page 36 of Chapter 5.

# Chapter 7

## GOALS

*to learn that, at Baptism, we are freed from sin, and we become members of the Church; to understand that the Sacrament of Confirmation completes Baptism and seals us with the Gift of the Holy Spirit*

## GETTING READY

**Opening Prayer:** *On the prayer table, place a Bible, a cross, and a bowl of holy water.*

**Materials Needed:** *markers (pages 48–49), writing paper for* ***Optional Activity*** *(page 52)*
*Make plans for a visit to the parish church.(See Liturgy Connection, page 51.)*

## Catechist Background

Our journey of faith begins at Baptism. This Sacrament of Christian Initiation is "the gateway to life in the Spirit, and the door which gives access to the other sacraments" (*CCC*, 1213). In Baptism we are cleansed of Original Sin and any personal sin. We become children of God and members of the Church. We receive the grace to lead lives of holiness. We are also given the hope of eternal life.

People of all ages may be baptized. When people are baptized, they are immersed in water, or water is poured on their heads three times in the name of the Father, and of the Son, and of the Holy Spirit. They are anointed with Chrism, holy oil, recalling the anointing of Jesus Christ.

## Opening Prayer

On the prayer table, place a bowl of holy water. Invite the students to process to the prayer space. Have them take turns placing the fingers of their right hands in the water and then making the Sign of the Cross. Then ask the students to listen to the following reading.

***Reader***: *A reading from the Book of the Prophet Isaiah*

*"I will pour out water upon the thirsty ground,*
*and streams upon the dry land;*
*I will pour out my spirit upon your offspring,*
*and my blessing upon your descendants."*

(Isaiah 44:3)

Then pray together: *May everything we do today be done in the name of the Father, of the Son, and of the Holy Spirit. Amen.*

# 7 The Church Offers Us New Life in Christ

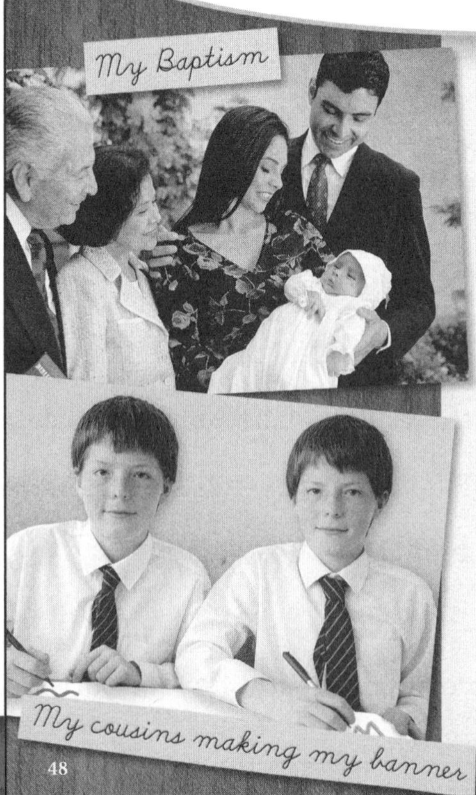


Hello. My name is Margaret. Yesterday I asked Dad questions about my Baptism: Who was there? Where was I baptized? What did everyone do after the Baptism? To help answer my questions, Dad found our family's treasure box. In the box we found many things from the day I was baptized: photographs, my baptismal certificate, a banner, and many other baptismal keepsakes.

I wanted to know about my Baptism because my Aunt Melissa and Uncle Kyle just adopted a baby. The baby's name is Michael, and he is going to be baptized. My parents and I, my grandparents, aunts, uncles, and cousins are going to my Aunt Melissa's parish church to celebrate Michael's Baptism. After the Baptism we are invited to my grandparents' house for a party.

The newly baptized are clothed with a white baptismal garment to symbolize putting on Christ, and they are given a candle to symbolize that they are to walk in the light of Christ.

We first receive the Gift of the Holy Spirit in Baptism. In the Sacrament of Confirmation we are sealed with the Gift of the Holy Spirit.

The Sacrament of Confirmation is usually celebrated during the Mass. After the Liturgy of the Word, the entire assembly renews their baptismal vows. Then the bishop extends his hands over the heads of the candidates and prays that they may receive the Gifts of the Holy Spirit. After this the bishop anoints the candidate's forehead with Chrism, praying, "Be sealed with the gift of the Holy Spirit."

## Reflection

"The Spirit of the LORD shall rest upon him:
a spirit of wisdom and of understanding,
A spirit of counsel and of strength,
A spirit of knowledge and of fear of the LORD.
And his delight shall be the fear of the LORD."

*(Isaiah 11:2–3)*

I asked Mom what I could do for Michael. Mom handed me the banner that was in our box and said, "Margaret, your twin cousins made this and gave it to you on the day of your Baptism." When I opened the banner, it was brightly decorated and had "Welcome, Margaret" printed in large letters. After seeing my banner, I decided to make a banner for Michael.

In the space above, help Margaret decorate her banner.

Who was at the celebration of your Baptism?

Have you ever been to a baptismal celebration of a family member or friend?

What do you remember about the celebration?

## Introduction ( __ min.)

Have volunteers read aloud the story "Welcome, Michael." Then give the students time to design a welcome banner.

Afterwards, discuss the questions that follow the story. Since it is likely that many of the students were baptized as infants, encourage them to talk about their Baptisms with family members. Emphasize the importance of the celebration because it was then that they were welcomed into the Church.

### We Will Learn...

Remind the students that sacraments are signs of God's love for us. Explain that in this chapter the students will learn about the Sacraments of Baptism and Confirmation. Ask a volunteer to read the three faith statements on the scroll.

# Presentation ( __ min.)

## 1 Baptism is the foundation of the Christian life.

*God the Father, God the Son, God the Holy Spirit, we believe in you.*

Discuss with the students the meaning of the word *foundation*. Point out that a foundation is a base and a support.

Ask the students: *What is a sacrament?* Also ask: *What are the three Sacraments of Christian Initiation?* Refer to Chapter 6.

Remind the students that through the Sacraments of Baptism, Confirmation, and Eucharist, we are born into the Church, strengthened, and nourished. Stress that the Sacrament of Baptism is the foundation of the Christian life.

Have a volunteer read the first paragraph. Point out that at Baptism we become children of God, members of Christ, and Temples of the Holy Spirit. Then read aloud the second paragraph and the explanation of the effects of Baptism: being freed from sin, becoming children of God, and being welcomed into the Church.

Help the students recall what they learned about Original Sin. (See Chapter 1, page 9.) Point out that Salvation is the forgiveness of sins and the restoring of friendship with God.

Ask the students to respond to the concluding question.

### 1 Baptism is the foundation of the Christian life.

Baptism is the first sacrament that we celebrate. In fact, we are unable to receive any other sacrament until we have first been baptized. Through Baptism we receive a share in God's own life, the life of grace. The grace of Baptism makes us children of God, members of Christ, and Temples of the Holy Spirit. It gives us the power to live and act as disciples of Jesus Christ.

Baptism leads us to the other two Sacraments of Christian Initiation, Confirmation and Eucharist. **Baptism** is the sacrament in which we:

- *Are freed from sin:* Jesus' victory over sin and death offers us Salvation. Salvation is the forgiveness of sins and the restoring of friendship with God. Baptism is necessary for Salvation. Baptism frees us from Original Sin and all our personal sins are forgiven.
- *Become children of God:* We become sisters and brothers with everyone else who has been baptized. Baptism makes us members of one family. God sees all of us as his children. He loves each one of us.
- *Are welcomed into the Church:* At Baptism we are welcomed into a community of believers led by the Holy Spirit. We become a part of the Body of Christ, the People of God. We are united with all those who have been baptized in Christ.

What are three things that happen when we are baptized?

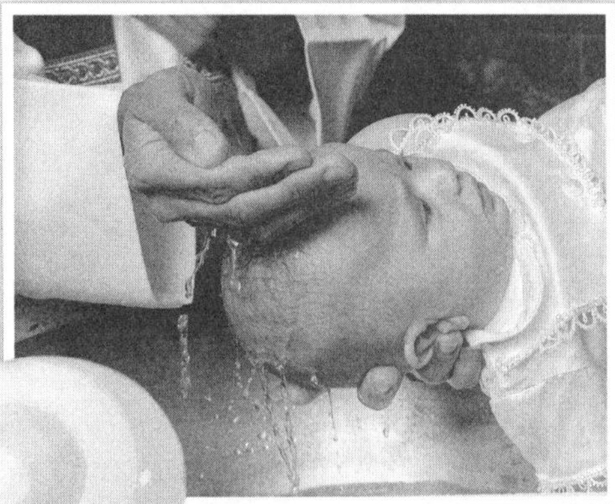

#### Do You Know?

At Baptism we are sealed, or marked forever, as belonging to Jesus Christ. This spiritual mark, called a character, can never be erased. Once we have received Baptism, no matter what may happen, we belong to Christ and the Church. Thus, Baptism is a sacrament that is never repeated. Once we have been baptized, we are marked forever with the sign of faith and have the hope of eternal life, living in happiness with God forever.



#### Do You Know?

Read aloud the feature. You may want to explain to the students that no sin committed after Baptism can erase the seal of Baptism. For your own reference, see paragraphs 1272–1274 in the *Catechism of the Catholic Church*.

## 2 We celebrate the Sacrament of Baptism.

Many people are baptized as infants or young children. Others are baptized as older children, adolescents, or adults. No one is ever too young or too old to begin a new life in Christ through Baptism.

In many parishes infants or young children receive the Sacrament of Baptism on Sunday, the day of Jesus Christ's Resurrection. The celebration of the sacrament on Sunday highlights the fact that through Baptism we rise to new life in Christ. The Sunday celebration allows parish members to participate in the celebration. The **celebrant** of Baptism is a bishop, priest, or deacon. He celebrates the sacrament for and with the community. Because Baptism is necessary for Salvation, when there is a serious need, anyone can baptize.

The actual Baptism can take place in two ways. The celebrant can immerse, or plunge, the child in water three times. Or the celebrant can pour water over the child's head three times.

While immersing or pouring, the celebrant says,

"N.[name], I baptize you in the name
of the Father,
and of the Son,
and of the Holy Spirit."

**Chrism** is perfumed oil blessed by the bishop. The celebrant anoints the newly-baptized child on the crown of the head with Chrism. This anointing is a sign of the Gift of the Holy Spirit. It shows that the newly-baptized child shares in the mission of Jesus Christ. This anointing also connects Baptism to the Sacrament of Confirmation during which another anointing with Chrism takes place.

When were you baptized?

Who took part in the celebration?

51

## 2 We celebrate the Sacrament of Baptism.

*God, we are your children.*

Point out to the students that people of all ages may be baptized. Have volunteers read the first two paragraphs. Explain that sometimes Baptism is celebrated during Mass.

Tell the students that the usual or "ordinary" celebrant of Baptism is a bishop, priest, or deacon. However, in the case of an emergency, any person can baptize (See *CCC*, 1284.)

Then have the students focus on the photographs on pages 50 and 51. Read aloud the third and fourth paragraphs, emphasizing the words of Baptism.

You may want to share the following information with the students. Explain that some people are baptized as older children or adults. These people participate in the Rite of Christian Initiation for Adults (RCIA) and enter the catechumenate, a period of formation or preparation for Christian initiation. It includes prayer, religious instruction, and service to others. Those who enter the catechumenate are called catechumens. They celebrate the three Sacraments of Christian Initiation in one celebration, usually at the Easter Vigil.

Read aloud the last paragraph. Stress that the anointing with Chrism is a sign of the Gift of the Holy Spirit.

**Note:** For more information about baptized Christians, refer to the paragraphs about our common vocation and the priesthood of the faithful (Unit 3: *More for You to Know*, page 66).

Ask the students to discuss the concluding questions with their families.

## Liturgy Connection

**If possible, take the students into the church. Show them the baptismal font or pool and the Easter candle. Invite a parish priest or deacon to explain the sacramental celebration of Baptism.**

**If time permits, provide materials for the students to make a welcome banner for the parish to display for the children who will be baptized in the coming month.**

## 3 We celebrate the Sacrament of Confirmation.

*Come, Holy Spirit.*

Begin by writing the word *Confirmation* on the board or a large sheet of paper. Circle the word *Confirm*. Ask the students what the word means. Invite a few volunteers to respond. Point out that one of the meanings of the word is "to strengthen."

Then ask volunteers to read the first three paragraphs. Stress that Confirmation strengthens our bond with Christ and the Church.

Ask the students to focus on the photograph on the page. Then read aloud the fourth through the seventh paragraphs. Refer to the Baptism and Confirmation sections on *The Seven Sacraments* chart on text pages 104–105.

Ask a volunteer to read the last paragraph. Read more about the Gifts of the Holy Spirit and the fruits of the Holy Spirit on text page 115.

Have volunteers respond to the concluding question. Responses should include: by praying and by learning more about our faith.

### 3 We celebrate the Sacrament of Confirmation.

Confirmation is the sacrament in which we receive the Gift of the Holy Spirit in a special way. Confirmation is a Sacrament of Christian Initiation. Confirmation strengthens our bond with Christ and the Church. All baptized members of the Church are called to receive this sacrament.

Those who are baptized as adults or older children often receive Baptism, Confirmation, and the Eucharist at one celebration, usually at the Easter Vigil. Those who are baptized as infants or young children usually receive Confirmation between the ages of seven and sixteen.

The parish community helps young people prepare for Confirmation through prayer, instruction in the faith, and opportunities for service. The people who are to be confirmed are called candidates. Candidates must profess their faith, be without serious sin, desire Confirmation, and be ready to live their faith.

A bishop from the diocese comes to the parish to confirm the candidates, often during a special Mass. When necessary, a bishop may designate a priest to confirm the candidates.

The bishop confirms each candidate by laying his right hand on the candidate's head and tracing the Sign of the Cross on the candidate's forehead with Chrism. As the bishop does this he calls the candidate by name, saying, "Be sealed with the Gift of the Holy Spirit."

The person confirmed responds, "Amen."

At Confirmation, the anointing with Chrism confirms and completes the baptismal anointing. Like the character or mark of Baptism, the seal of Confirmation is with a person always. Because of this, a person receives Confirmation only once.

When we are baptized, the Holy Spirit shares seven spiritual gifts with us to help us to live as faithful followers of Jesus Christ. At Confirmation the Holy Spirit strengthens these gifts within us so that throughout our lives we can be witnesses to our faith in our words and actions. The Gifts of the Holy Spirit are: wisdom, understanding, counsel (right judgment), fortitude (courage), knowledge, piety (reverence), and fear of the Lord (wonder and awe).

How does a person prepare for the Sacrament of Confirmation?

52

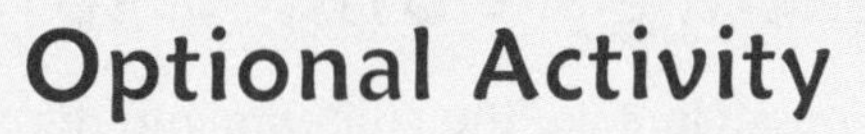

## Optional Activity

**Have the students work in small groups. Ask each group to write a prayer for the parish candidates who are preparing for the Sacrament of Confirmation. When the groups are finished, ask the students to gather in the prayer space. Have a representative of each group read aloud the group's prayer.**

## Review

**Write *True* or *False* next to the following sentences. On a separate piece of paper, change the false sentences to make them true.**

1. True At Baptism we are freed from Original Sin.
2. False We ~~may~~ receive the Sacrament of Confirmation ~~more than~~ only once.
3. False We celebrate the Sacraments of Baptism and Confirmation ~~in private~~ with our community.
4. True At Baptism and Confirmation a person is anointed with Chrism.

**Discuss the following.** (See side column.)

5. Why is it appropriate for parish communities to celebrate Baptism on Sunday?
6. What do we become at Baptism?
7. What do the seven Gifts of the Holy Spirit help us to do?

Baptism (page 50)
celebrant (page 51)
Chrism (page 51)
Confirmation (page 52)

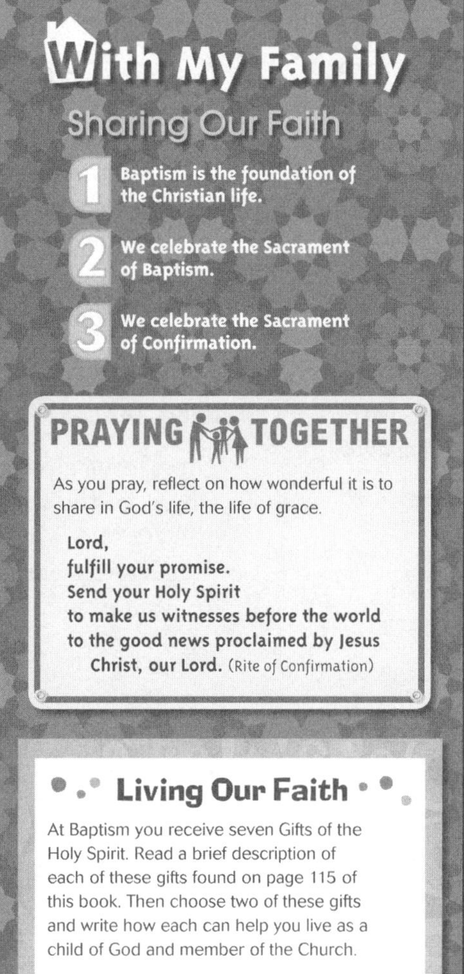

## With My Family

### Sharing Our Faith

1. Baptism is the foundation of the Christian life.
2. We celebrate the Sacrament of Baptism.
3. We celebrate the Sacrament of Confirmation.

### PRAYING TOGETHER

As you pray, reflect on how wonderful it is to share in God's life, the life of grace.

**Lord,**
**fulfill your promise.**
**Send your Holy Spirit**
**to make us witnesses before the world**
**to the good news proclaimed by Jesus Christ, our Lord.** (Rite of Confirmation)

### Living Our Faith

At Baptism you receive seven Gifts of the Holy Spirit. Read a brief description of each of these gifts found on page 115 of this book. Then choose two of these gifts and write how each can help you live as a child of God and member of the Church.

53

# Conclusion (__ min.)

## Review

Provide five to ten minutes for the students to work independently to complete the first part of the *Review*. Check the students' answers. Clarify any misconceptions. Then discuss the questions in the second part of the *Review*. Possible responses follow.

**5.** It is appropriate for parish communities to celebrate Baptism on Sunday, the day of Christ's Resurrection, because through Baptism we rise to new life in Jesus Christ. The Sunday celebration also allows parish members to participate in the celebration.

**6.** At Baptism we become children of God, members of Christ, and Temples of the Holy Spirit.

**7.** The Gifts of the Holy Spirit help us to live as faithful followers and witnesses of Jesus Christ.

### *Faith Words*

Have the students work in pairs. Ask each pair to write clues for each Faith Word (for example, sacrament that is the foundation of the Christian life). Then have the pairs take turns presenting their clues and having the students in the group guess the Faith Words.

## With My Family

### *Sharing Our Faith*

Encourage the students to share with their families what they have learned about the Sacraments of Baptism and Confirmation.

### *Praying Together*

Encourage the students to share this prayer with their families.

### *Living Our Faith*

Encourage the students to work with their families to complete the activity.

## CATECHISM FOCUS

"Confirmation perfects Baptismal grace; it is the sacrament which gives the Holy Spirit in order to root us more deeply in the divine filiation, incorporate us more firmly into Christ, strengthen our bond with the Church, associate us more closely with her mission, and help us bear witness to the Christian faith in words accompanied by deeds." (*CCC*, 1316)

# Chapter 8

## GOALS

*to learn that Jesus is truly present in the Eucharist; to be thankful for Jesus' gift of himself in the Eucharist*

## GETTING READY

**Opening Prayer:** *Have lyrics available for a well-known hymn of thanksgiving. Place an empty basket on the prayer table. Have index cards available.*

**Materials Needed:** *highlighters or colored pencils, costumes and props for* ***Optional Activity*** *(page 56)*

## Catechist Background

On the night before he died, Jesus did a most extraordinary thing. He gave himself, his own Body and Blood, to his disciples. "While they were eating, he took bread, said the blessing, broke it, and gave it to them, and said, 'Take it; this is my body.' Then he took a cup, gave thanks, and gave it to them, and they all drank from it. He said to them, 'This is my blood of the covenant, which will be shed for many.'" (Mark 14:22–23)

Thus, Jesus gave us the Sacrament of the Eucharist, which is "the source and summit of the Christian life" (*CCC*,1324). When we celebrate the Eucharist, we carry out Jesus' command at the Last Supper to "do this in memory of me" (Luke 22:19).

## Opening Prayer

Invite the students to reflect silently on all the people and gifts for which they are thankful. Give each student an index card. Ask the students to write the names of these people and gifts on the cards.

Place an empty basket on the prayer table. Ask the students to place their cards in the basket as they gather in the prayer space.

When the students have gathered, hold up the basket, and say: *God has given us so many wonderful gifts. Let us thank him together.* Read the following psalm verse:

*"Give thanks to the LORD, who is good,*
*whose love endures forever."*
(Psalm 106:1)

Then sing a hymn of thanksgiving. You may want to choose the traditional hymn "Now Thank We All Our God." (See the parish missalette.)

# 8 We Are Nourished by the Body and Blood of Christ

## Gifts to Treasure

Last Saturday Eric went to his Grandmom Lily's house to help her pack. She was going to move to a neighboring town. When Eric got to the house, Grandmom Lily was in the kitchen. She was going through boxes that she had brought up from the basement. Grandmom Lily said to Eric, "Look at two treasures I just found."

Eric thought his grandmother was going to show him a necklace or some other pieces of jewelry. But Grandmom Lily handed him a book of coupons. She said, "When your father was your age, he gave me these coupons for my birthday."

Eric laughed when he read the coupons aloud. The first one read, "I will clean my room before you ask me." Another one read, "I will not complain once this week."

Then Grandmom Lily held up a seashell. She told Eric, "Your Aunt Lee gave this shell to me that same year. It was her favorite shell from the collection she had. Out of all the birthday gifts I received that year, these two were my favorites."

Eric asked, "Why were these gifts your favorites, Grandmom?"

Grandmom Lily answered, "Because they were gifts of love. Eric, always remember that some of the most meaningful gifts you can give cannot be bought in a store. When we love others, we give them our time and attention. We listen to them. We spend time with them. We try to help them. In fact, you're giving me a gift right now—the gift of your time and love."

Eric's grandmother put the coupons and the shell in a small box. She said, "I'm going to make room for these two treasures in my new home."

The Eucharist is a memorial of Christ's sacrifice on the cross, a memorial and celebration of Christ's suffering, Death, Resurrection, and Ascension. At each Mass, these events become present to us so we can be changed by them.

The Eucharist is "the Sacrament of sacraments" (*CCC*, 1330). Through the words and actions of the priest and by the power of the Holy Spirit, the bread and wine become the Body and Blood of Christ. Receiving the Eucharist unites us with Christ and with one another, forming us into the Body of Christ. The Eucharist is our spiritual nourishment on earth, preparing us for the banquet of glory to come.

## Reflection

Jesus said, "I am the bread of life. . . . I am the living bread that came down from heaven; whoever eats this bread will live forever; and the bread that I will give is my flesh for the life of the world".

*(John 6:48, 51)*

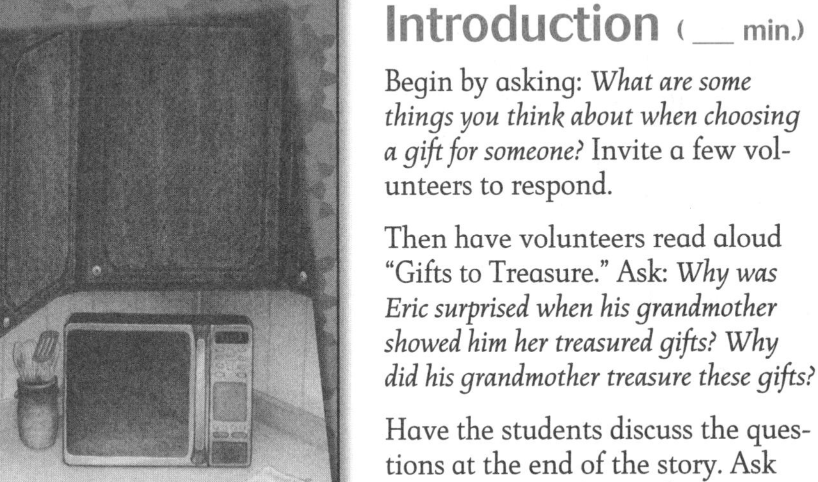


What is the most meaningful gift someone has given to you?

What is the most meaningful gift you have given to someone?

### We Will Learn...

1 Jesus gave us himself in the Eucharist.

2 The Eucharist is a memorial, a meal, and a sacrifice.

3 The Mass is the celebration of the Eucharist.

55

## Introduction ( ___ min.)

Begin by asking: *What are some things you think about when choosing a gift for someone?* Invite a few volunteers to respond.

Then have volunteers read aloud "Gifts to Treasure." Ask: *Why was Eric surprised when his grandmother showed him her treasured gifts? Why did his grandmother treasure these gifts?*

Have the students discuss the questions at the end of the story. Ask the students to share what was meaningful about these gifts.

### We Will Learn...

**Explain to the students that, in this chapter, they will be learning about the third Sacrament of Christian Initiation, the Eucharist. Then read the three statements.**

## Presentation (__ min.)

### 1 Jesus gave us himself in the Eucharist.

*For all you have done for us, we thank you, Jesus.*

Begin by asking the students to recall what happened on the night before Jesus died. Ask the students to turn to pages 20–21 in Chapter 3 of their texts. Have volunteers share their responses.

Direct the students to focus on the art on page 56 as a volunteer reads the first two paragraphs. Stress that through the Eucharist Jesus remains with us forever.

Point out to the students that the Church teaches that the Eucharist is "the heart and summit of the Church's life" (*CCC*, 1407). Emphasize that, under the appearances of bread and wine, Jesus is truly present to us in the Sacrament of the Eucharist. Then read aloud the third and fourth paragraphs. Have the students highlight or underline the fourth paragraph.

Remind the students that the Sacrament of the Eucharist is a Sacrament of Christian Initiation. Through this sacrament we complete our initiation into the Church. Then ask a volunteer to read the last two paragraphs.

Discuss the concluding question. Point out that we receive Jesus himself in Holy Communion. We are nourished and strengthened to be his followers. We are united with the Church.

### 1 Jesus gave us himself in the Eucharist.

Jesus wanted to remain present with his disciples. So at the Last Supper on the night before he died, Jesus gave his disciples a special way to remember him and to be with him. "While they were eating, he took bread, said the blessing, broke it, and gave it to them, and said, 'Take it; this is my body.' Then he took a cup, gave thanks, and gave it to them, and they all drank from it. He said to them, 'This is my blood of the covenant, which will be shed for many.'" (Mark 14:22–24)

Jesus' breaking of the bread and sharing of the cup was an offering of himself for our Salvation. At the Last Supper Jesus gave us the gift of himself and instituted the Eucharist. Through the Eucharist Jesus remains with us forever.

The **Eucharist** is the sacrament of the Body and Blood of Christ. The Mass is the celebration of the Eucharist.

Through the power of the Holy Spirit and the words and actions of the priest, Jesus truly becomes present to us in the Sacrament of the Eucharist. He is truly present to us under the appearances of bread and wine. We receive Jesus Christ himself in Holy Communion.

When we receive the Eucharist, we share in God's own life—the life of the Father, the Son, and the Holy Spirit. Our relationship with Christ and one another is strengthened. Christ unites all the faithful in one body, the Body of Christ, the Church.

In the Sacrament of the Eucharist we complete our Christian Initiation into the Church. The Eucharist nourishes us to be faithful members of the Church. Thus, it is the only Sacrament of Christian Initiation that we receive again and again.

Why do you think the Eucharist is at the center of our lives?

56

## Optional Activity

**Read aloud the story of Jesus' appearance on the road to Emmaus (Luke 24:13–35). After you have finished reading, stress that the disciples recognized Jesus when he broke the bread and shared it with them. Invite the students to act out the story.**

## 2 The Eucharist is a memorial, a meal, and a sacrifice.

*The Eucharist is a memorial.*

When Jesus gave his disciples the Eucharist, he told them, "do this in memory of me" (Luke 22:19). When we gather and celebrate the Sacrament of the Eucharist, we are remembering Jesus who is present to us in this celebration. We are remembering the new life we have because of Jesus Christ's Death and Resurrection.

*The Eucharist is a meal.*

At the Last Supper Jesus and his disciples were eating and celebrating a special meal. In the Eucharist we share in a meal. In the Eucharist we, too, are nourished. We are nourished by the Body and Blood of Jesus Christ. As Jesus told us, "For my flesh is true food, and my blood is true drink. Whoever eats my flesh and drinks my blood remains in me and I in him" (John 6:55–56).

*The Eucharist is a sacrifice.*

A sacrifice is a gift offered to God by a priest in the name of all the people. During the celebration of the Eucharist, Jesus acts through the priest. At each celebration, Jesus' sacrifice on the cross, his Resurrection, and his Ascension into Heaven are made present again through the words and actions of the priest.

Through this sacrifice we are saved. This sacrifice is offered for the forgiveness of the sins of the living and the dead. Through it we are reconciled with God and one another. Our less serious sins are forgiven, and we are strengthened to avoid serious sin.

In the Eucharist Jesus offers his Father praise and thanksgiving. This thanks and praise is for all the gifts of Creation. The word *eucharist* means "to give thanks." In every celebration of the Eucharist, the whole Church offers thanks and praise. When we celebrate the Eucharist, we pray to the Father, through the Son, in the unity of the Holy Spirit. We join Jesus in offering ourselves to God the Father. We offer all our joys and concerns. We offer our willingness to live as Jesus' disciples.

What will you remember about Jesus the next time you celebrate the Eucharist?

What joys and concerns will you offer to God?

57

## 2 The Eucharist is a memorial, a meal, and a sacrifice.

*Jesus, we believe you are truly present in the Eucharist.*

You may want to point out to the students that the early Christians called the Eucharist "the breaking of the bread." Read Acts of the Apostles 2:42: "They devoted themselves to the teaching of the apostles and to the communal life, to the breaking of the bread and to the prayers."

Have the students read the faith statement at the top of page 57. Ask volunteers to read the first two paragraphs.

Explain the meaning of the word *sacrifice* as defined in the first sentence of the third paragraph. Stress that Jesus acts through the priest during each celebration of the Eucharist. Have volunteers read the third and fourth paragraphs.

Explain that the word *eucharist* means "to give thanks." Then have a volunteer read aloud the last paragraph.

Read the concluding questions. Provide a brief period of silence in which the students can reflect on their responses.

### About Altar Breads

Altar breads, or unconsecrated hosts, are the small round wafers of bread that when consecrated at Mass, become the Body of Christ. These hosts are often made by members of religious communities dedicated to a life of prayer.

The hosts are made of wheat flour and water. Because Jesus used unleavened Passover bread at the Last Supper, the dough for the Eucharist bread is unleavened. It is made without yeast so it does not rise.

## 3 The Mass is the celebration of the Eucharist.

*O God, we sing your praises.*

Point out that every Mass is a celebration of the Sacrament of the Eucharist. The Mass is the Church's great act of worship. Then invite a volunteer to read aloud the first two paragraphs.

Stress that Jesus is with us when we gather for Mass with our parish community. Then read aloud the third paragraph. Have the students highlight or underline the paragraph.

Point out that the Church recommends that we receive Holy Communion each time we participate in the Mass. Stress that to be worthy to receive Holy Communion, we must be in the state of grace. Therefore, if we have committed serious sin, we must first receive the Sacrament of Penance.

Read aloud the concluding question. Pause to allow students to reflect quietly on their responses.

Please note that the parts of the Mass are explained in Chapter 9 and on pages 106–107.

### 3 The Mass is the celebration of the Eucharist.

The Mass is the Church's great act of worship. The celebration of the Eucharist, the Mass, is the center of the Church's life. For this reason the Church requires all members to participate in Mass every Sunday or Saturday evening.

When we participate in the Mass, we show that we appreciate the great gift Jesus has given us—the gift of himself. Some of the ways that we participate are by singing, praying the responses, listening and responding to readings from the Bible, and receiving Holy Communion.

During Mass Jesus is among us. He offers himself so that we can grow in God's friendship and love. Jesus is present to us in the Word of God, in those who have gathered in his name, in the priest celebrant, and most importantly, in his Body and Blood which we receive in Holy Communion.

The Church recommends that each time we participate in the Mass, we receive Holy Communion. The Church requires us to receive Holy Communion at least once a year.

How will you participate in next Sunday's Mass?

#### Do You Know?

The Church has many feast days, including very special ones called Holy Days of Obligation. The Church requires that we participate in Mass on these days. In addition to Sundays, in the United States the Holy Days of Obligation are:

Solemnity of Mary, Mother of God (January 1)

Ascension (when celebrated on Thursday during the Easter season)

Assumption of Mary (August 15)

All Saints' Day (November 1)

Immaculate Conception (December 8)

Christmas (December 25)

58

#### Do You Know?

Have a volunteer read the feature. Explain that the Church considers every Sunday as a Holy Day of Obligation. Then ask the students to identify from the list the holy day that the Church will be celebrating next.

You may want to refer to the following pages in Chapter 14 to find out more about All Saints' Day (page 94), and the feasts of the Immaculate Conception and the Assumption (page 95).

## Review

**Complete the following sentences.**

1. Jesus gave us the gift of himself in the Eucharist at ___the Last Supper___.
2. The word *eucharist* means "___to give thanks___."
3. In the Eucharist Jesus is truly present to us under the appearances of ___bread and wine___.
4. The Eucharist is a memorial, a meal, and a ___sacrifice___.

**Discuss the following.** (See side column.)

5. What happens to us when we receive the Eucharist?
6. How is Jesus present to us at Mass?
7. In what ways do we participate at Mass?

Eucharist (page 56)
sacrifice (page 57)

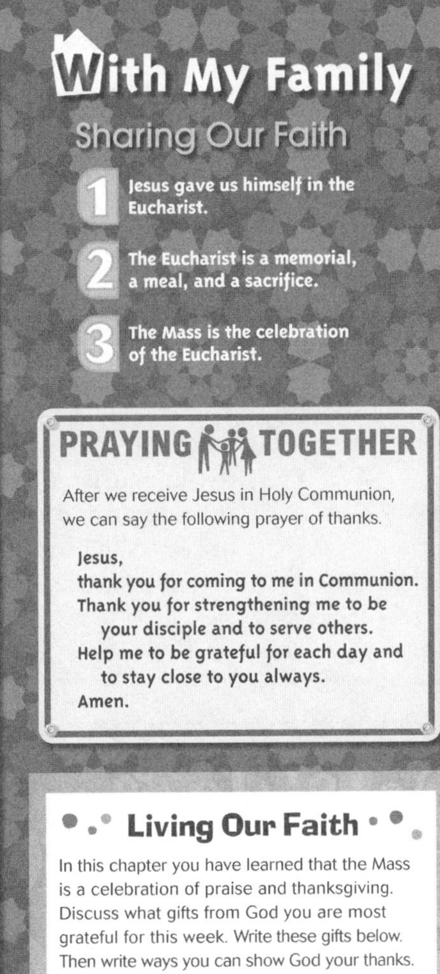

## With My Family

### Sharing Our Faith

1. Jesus gave us himself in the Eucharist.
2. The Eucharist is a memorial, a meal, and a sacrifice.
3. The Mass is the celebration of the Eucharist.

### PRAYING TOGETHER

After we receive Jesus in Holy Communion, we can say the following prayer of thanks.

Jesus,
thank you for coming to me in Communion.
Thank you for strengthening me to be
your disciple and to serve others.
Help me to be grateful for each day and
to stay close to you always.
Amen.

### Living Our Faith

In this chapter you have learned that the Mass is a celebration of praise and thanksgiving. Discuss what gifts from God you are most grateful for this week. Write these gifts below. Then write ways you can show God your thanks.

| Gift | Way to give thanks |
|---|---|
| Our food | Try not to waste food. Donate food to a pantry. |
| | |
| | |
| | |

59

# Conclusion (__ min.)

### Review

Provide five to ten minutes for the students to work independently to complete the first part of the *Review*. Check the students' answers. Clarify any misconceptions. Then discuss the questions in the second part of the *Review*. Possible responses follow.

**5.** When we receive the Eucharist, we share in God's own life, grace. Our relationship with Christ and one another is strengthened.

**6.** Jesus is present to us at Mass in the Word of God, in those who have gathered in his name, in the priest celebrant, and most importantly, in his Body and Blood which we receive in Holy Communion.

**7.** We participate at Mass by singing, praying the responses, listening and responding to readings from the Bible, and receiving Holy Communion.

***Faith Words***

Have the students find the definitions of the words in the *Glossary* in their texts. Then have students write one sentence using both words.

## CATECHISM FOCUS

**"The command of Jesus to repeat his actions and words 'until he comes' does not only ask us to remember Jesus and what he did. It is directed at the liturgical celebration, by the apostles and their successors, of the memorial of Christ, of his life, of his death, of his Resurrection, and of his intercession in the presence of the father."**
**(*CCC*, 1341)**

**For additional reference and reflection, see *CCC*, 1406–1419.**

### With My Family

***Sharing Our Faith***

Encourage the students to share with their families what they have learned about the Sacrament of the Eucharist.

***Praying Together***

As you pray these words together, replace the pronoun *me* with *us*. Encourage the students to share this prayer with their families.

***Living Our Faith***

Encourage the students to work with their families in completing the list. Also encourage the students to perform the acts of thanksgiving.

# Chapter 9

## GOALS

*to learn about the four parts of the Mass; to deepen appreciation for the Mass*

## GETTING READY

**Opening Prayer:** *On the prayer table, place a Bible, a battery-operated candle, and wheat and grapes.*

**Materials Needed:** *highlighters or colored pencils Ask the pastor if it is possible to show the students the parish's Lectionary and the Book of the Gospels.* *(See page 62.)*

## Catechist Background

In the Mass, the Liturgy of the Word and the Liturgy of the Eucharist form one single act of worship. The Mass is the central communal worship of the Church. In this liturgical action the priest celebrant leads the assembly in prayer. We each have an active part, whether that be reading, listening, singing, or praying the responses together.

The individual parts of the Mass are: the Introductory Rites, the Liturgy of the Word, the Liturgy of the Eucharist, and the Concluding Rites. In the Introductory Rites the Church gathers us together in prayer. We pray the Sign of the Cross, we ask forgiveness of our sins, and we praise God.

In the Liturgy of the Word, the Church shares the story of our faith through the Scripture readings,

## Opening Prayer

Choose one student to carry a crucifix and another student to carry an open Bible as they lead the other students in a procession to the prayer space. Then have the two procession leaders place the crucifix and the Bible on the prayer table.

Lead the students in prayer with the following words: *On the night before Jesus died, on the night he gave himself to us in the Eucharist, he talked to his disciples about many things. He told them: "Remain in me as I remain in you . . . . I am the vine, you are the branches"* (John 15:4, 5).

Invite the students to join hands. Pray: *Jesus, you are the vine. We are the branches. You nourish us and unite us through the Sacrament of the Eucharist. May we always remain in you and continue to grow in your love.*

Ask the students to respond: *Jesus, you are the vine. We are the branches.*

## 9 We Gather for Mass

### Family Celebrations

Think about your family's celebrations.

Which recent celebration was your favorite?

____________________________

When was the celebration?

____________________________

Who was there?

____________________________

____________________________

____________________________

____________________________

HAPPY BIRTHDAY

especially the Gospel. We profess our faith in the Blessed Trinity and the teachings of the Church. We pray together for the needs of the Church and the world.

During the Liturgy of the Eucharist, we prayerfully listen as the priest prays the Eucharistic Prayer. At the Consecration, through the words and actions of the priest and by the power of the Holy Spirit, the bread and wine become the Body and Blood of Christ. We pray the Lord's Prayer, we offer each other a Sign of Peace, and we ask for God's mercy. We then receive the Body and Blood of Christ in Holy Communion.

During the last part of the Mass, the Concluding Rites, the priest or deacon blesses us and then sends us out to love and serve the Lord.

## Reflection

"The parish Sunday Mass. . . .is the whole parish community's central act of worship, through which Christ unites the faithful to himself and to one another in his perfect sacrifice of praise."

*(National Directory for Catechesis, 36A3b)*

Check the celebration activities in which you participated. Add your own.

_____ sharing a meal

_____ telling family stories

_____ listening to family stories

_____ singing

_____ dancing

_____ taking photos or a video

_____ ____________________

How will you remember the celebration?

_____ look at photos or watch the video

_____ make scrapbook pages

_____ write about the celebration in a diary or journal

_____ talk about the celebration with family and friends

### We Will Learn...

1 At Mass we praise God, and we listen to his Word.

2 We offer gifts, and the Eucharistic Prayer begins.

3 We receive Holy Communion, and we are sent to bring God's love to others.



## Introduction ( ___ min.)

On the board or on a large sheet of paper, write the word *celebration*. For about three minutes, have the students brainstorm words that they associate with *celebration* and list them on the paper. Remind the students that when brainstorming, we do not judge, comment on, or edit responses until the time elapses. When the three minutes have passed, ask the students to help you to edit the list. Cross out any inappropriate words.

Then have the students write their responses to the "Family Celebration" questions. Invite volunteers to share their responses.

### We Will Learn...

**Remind the students that the Mass is the celebration of the Sacrament of the Eucharist. Point out that in this chapter the students will be learning about the parts of this celebration.**

## Presentation ( __ min.)

### 1 At Mass we praise God, and we listen to his Word.

*Glory to God in the highest!*

You may want to begin by discussing what is special about gathering with friends and family for celebrations. Then ask the students to think about gathering for the celebration of Mass. Explain that the group of people who gather is called the assembly. Stress that it is important that each person in the assembly participate in the Mass. Point out that the priest who leads the assembly in the celebration is the presider or celebrant.

Explain that there are four parts of the Mass. Then ask a volunteer to read the first two paragraphs. Ask the students: *What happens when Mass begins?*

If possible show the students the parish Lectionary and the *Book of the Gospels*. Explain that the reader reads the first two readings from the Lectionary. The priest or deacon reads the Gospel from the *Book of the Gospels*.

Summarize and present the third paragraph and the explanation of the readings. Point out the importance of listening carefully to the readings and the Gospel.

Have a volunteer read the last paragraph. You may want to have the students pray the Nicene Creed which may be found on page 120.

You may also want the students to read about the specific prayers and readings of the Introductory Rites and the Liturgy of the Word on page 106.

Read aloud the concluding question. Have the students work in pairs to prepare an explanation for younger children.

### 1 At Mass we praise God, and we listen to his Word.

The Mass is the celebration of the Eucharist. The community of people who gather for this celebration is called the liturgical **assembly**. Only an ordained priest can preside at Mass. He leads the assembly in the celebration of the Mass. The Mass has four parts: the Introductory Rites, the Liturgy of the Word, the Liturgy of the Eucharist, and the Concluding Rites.

The part of the Mass that unites us as a community is the **Introductory Rites**. It prepares us to hear God's Word and to celebrate the Eucharist. During the Introductory Rites, we make the Sign of the Cross with the priest, who greets us in Jesus' name. Together we recall our sins and ask for God's mercy. Then, on most Sundays of the year, we praise God by saying or singing the Gloria—a prayer giving glory to God. The priest prays the Opening Prayer, known as the *Collect*. It is prayed to God the Father through Christ in the Holy Spirit.

Then we participate in the **Liturgy of the Word**, which is the part of the Mass when we listen and respond to God's Word. We hear about God's great love for his people. We hear about the life and teaching of Jesus Christ. On Sunday, we listen to three readings from the Bible, the Word of God.

- The first reading is usually from the Old Testament. We respond to this reading by singing or praying a psalm.
- The second reading is from the New Testament, most often from one of the letters of Saint Paul.

- The last reading is always taken from one of the four Gospels. These are accounts of the Good News of Jesus Christ in the New Testament according to: Matthew, Mark, Luke, or John. We stand to listen as the priest or deacon proclaims the Gospel.

After the readings and the Gospel, the priest, or deacon gives a *homily*. We listen as he explains the meaning of the readings and teaches us about our Catholic faith. Then, together, we say the Creed, stating our beliefs in God and in all that the Church teaches. Next, we pray together the Prayer of the Faithful for the needs of the Church, the world, and our local community.

How would you explain the Introductory Rites and the Liturgy of the Word to a younger child?

62

### The Liturgical Year

**At this time you may want to present *The Liturgical Year*, pages 102 and 103. Explain that the special clothes the priests and deacons wear are vestments. The color of the priest's outer vestment, the chasuble, is the same color used in the church for the current liturgical season. There are special readings and Gospels for each season.**

## We offer gifts, and the Eucharistic Prayer begins.

The Liturgy of the Eucharist is the third part of the Mass. The **Liturgy of the Eucharist** is the part of the Mass when the bread and wine become the Body and Blood of Christ, which we receive in Holy Communion.

The Liturgy of the Eucharist begins as the deacon or priest prepares the altar and the gifts that we offer. Members of the assembly present to the priest gifts of wheat bread and grape wine and our collection for the Church and the poor. These gifts are a sign that we give to God all that we are and all that we do. The priest then gives thanks to God for the gifts. We respond, "Blessed be God for ever."

Then the priest in the name of the entire community prays the Eucharistic Prayer, the Church's greatest prayer of praise and thanksgiving.

During this prayer the priest says and does what Jesus said and did at the Last Supper. As the priest takes the bread, he says,

"Take this, all of you, and eat it:
this is my body which will be given up
for you."

As the priest takes the cup of wine,
he says:

"Take this, all of you, and drink from it:
this is the cup of my blood...."

This part of the Eucharistic Prayer is called the *Consecration*. Through these words and actions of the priest, by the power of the Holy Spirit, the bread and wine become the Body and Blood of Christ. This change that the bread and wine undergo is called *transubstantiation*.

At the end of the Eucharistic Prayer, we say or sing "Amen." Together we are saying "Yes, we believe."

Explain what happens during the Eucharistic Prayer.

63

## We offer gifts, and the Eucharistic Prayer begins.

*Blessed be God forever.*

Ask the students: *How would you feel if someone from the parish leadership team called and asked your family to carry the gifts to the priest next Sunday at Mass?* Have a few volunteers share their responses. Explain that carrying the gifts takes place during the Liturgy of the Eucharist.

Have volunteers read the first two paragraphs. Ask the students to highlight or underline the response in the last sentence in the second paragraph.

Write *Eucharistic Prayer* on the board or on a large sheet of paper. Stress that this is the Church's greatest prayer of praise and thanksgiving. Read aloud the remaining paragraphs. Have the students highlight or underline the words of the priest at the Consecration. Emphasize that Jesus is truly present in the Eucharist.

Ask a few volunteers to explain what happens during the Eucharistic Prayer. You may want the students to read about the Preparation of the Gifts and the Eucharistic Prayer on pages 106–107.

### Optional Activity

Have the students work in pairs. Ask the students in each pair to write captions for the photos on pages 62–63. Then have the pairs take turns sharing the captions with the entire group.

## 3 We receive Holy Communion, and we are sent to bring God's love to others.

*Jesus, grant us your peace.*

Explain to the students that the Liturgy of the Eucharist continues as we prepare to receive Holy Communion. We pray the Lord's Prayer and exchange a Sign of Peace. Have volunteers read the first two paragraphs. You may want the students to read about the Communion Rite on page 107.

Emphasize that we should be prayerful and respectful as we go forward to receive Holy Communion. We should also be respectful and prayerful as we receive Holy Communion.

Have volunteers read the last two paragraphs. Stress the importance of remaining in church for the Concluding Rites.

Read aloud the concluding question. Discuss with the students specific ways they can live the message of the Eucharist by sharing their time and talents with others this week. Pause briefly to have the students reflect quietly on their personal responses to the question.

At this time you may want to explain *Visits to the Most Blessed Sacrament* and *Benediction* on page 120.

### 3 We receive Holy Communion, and we are sent to bring God's love to others.

The Liturgy of the Eucharist continues as we prepare to receive Jesus Christ in Holy Communion. Together we pray the Lord's Prayer, also called the Our Father. We offer a Sign of Peace to each other. We say aloud or sing the Lamb of God, asking for God's mercy and peace. Then the priest breaks the large Host.

At the proper time we come forward to receive Holy Communion. We sing to show our unity with Christ and one another. We receive the Body and Blood of Christ in Holy Communion.

During the last part of Mass, the **Concluding Rites**, the priest blesses us. Then he or the deacon says these or similar words, "Go in peace to love and serve the Lord."

We have been nourished by the celebration of the Eucharist. Now we are sent to love and serve the Lord each day by bringing the peace and love of Jesus to everyone we meet. We can share our time and talents. We can care for the poor, sick, and lonely people we see around us. As members of the Church, we are called to share the Gospel of Jesus Christ with those around us. This is what it means to live the message of the Eucharist we have celebrated, and what it means to be followers of Christ.

How will you share your time and talents with others this week?

#### Do You Know?

The Church urges us to receive Holy Communion each time we participate in the Mass. To receive Holy Communion we must be in the state of grace. Therefore, if we have committed serious sin, we must first receive God's forgiveness in the Sacrament of Penance.

The Church requires us to receive Communion at least once a year. When we receive Communion, our unity with Jesus Christ and the Church, the Body of Christ, is strengthened.

64

#### Do You Know?

Have a volunteer read aloud the feature. Explain that as a sign of respect for Jesus in the Eucharist, we should not take any food or drink for one hour before receiving Holy Communion. This is called the eucharistic fast. When necessary, water and medicine may be taken during this fast.

## Review

Complete the following sentences by writing the correct part of the Mass.

1. Members of the assembly present gifts of bread and wine during the Liturgy of the Eucharist.
2. We sing or say the Gloria during the Introductory Rites.
3. We are sent to serve God and others during the Concluding Rites.
4. Bread and wine become the Body and Blood of Christ during the Liturgy of the Eucharist and/or Eucharistic Prayer and/or Consecration.
5. The priest or deacon proclaims the Gospel during the Liturgy of the Word.

Discuss the following. (See side column.)

6. Explain what happens during the Introductory Rites of Mass.
7. Explain what happens during the Liturgy of the Word.
8. Explain what happens during the Liturgy of the Eucharist.

### Faith Words

assembly (page 62)
Introductory Rites (page 62)
Liturgy of the Word (page 62)
Liturgy of the Eucharist (page 63)
Concluding Rites (page 64)

## With My Family

### Sharing Our Faith

1. At Mass we praise God, and we listen to his Word.
2. We offer gifts, and the Eucharistic Prayer begins.
3. We receive Holy Communion, and we are sent to bring God's love to others.

### PRAYING TOGETHER

At the beginning of the Liturgy of the Eucharist, the priest invites us to lift up our hearts. We respond, "We lift them up to the Lord." Then we praise God by praying or singing:

**Holy, holy, holy Lord,**
**God of power and might,**
**heaven and earth are full of your glory.**
**Hosanna in the highest.**
**Blessed is he who comes in**
**the name of the Lord.**
**Hosanna in the highest.**

### Living Our Faith

In the Concluding Rites at Mass, we are sent to live out the message of the Eucharist. Write ways you can do this.

at home

at school

in the neighborhood

65

## CATECHISM FOCUS

"The Eucharistic celebration always includes: the proclamation of the Word of God; thanksgiving to God the Father for all his benefits, above all the gift of his Son; the consecration of bread and wine; and participation in the liturgical banquet by receiving the Lord's body and blood. These elements constitute one single act of worship." (*CCC*, 1408)

## Conclusion (__ min.)

### Review

Provide five to ten minutes for the students to work independently to complete the first part of the *Review*. Check the students' answers. Clarify any misconceptions. Then discuss the questions in the second part of the *Review*. For possible responses check the pages and paragraphs given below.

**6.** See page 62, paragraph 2.

**7.** See page 62, paragraphs 3 and 4.

**8.** See page 63 and paragraphs 1 and 2 on page 64.

### *Faith Words*

Have the students work in small groups. Ask each group to write a set of clues for the Faith Words. Then have the groups take turns challenging the others by reading aloud their clues and having the other groups guess the appropriate words.

### *More for You to Know*

On page 66 you will find *More for You to Know* for Unit 3. The articles on this page provide additional or supplemental information about the doctrinal concepts presented in Chapters 7–9. These articles are about the liturgy, our common vocation, and the priesthood of the faithful.

### With My Family

#### *Sharing Our Faith*

Encourage the students to share with their families what they have learned about the four parts of the Mass.

#### *Praying Together*

Have a volunteer read the introductory paragraph. Then have the students stand and read the prayer together.

#### *Living Our Faith*

Encourage the students to discuss with their families ways to live out the message of the Eucharist.

# MORE for You to Know

**THE LITURGY** The liturgy is the official public prayer of the Church. The liturgy includes the celebration of the Eucharist and the other sacraments. It also includes the Liturgy of the Hours. We each bring our own selves and our relationship with God to every celebration of the liturgy. We join together as Jesus' true friends and disciples, just as Jesus' first followers did. We proclaim the Good News of Jesus Christ and celebrate his Death and Resurrection. Whenever the liturgy is celebrated, the whole Church is celebrating.

**OUR COMMON VOCATION** A vocation is a calling to a way of life. As baptized Christians we share a common vocation. Our common vocation is a call from God to grow in holiness and to spread the message of Jesus' life and saving work.

**PRIESTHOOD OF THE FAITHFUL** When Jesus was baptized by John the Baptist, the Spirit of the Lord came upon him. This baptismal anointing by the Spirit made it known that Jesus Christ is the Messiah, the Anointed One. Jesus' relationship with God his Father was revealed, and God the Holy Spirit came upon Jesus, marking him as Priest, Prophet, and King.

In the Sacrament of Baptism, we too are anointed. We are called to share in Christ's priestly mission. As baptized members of the Church, we share in Christ's priesthood. This priesthood is not the ordained priesthood but is known as the *priesthood of the faithful.*

As sharers in the priesthood of the faithful, we can all participate in the liturgy, especially the Eucharist, in prayer, and in offering our lives to God.

# UNIT 3 Assessment

**Match the columns.**

1. ___c___ Liturgy of the Eucharist
2. ___d___ Liturgy of the Word
3. ___b___ Introductory Rites
4. ___a___ Concluding Rites

a. The priest blesses us, and we go out to bring God's peace and love to others.

b. We prepare to hear God's Word, and to celebrate the Eucharist as a community.

c. The bread and wine become the Body and Blood of Christ which we receive in Holy Communion.

d. We listen and respond to God's Word.

**Write the term that best fits each statement.**

5. During this sacrament the bishop says, "Be sealed with the Gift of the Holy Spirit." **Confirmation**
6. We are anointed with this oil at both Baptism and Confirmation. **Chrism**
7. This is the Church's great act of worship. **the Mass**
8. Through this sacrament, we become children of God and are freed from sin. **Baptism**
9. In this sacrament we receive the Body and Blood of Christ. **Eucharist**

**Write your responses on a separate piece of paper.**

10. What happens during the Eucharistic Prayer of the Mass? **Through the words and actions of the priest and the power of the Holy Spirit, the bread and wine become the Body and Blood of Jesus.**
11. Write two reasons why the Sacrament of Baptism is so important. **See page 50 of Chapter 6.**
12. Name two ways we participate at Mass. **See Chapter 9.**
13. What are some ways we can love and serve the Lord? **See page 64 of Chapter 9.**
14. What action connects the Sacraments of Baptism and Confirmation? **The anointing with Chrism connects Baptism and Confirmation.**
15. Why is the celebration of the Eucharist, the Mass, at the center of the Church's life? **The Eucharist is the sacrament of the Body and Blood of Christ. We receive Jesus himself.**

# Chapter 10

## GOALS

*to focus on the Ten Commandments as ways to live in God's love; to appreciate that by following God's law, we can find true happiness*

## GETTING READY

**Opening Prayer:** *On the prayer table, place a Bible opened to the Book of Exodus.*

**Materials Needed:** *crayons or markers (page 69), Bible, highlighters or colored pencils, writing paper for **Optional Activity** (page 70)*

## Catechist Background

When God freed the Israelites from their captivity in Egypt, they began their journey through the desert to Canaan, the land God had promised to them. On their journey and in Canaan, the Israelites were to live as a holy people according to the covenant God made with them. (See Exodus 6:2–8.)

To celebrate and safeguard the freedom of the faith community, God gave the Ten Commandments to Moses on Mount Sinai. Through these commandments God made his will known.

Jesus was Jewish and lived out his faith by embracing and following the Ten Commandments. He wanted his disciples to follow his example.

## Opening Prayer

Begin by pausing for a few minutes of silence. Ask the students to reflect quietly on some of the things they did yesterday. Then ask them to reflect on some of the things they will be doing today.

Invite the students to gather in the prayer space. Pray together the Lord's Prayer. Then ask the students to open their hands in front of them, holding palms up in a prayerful gesture. Then read each line of the following prayer, pausing at the break marks. Ask the students to repeat the line during each pause.

*O God, we offer to you today/all we think, and do, and say/uniting it with what was done/on earth by Jesus Christ, your Son.*

Encourage the students to pray these or similar words as they begin each day.

# 10 The Ten Commandments Guide Us

## Following Rules

What rules might the children in the photographs be following?

What are some rules that you follow at home? in school? in the neighborhood?

How do rules or laws help us?

In the space provided, write about or draw yourself following one of these rules.

68

In the first three commandments we are called to love, honor, and worship God above all else. In the Fourth through Tenth Commandments, we are called to love our neighbors as ourselves. As Jesus showed us, the disciple who lives by the Ten Commandments will live in true freedom, the freedom of the sons and daughters of God. This is our human dignity because we are made in the image and likeness of God. The gift of the Ten Commandments is a path to that true freedom.

## Reflection

"Happy those whose way is blameless,
who walk by the teaching of the
LORD.
Happy those who observe God's decrees,
who seek the LORD with all
their heart."

*(Psalm 119:1–2)*

## Introduction ( __ min.)

Point out to the students that people of all ages follow laws and rules each day. Ask the students to think of ones that they have followed today. Invite a few volunteers to share their responses.

Then direct the students' attention to the photographs on pages 68 and 69. Talk with the students about the rules the young people in the photographs are following. Also discuss rules and laws the students follow at home, in school, and in the neighborhood. Ask the students to draw or write about a specific law in the space provided. Then help the students identify how laws and rules help us.

### We Will Learn...

**Read the three statements aloud. Point out that the students will be learning about the Ten Commandments and how following them helps us to live in God's love.**

# Presentation (__ min.)

## 1 God gave us the Ten Commandments to help us to live in his love.

*God, we know that you want us to live in true freedom.*

Begin by explaining that the Israelites were in Egypt because they had come there when there was a great famine in their land. But over time the Egyptians began treating the Israelites as slaves.

Read aloud the story of the Ten Commandments as presented in the second through the fourth paragraphs on page 70. Point out that God gave the commandments to Moses and the Israelites when they were traveling in the desert on their way to the land God had promised them. Explain that the commandments were written on stone tablets. You may want to read the following passages or summarize them for the students: Exodus 24:12–18, Exodus 32:1–29, and Exodus 34:1–11.

**Note:** The wording of the commandments is the *Traditional Catechetical Formula* in the *Catechism of the Catholic Church.*

Draw the students' attention to the Ten Commandments chart. Have the students form two groups. Have one group read the First Commandment. Have the second group read what the First Commandment means for us. Do the same for each commandment.

In your discussion of the concluding question, stress that when we obey the commandments, we find true happiness and freedom.

### 1 God gave us the Ten Commandments to help us to live in his love.

In the Bible we read that God gave the people of Israel the Ten Commandments, or laws, for their safety and freedom. This is the story of the Ten Commandments.

Thousands of years ago the people of Israel lived as slaves in Egypt. But God had chosen the Israelites to be his own people—the ones who would know and worship the one true God. This was hard for them because they were slaves of the Egyptians, who worshiped many false gods. To help the Israelites, God gave them a great leader named Moses.

Through Moses God helped the Israelites escape from Egypt. He led them to safety and freedom in the desert. In return God asked the Israelites to join in a special agreement, or covenant. A **covenant** is a special agreement between God and his people. God said, "If you hearken to my voice and keep my covenant, you shall be my special possession, dearer to me than all other people" (Exodus 19:5).

The people promised to obey God and keep the covenant. Then God gave Moses the laws of the covenant called the **Ten Commandments**. The Ten Commandments would help God's people to remain faithful to the one true God and to be truly safe and free.

How do you think the Ten Commandments help us to be safe and free?

| The Ten Commandments | What the Commandments Mean for Us |
|---|---|
| 1. I am the LORD your God: you shall not have strange gods before me. | God must come first in our lives. No person and no thing can be more important to us than God. |
| 2. You shall not take the name of the LORD your God in vain. | We must respect God's name, the name of Jesus, and holy places. |
| 3. Remember to keep holy the LORD'S Day. | We must worship God on Sundays and holy days, and must rest from work. |
| 4. Honor your father and your mother. | We must love, honor, and obey our parents and guardians. |
| 5. You shall not kill. | We must respect and care for the gift of life. |
| 6. You shall not commit adultery. | We must respect our own bodies and the bodies of others in thought, word, and deed. |
| 7. You shall not steal. | We must not take or destroy what belongs to others. |
| 8. You shall not bear false witness against your neighbor. | We must respect the truth. |
| 9. You shall not covet your neighbor's wife. | We must protect the holiness of marriage and the sacredness of human sexuality. |
| 10. You shall not covet your neighbor's goods. | We must respect the rights and property of others. |

70

## Optional Activity

Have the students work in pairs. Ask each pair to write a prayer to thank God for giving us the Ten Commandments. When the students are finished writing, have each set of partners share the prayer with the group. Collect the prayers and clip or staple them together. Place the collection in the prayer space.

## 2 The first three commandments call us to love God.

The First Commandment states that God must come before everyone and everything else in our lives. The Second Commandment reminds us that God's name is holy and must be used with love and respect.

The Third Commandment states that we are to keep holy the Lord's Day. For Catholics, Sunday is the Lord's Day because it was on a Sunday that Jesus Christ rose from the dead. On Sundays we gather with our parish community to celebrate the Mass. Participating in the Mass is the most important way of keeping the Lord's Day holy because the Sacrament of the Eucharist is at the very center of the Christian life. Catholics must participate in Mass on Sunday or Saturday evening and on Holy Days of Obligation. (See list on page 58.)

On Sunday we must also rest from work or other activities so that we can keep the Lord's Day holy.

How does keeping the first three commandments show that you love God?

### Do You Know?

When Jesus was growing up in Nazareth, he studied the teachings of the Old Testament. He treasured the covenant God made with his people. He studied the Ten Commandments and obeyed them. When Jesus was older, his followers saw that Jesus lived according to the covenant. One day as Jesus was teaching, he explained, "Do not think that I have come to abolish the law or the prophets. I have come not to abolish but to fulfill" (Matthew 5:17).

71

## 2 The first three commandments call us to love God.

*God, we love you above all things.*

Have the students use a specific color to highlight or underline the first three commandments on the chart on page 70.

Ask a volunteer to read the first paragraph on page 71. Ask: *What are some things people put first in their lives?* Help the students conclude that sometimes people put sports, friends, music, celebrities, money, and possessions before anyone or anything. Explain that this is not what we are asked to do in the First Commandment.

Explain to the students that the names of the three Persons of the Blessed Trinity should always be spoken with respect. Ask the students to identify the names we use to address the three Persons of the Trinity. List these names on the board or on a large sheet of paper. Possible responses include: Lord, God the Father, Jesus, Jesus Christ, Jesus our Savior, Holy Spirit.

Then read aloud the second paragraph. Stress that participating in the celebration of Mass with our parish community is the most important way of keeping the Lord's Day holy. Point out that some people have jobs that require them to work on Sunday. Explain that to help people fulfill their obligation many parishes have Masses scheduled on Saturday evening or a few during the day on Sunday.

Discuss with the students ways we can help make Sunday a special day for our families: help to prepare a special family meal, spend more time with our families, watch younger brothers and sisters to give parents a chance to rest, contact family members who live at a distance.

Read the concluding question, and ask the students to reflect quietly on their responses.

### Do You Know?

Have a volunteer read the feature aloud. Point out that Jesus thought it was very important to follow the Ten Commandments. You may want to read the story of Jesus and the Rich Young Man (Matthew 19:16–21).

## 3 The Fourth through the Tenth Commandments call us to love others and ourselves.

*God, may we live according to your law.*

Remind the students that the first three commandments are guides for us in loving God. Then explain that the other seven commandments guide us in loving others and ourselves.

Have volunteers read the paragraphs about these seven commandments. Pause after each paragraph to have the students tell in their own words what we are called to do in following the particular commandment or commandments.

For the Fourth Commandment, you may want to point out that in Jesus' early life within the Holy Family, Jesus respected Mary and Joseph (Luke 2:51). Jesus also taught that we should obey civil authority (Matthew 22:19–22).

For the Fifth Commandment, you may want to explain that Jesus asks us to use positive ways to deal with anger (Matthew 5:21–22). Discuss with the students positive ways of dealing with anger. Possible suggestions: talking things over, not bullying, removing oneself from a setting while being angry.

For the Sixth and Ninth Commandments, you may want to refer to the explanation of the human virtues of chastity and modesty (Unit 4: *More for You to Know*, page 98).

For the Seventh and Tenth Commandments, you may want to explain that we follow these commandments by being grateful for what we own and sharing these gifts with others.

Have a volunteer read the last paragraph. Emphasize that God has given us the commandments to help us to live peaceful and loving lives.

### 3 The Fourth through the Tenth Commandments call us to love others and ourselves.

The Fourth Commandment states that we are to honor our parents. Our parents have given us life. We owe them love, respect, and care. We should also show respect for our guardians, our teachers, older members of the community, and all those in positions of authority.

The Fifth Commandment reminds us that all life is a gift from God, from the moment of conception until natural death. Thus, the Fifth Commandment forbids abortion, suicide, and murder, which includes euthanasia. We must not do anything that would harm others or harm our own bodies and minds.

The Sixth and Ninth Commandments remind us that our human sexuality is something sacred. We must respect our bodies and the bodies of others in thought, word, and deed.

The Seventh Commandment forbids destroying or stealing what belongs to others. We must return items or repay others if we have taken their property. The Tenth Commandment forbids envy, or jealousy of what others own.

The Eighth Commandment requires us to tell the truth. It forbids lying and gossip that hurts others. If we have hurt the good name of others we must try to repair it.

The Ten Commandments show us how to remain faithful to God in this life and to attain eternal life. The commandments help us to live together in peace and love. God has given us these laws for our safety and our freedom.

How does keeping the Fourth through the Tenth Commandments show that you love God and others?

72

## Optional Activity

Have the students work in small groups. Ask each group to prepare a TV talk show segment about the importance of the Ten Commandments in our lives. Then ask the members of the groups to take turns presenting their segments to all the students.

## Review

**Write *True* or *False* for the following sentences. On a separate piece of paper, change the false sentences to make them true.**

1. False Through ~~Jesus,~~ Moses God led the Egyptians out of slavery.
2. True Catholics keep Sunday as the Lord's Day.
3. True When we keep the first three commandments, we are showing love for God.
4. True God gave us the Ten Commandments for our safety and our freedom.

**Discuss the following.** (See side column.)

5. How did the Israelites keep their covenant with God?
6. What are ways we can keep the Lord's Day holy?
7. What are some ways we show love for ourselves and others by keeping the Fourth through the Tenth Commandments?

covenant (page 70)

Ten Commandments (page 70)

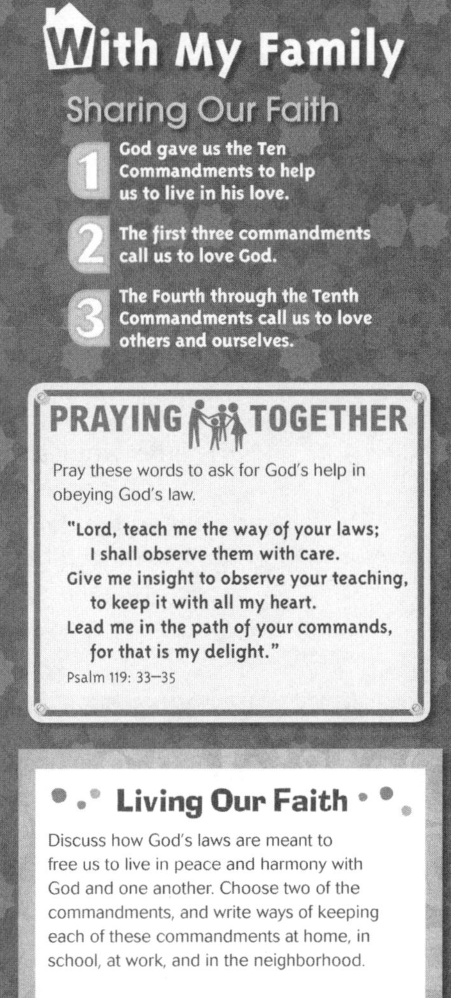

## With My Family

### Sharing Our Faith

1. God gave us the Ten Commandments to help us to live in his love.
2. The first three commandments call us to love God.
3. The Fourth through the Tenth Commandments call us to love others and ourselves.

### PRAYING TOGETHER

Pray these words to ask for God's help in obeying God's law.

"Lord, teach me the way of your laws;
I shall observe them with care.
Give me insight to observe your teaching,
to keep it with all my heart.
Lead me in the path of your commands,
for that is my delight."

Psalm 119: 33–35

### Living Our Faith

Discuss how God's laws are meant to free us to live in peace and harmony with God and one another. Choose two of the commandments, and write ways of keeping each of these commandments at home, in school, at work, and in the neighborhood.

______________________________

______________________________

______________________________

Talk together about following these ways, and how they can promote peace and harmony in your lives.

73

## CATECHISM FOCUS

"In fidelity to Scripture and in conformity with Jesus' example, the tradition of the Church has always acknowledged the primordial importance and significance of the Decalogue." (CCC, 2078)

(Decalogue: the Ten Commandments given to Moses on Mount Sinai)

# Conclusion (_ min.)

## Review

Provide five to ten minutes for the students to work independently to complete the first part of the *Review.* Then discuss the questions in the second part of the *Review*. Possible responses follow.

**5.** God promised the Israelites that if they listened to him, followed the commandments, and were faithful to him, he would guide and protect them.

**6.** We can keep the Lord's Day holy by gathering with our parish community for Mass. We should try to rest from work and other strenuous activities.

**7.** Accept reasonable responses. See page 72.

### *Faith Words*

Ask the students to write a sentence that includes both words.

## With My Family

### *Sharing Our Faith*

Encourage the students to share with their families what they have learned about the Ten Commandments.

### *Praying Together*

Pray together the psalm verse. Ask the students to share the verse with their families this week.

### *Living Our Faith*

Ask a volunteer to read the activity directions. Encourage the students to do the activity together with their families this week.

Chapter 11

# Catechist Background

Through the voice of the Prophet Isaiah, God promised the Israelites a "Teacher" who would guide them by saying "This is the way; walk in it" (Isaiah 30:21). They would see this teacher with their own eyes and know that his instruction was trustworthy. We know that Jesus is the fulfillment of Isaiah's prophecy. In his Sermon on the Mount (Matthew 5:1–12), Jesus illuminates the road his disciples are to follow in the Beatitudes.

The Beatitudes echo God's promises to Abraham and clarify the fulfillment of these promises in the Kingdom of God. In the first three Beatitudes we are reminded that Jesus identified himself with the poor, the alienated, and the helpless of society.

## GOALS

*to learn that following Jesus' teaching leads to true happiness; to respond to the Great Commandment by following it in our everyday lives*

## GETTING READY

**Opening Prayer:** *On the prayer table, place a Bible and a battery-operated candle.*

**Materials Needed:** *large sheet of paper (page 76), poster board for **Sharing Scripture** (page 76), highlighters or colored pencils*

## Opening Prayer

Invite the students to remain seated. You may wish to use the following script to guide the students in reflective prayer about the Sermon on the Mount (Matthew 5—7).

*Close your eyes. Visualize yourself sitting on a mountainside on a warm day. You are one person among thousands listening to Jesus teach. Yet you feel he is speaking directly to you.*

*You listen closely as Jesus talks about God's Kingdom, about helping poor people, and about judging others. You tell yourself you want to remember how Jesus wants people to pray.*

*You are amazed by Jesus' challenging words —to be peacemakers, to be light for others by doing good deeds, and to treat others the way that you would have them treat you. You think that you will never forget Jesus' words.*

Ask the students to reflect on ways they will answer Jesus' challenge.

# 11 Jesus Teaches About True Happiness

"Tomorrow's the big day!" Caroline said to her friend Mia when they were having lunch on Friday.

"Yes! My sleeping bag is packed, and I'm ready to go," replied Mia. The two friends were going with the Junior Wilderness Club on their first overnight camping trip. They had been looking forward to it for months.

Later that evening the phone rang at Caroline's apartment. It was Mia. "I can't go camping tomorrow," she whispered. Mia explained that her grandfather had gone into the hospital. Mia said, "Mom is needed at the hospital. She would feel better if I were not so far away. I'm worried about Grandpop, and I don't think I would enjoy the trip. I'll talk to you on Monday. Have a good time."

Caroline told her parents what had happened. Caroline said, "I don't want to go camping now. I won't have any fun without Mia."

We live these Beatitudes when we acknowledge our dependence on God.

In the remaining five Beatitudes we are called to walk the path of justice and mercy. We are directed on the road of peacemaking and integrity. We are challenged to serve the cause of the Kingdom, as individuals and as a community, despite persecution or hatred.

In following the road to true happiness, we follow Jesus' Great Commandment . If we heed Jesus' command, we love God with our entire being. We love others as we love ourselves. Sometimes we may find that loving God, others, and ourselves as Jesus has asked us to do can be quite challenging. We may get detoured, but if we do, God will always seek us out. He will never take away his invitation to eternal happiness.

## Reflection

"At present we see indistinctly, as in a mirror, but then face to face. At present I know partially; then I shall know fully, as I am fully known. So faith, hope, love remain, these three; but the greatest of these is love."

*(1 Corinthians 13:12–13)*

Caroline's dad said, "I have an idea. Why don't you invite Mia to spend Saturday night with us? You can camp out here."

Caroline's mom called Mia's mom and said, "On your way to the hospital, you can drop off Mia for a camp out here. I'll call the troop leader and explain." Both Mia and her mom were very happy about this plan.

On Saturday the two girls set up a tent in Caroline's room. They made a giant get-well card for Mia's grandfather. After supper they sang camping songs, and told scary stories.

Before the friends fell asleep, Caroline said, "This is great! I'm sure having fun at our own camp out."

Mia agreed and said, "Caroline, I am so happy that you are my friend. You and your family are helping me and my mom. And I'm sure Grandpop will like the card we made."

...

**Has something ever happened that you thought would spoil your happiness but instead actually added to it?**

**What makes you happy?**

**How can you help others to be happy?**

**We Will Learn...**

1 Jesus teaches his disciples about loving God and others.

2 Jesus teaches us the Beatitudes.

3 We are called to live in faith, hope, and love.



## Introduction ( __ min.)

Have volunteers read the story "Camping Out." Then ask: *How do you think Mia felt when she found out about her grandfather? How did Caroline feel when she found out that Mia couldn't come to the camp out?*

Then talk about the end of the story. Ask: *How did both girls turn their disappointment into a positive experience?* Point out that by thinking of others, they were still able to have fun even though the camp out was not with the entire Wilderness group.

Discuss the questions at the end of the story.

### We Will Learn...

Read the three statements. Point out to the students that in this chapter they will be studying Jesus' teaching about loving God and others.

## Presentation ( __ min.)

### 1 Jesus teaches his disciples about loving God and others.

*Jesus, our Teacher, we are your disciples.*

Have the students look at the illustration on pages 76 and 77. As the students focus on the illustration, ask a volunteer to read the first paragraph.

Have a volunteer read the second paragraph. Remind the students that, in the Ten Commandments, the first three commandments pertain to showing love for God. The other seven commandments pertain to showing love for others and ourselves. Thus, the Great Commandment sums up the Ten Commandments.

On the board or on a large sheet of paper, make a three-column chart. At the top of the left column, write *God*. At the top of the middle column, write *others*; at the top of the right column, write *ourselves*. Have the students suggest ways of loving God, others, and ourselves. List the suggestions in the appropriate columns. When you have completed the chart, you may want to consider displaying it in the prayer space.

Read the concluding question. Pause briefly to allow the students to reflect quietly about their responses.

### 1 Jesus teaches his disciples about loving God and others.

Jesus went from town to town teaching and showing people how much God loves us. He lived by the Ten Commandments and urged his disciples to follow his example. One day someone asked Jesus, "Teacher, which commandment in the law is the greatest?" Jesus said to the man, "You shall love the Lord, your God, with all your heart, with all your soul, and with all your mind" (Matthew 22:36–37). Jesus also told the man, "You shall love your neighbor as yourself" (Matthew 22:39).

We call Jesus' answer the Great Commandment. Following the Great Commandment helps us to show our love for God, ourselves, and others. It helps us find true happiness in the Kingdom of God.

How will you follow the Great Commandment?

76

## Sharing Scripture

In 1 Corinthians 13 we read Saint's Paul's definition of love. Read aloud verses one through eight. Then reread verses four through seven. Help the students to make a chart. In the first column list what love is, and in the second column list what love is not. Have the students add their own entries for both columns.

## 2 Jesus teaches us the Beatitudes.

One day many people were gathered to listen to Jesus teach. He taught them the Beatitudes. The **Beatitudes** are Jesus' teachings that describe the way to live as his disciples. When we live as Jesus' disciples, we can find true happiness. In the Beatitudes the word *blessed* means "happy." This is a good clue to what the Beatitudes are all about.

Jesus taught us the Beatitudes as guidelines for being truly happy, and reaching our final goal: life in God's Kingdom forever as his sons and daughters. Look at the chart on this page. It names each Beatitude and states how observing each one helps us to spread the Kingdom of God.

How can we thank Jesus for teaching us ways to find true happiness?

| The Beatitudes | What the Beatitudes Mean for Us |
|---|---|
| "Blessed are the poor in spirit, for theirs is the kingdom of heaven." | We are "poor in spirit" when we depend on God for everything. No person or thing is more important to us than God. We remember that God created us, and our goal in life is to be happy with him forever in Heaven. |
| "Blessed are they who mourn, for they will be comforted." | We "mourn" when we are sad because of the sin, evil, and suffering in the world. We trust that God will comfort us. |
| "Blessed are the meek, for they will inherit the land." | We are "meek" when we show respect, gentleness, and patience to all people, even those who do not respect us. |
| "Blessed are they who hunger and thirst for righteousness, for they will be satisfied." | We "hunger and thirst for righteousness" when we are fair and just toward others. |
| "Blessed are the merciful, for they will be shown mercy." | We are "merciful" when we are willing to forgive others, and do not take revenge on those who hurt us. |
| "Blessed are the clean of heart, for they will see God." | We are "clean of heart" when we are faithful to God's teachings, and try to see God in all people and in all situations. |
| "Blessed are the peacemakers, for they will be called children of God." | We are "peacemakers" when we treat others with love and respect, and when we help others to stop fighting and make peace. |
| "Blessed are they who are persecuted for the sake of righteousness, for theirs is the kingdom of heaven." Matthew 5:3–10 | We are "persecuted for the sake of righteousness" when we are ignored or insulted for following Jesus' example. |

77

## 2 Jesus teaches us the Beatitudes.

*Jesus, you show us the way to true happiness.*

Ask the students: *What is the Kingdom of God?* Refer the students to Chapter 2, page 16. Have a few volunteers share their responses. Stress that the Kingdom of God is the power of God's love active in our lives and in the world.

Ask: *What are other words for* happy? Have a few volunteers share their responses. Explain that *blessed* is another word for *happy*. Then read aloud the first paragraph. Ask the students to highlight or underline the third sentence.

Point out that the Beatitudes are guidelines. Assign each student to one of two groups. Have the students look at the chart on page 77. Ask Group 1 to read each Beatitude and Group 2 to read the explanation for each Beatitude. Then discuss ways that the students can put the Beatitudes into practice at home, in school, or in the world at large.

Read the concluding question. Have a few volunteers share their responses. Possible responses include: saying prayers of thanks, putting the Beatitudes into practice, sharing with others what they have learned about the Beatitudes.

## Optional Activity

Have the students work in small groups. Ask each group to prepare a role-play in which the members show ways to live out the Beatitudes. When the students have finished preparing, have them take turns presenting their role-plays for the other groups. Have the other students guess the appropriate Beatitude.

## 3 We are called to live in faith, hope, and love.

*Holy Spirit, help us to be people of faith, of hope, and of love.*

Ask the students: *What are good habits that we can develop?* Have a few volunteers share their responses. Possible responses include: being polite, obeying safety rules, getting enough exercise, and eating healthy foods.

Explain that a virtue is a good habit. Have a volunteer read aloud the first paragraph. Stress that the theological virtues of faith, hope, and charity, or love, are given to us by God.

Ask a volunteer to read the paragraph about faith. Have the students highlight or underline the first sentence. Then pray together the Apostles' Creed on page 121.

Ask volunteers to read the paragraphs about hope and charity, which is another name for love. Have the students highlight or underline the sentences explaining what these virtues are.

Have the students reflect quietly on ways they can be people of faith, hope, and charity. Then invite volunteers to share their responses. Possible responses include: by living according to the teachings of Jesus Christ and the Church; by trusting in Jesus' promises that we would share in God's life forever; by showing our love for God and others in our thoughts, words, and actions.

### 3 We are called to live in faith, hope, and love.

A **virtue** is a good habit that helps us to act according to God's love for us. Virtues help guide our conduct with the help of God's grace. The virtues of faith, hope, and charity are *theological virtues.* They are gifts given to us directly by God.

- **Faith** is the virtue that enables us to believe in God and all that the Church teaches us. We live as people of *faith* by believing in all that God has told us about himself and all that he has done. Faith is necessary in order to be saved. We profess our faith in the words of the Apostles' Creed and by living according to the teachings of Jesus Christ and the Church. The Holy Spirit helps us to have faith in God and to strive for our greatest goal, life forever with God in Heaven.
- **Hope** is the virtue that enables us to trust in God's promise to share his life with us forever. We live as people of *hope* by trusting in Jesus and his promises of the Kingdom of God and of eternal life.
- **Charity**, or love, is the greatest of all virtues. It enables us to love God and to love our neighbor. We live as people of *charity*, or love, by loving God above all things and our neighbors as ourselves.

When we live with faith, hope, and charity, we gradually come to understand and live the happiness that Jesus was teaching in the Beatitudes.

Name one way you can be a person of faith, a person of hope, and a person of charity.

### Do You Know?

By our Baptism we are all called to share the Good News of Jesus Christ by what we say and do. This is known as *evangelization.* Evangelization takes place in our everyday lives. Through our words and actions we evangelize those who have not heard the message of Jesus Christ. We can also evangelize those who have heard the message but need encouragement to live out the gift of faith that is theirs.

78

### Do You Know?

Before explaining what evangelization is, you may want the students to refer to Chapter 2, page 15. Read aloud the second paragraph about the ways Jesus shared the Good News of God's love.

Ask a volunteer to read aloud the feature. Point out that we can evangelize through our actions as well as our words.

## Review

**Fill in the blanks.**

1. In the Beatitudes the word **blessed** means "happy."
2. The Beatitudes are teachings of Jesus that describe the way to live as his **disciples**.
3. A **virtue** is a good habit that helps us to act according to God's love for us.
4. Following the Great Commandment helps us to show our love for **God**, **others**, and **ourselves**.

**Discuss the following. (See side column.)**

5. Choose one of the Beatitudes and explain what it means.
6. How do the virtues of faith, hope, and charity help us to live as disciples of Jesus?

Beatitudes (page 77)
virtue (page 78)
faith (page 78)
hope (page 78)
charity (page 78)

## With My Family

### Sharing Our Faith

1. Jesus teaches his disciples about loving God and others.
2. Jesus teaches us the Beatitudes.
3. We are called to live in faith, hope, and love.

### PRAYING TOGETHER

The following is a traditional prayer of the Church. Read and reflect on the meaning of the words. Pray these words every day this week.

**An Act of Love**

**O Lord God, I love you above all things and I love my neighbor for your sake because you are the highest, infinite and perfect good, worthy of all my love. In this love I intend to live and die. Amen.**

### Living Our Faith

As a family, identify people you know or have read about who live or lived according to the Beatitudes. Then ask each family member to decide what he or she can do to be more of a "Beatitude person" today. Write some ways here.

______________________________

______________________________

______________________________

______________________________

79

# Conclusion (__ min.)

### Review

Have the students work independently to complete the first part of the *Review*. Check the students' answers. Then discuss the questions in the second part of the *Review*.

**5.** Refer to the chart on page 77.

**6.** Faith helps us to believe in all that God has told us about himself and all that he has done. It helps us to live according to the teachings of Jesus. Hope enables us to trust in Jesus and his promises of the Kingdom of God and eternal life. Charity enables us to love God above all things and our neighbors as ourselves.

***Faith Words***

Scramble the letters of the Faith Words. Write the scrambles on the board or a large sheet of paper. You may wish to have the students unscramble: **tibaedtuse** for *Beatitudes*, **rytihac** for *charity*, **ohep** for *hope*, **iatfh** for *faith*, and **uviert** for *virtue*.

### With My Family

***Sharing Our Faith***

Ask the students to share with their families what they have learned about the Great Commandment, the Beatitudes, and the theological virtues.

***Praying Together***

Read the prayer together. Explain that the word *infinite* means "endless" or "immeasureable." Encourage the students to share the prayer with family members.

***Living Our Faith***

Discuss with the students what it means to live according to the Beatitudes. Encourage the students to work on the activity with their families.

## CATECHISM FOCUS

**"The Beatitudes teach us the final end to which God calls us: the Kingdom, the vision of God, participation in the divine nature, eternal life, filiation, rest in God." (CCC, 1726)**

**For additional reference and reflection, see *CCC*, 1725, 1727–1729, 1833–1844.**

# Chapter 12

**GOALS**

*to learn that Jesus Christ offers God's forgiveness; to appreciate the healing power of Jesus Christ that we receive in the Sacrament of Penance*

**GETTING READY**

**Opening Prayer:** *On the prayer table, place the Bible and a battery-operated candle.*

**Materials Needed:** *parish bulletin for **Liturgy Connection** (page 83), highlighters or colored pencils, strips of light-colored construction paper (one strip per student) and tape or stapler for **Optional Activity** (page 84)*

## Catechist Background

What words do you associate with the words *sin* and *forgiveness*? One word Jesus associated with these terms was *joy*: "I tell you . . . there will be more joy in heaven over one sinner who repents than over ninety–nine righteous people who have no need of repentance" (Luke 15:7).

Forgiveness is at the core of a life of discipleship. Because all of us are born with Original Sin, the potential to commit personal sin is always with us. But when we sin, we can always seek God's forgiveness.

By his actions and in his parables, Jesus showed that God always welcomes us back and forgives our sins. This is what we celebrate in the Sacrament

## Opening Prayer

Pause and ask the students to reflect quietly on what they have learned about the Ten Commandments, the Great Commandment, and the Beatitudes.

Then invite the students to gather in the prayer space. Ask a volunteer to read the following prayer aloud. Have the volunteer pause at the indicated breaks. Ask the other students to repeat the prayer words.

*Jesus, I believe that you are with me always./Help me to remember your example/when I have a decision to make./Help me to decide to do the right thing/and to remember you as I make my choice./Guide my words and actions so that they may have a positive effect on others./Amen.*

of Penance and Reconciliation. Trusting in God's love and mercy, we confess our sins to the priest. We express our sorrow, our contrition for what we have done. We are given a penance, an action to do or prayer to say, to help fashion us into more loving people. Finally, we receive absolution from the priest. Repentant and absolved, we are restored or strengthened in our right relationship with God and the Church.

When we ask and receive forgiveness, when we offer it to others, our brokenness is transformed into a means of grace, so that "where sin increased, grace overflowed all the more" (Romans 5:20). This is Christ's victory over sin. We celebrate with great joy the grace and forgiveness in which we all share.

## Reflection

"Awareness of our own sinfulness, including that which is inherited, is the first condition for salvation; the next is the confession of this sin before God, who desires only to receive this confession so that he can save man. To save means to embrace and lift up with redemptive love, with love that is always greater than any sin."

*Pope John Paul II in Crossing the Threshold of Faith*

## Introduction ( ___ min.)

Ask volunteers to read "Best Friends." Then ask: *Why do you think Adam's feelings were hurt when Carlos laughed at him? How did Carlos know that he had hurt his friend's feelings?* Focus on how knowing that he had hurt Adam's feelings caused Carlos to feel badly too.

Ask: *What do you think Carlos should say to Adam? How do you think Adam should respond?* Provide about five minutes for the students to write their responses on the lines provided. Then ask volunteers to share their responses.

Read aloud the questions following the story. Help the students to conclude that it is important for friends to ask for forgiveness and to forgive.

### We Will Learn...

**Have a volunteer read the three statements. Emphasize God's great love for us and his willingness to forgive us.**

## Presentation ( __ min.)

### 1 Jesus taught us about God's love and forgiveness.

*God, we turn to you in trust and love.*

You may want to begin by reading the parable of the prodigal son (Luke 15: 11–24) or the story of Jesus and Zacchaeus (Luke 19: 1–10). Emphasize the way the son or Zacchaeus had a change of heart.

Then write the word *conversion* on the board or a large sheet of paper. Explain that it comes from a Latin word that means "to turn toward." Point out that Jesus called people to turn away from sin, to convert or turn back to God. Then read the first and second paragraphs.

Remind the students that when we are baptized, we are freed from Original Sin. Then read the third paragraph.

On the board or a large sheet of paper, write the words *penance* and *reconciliation*. Explain that *penance* comes from a word that means "to show sorrow," and *reconciliation* comes from a word that means "the act of restoring harmony or friendship." Then read aloud the last paragraph.

Ask the concluding question. Help the students to conclude that when we are reconciled with God, our sins have been forgiven. Our friendship with God has been strengthened or restored.

### 1 Jesus taught us about God's love and forgiveness.

By the way he lived and the things he did, Jesus helped people to turn to God his Father and to follow God's law. Jesus wanted people to turn away from sin and grow closer to God.

During his ministry, Jesus helped his followers turn to God his Father with love and trust. He called them to conversion. **Conversion** is turning back to God with all one's heart. Jesus made their conversion possible by actually forgiving people's sins. They were then reconciled, or brought together again, with God.

As Jesus' followers today, we first receive God's forgiveness in the Sacrament of Baptism. We are freed from Original Sin, and forgiven any personal sins we may have committed. We begin our new life in Jesus Christ.

Yet, after Baptism, we sometimes make choices that do not show love for God, ourselves, and others. Just as he did two thousand years ago with those who followed him, Jesus today forgives those who are truly sorry. He does this through the Church in the Sacrament of Penance and Reconciliation. We can call this sacrament the Sacrament of Penance. It has also been called the sacrament of conversion, of confession, of forgiveness, and of Reconciliation.

What does it mean to be reconciled with God?

### Do You Know?

We prepare to celebrate the Sacrament of Penance by making an examination of conscience. We think about our choices and determine whether or not we have followed God's law and the teachings and example of Jesus. Doing this helps us to judge our decisions and actions and to know what we need to confess. Serious sins need to be confessed because they completely break our friendship with God. These sins must be forgiven so that we can again share in God's grace. We also confess our less serious sins. The forgiveness of these sins strengthens our weakened friendship with God, and helps us continue loving God and others. If we have committed serious sin, we must receive God's forgiveness in the Sacrament of Penance before receiving Holy Communion.

82

### Do You Know?

Explain that our conscience is a gift from God that helps us to know the difference between right and wrong. Then read aloud the paragraph.

You may want to refer the students to the examination of conscience on page 109 of the text.

## 2 We celebrate the Sacrament of Penance and Reconciliation.

Our conscience is our ability to know the difference between good and evil, right and wrong. When we think and do things that lead us away from God or fail to do the good that we can do, we sin. Sin is a thought, word, deed, or omission against God's law.

Every sin weakens our friendship with God and can lead to sinful habits. Less serious sin, *venial sin*, does not turn us completely away from God. Very serious sin, *mortal sin*, does completely turn us away from God because it is a choice that we freely make to do something that we know is seriously wrong. If we do not confess mortal sins before we die, we risk eternal separation from God which is called *Hell*.

God never stops loving us, even when we sin. He will always forgive us if we are sorry. We can receive God's forgiveness in the Sacrament of Penance. The sacrament has four main parts:

- Contrition—We express our heartfelt sorrow for our sins. We pray an Act of Contrition as a sign of sorrow and intention to sin no more.
- Confession—We confess, or tell, our sins to the priest.
- Penance—The priest gives us a penance, an action that shows we are sorry for our sins. It is sometimes a prayer or an act of service. Accepting this penance is a sign that we are turning back to God and are willing to change our lives.
- Absolution—Our sins are absolved, or forgiven. In the name of Christ and the Church and through the power of the Holy Spirit, a priest grants the forgiveness of sins. As a sign that our sins are being forgiven, the priest extends his hand and prays the words of absolution. We respond, "Amen."

Whether we celebrate the Sacrament of Penance individually or in a communal penance service, we always confess our sins individually to the priest and receive absolution from him. And each time we celebrate the Sacrament of Penance, whether individually or in a group, we are joined to the whole Church.

In the Sacrament of Penance, the priest, who has received the Sacrament of Holy Orders, acts in the name of Jesus Christ and the Church and through the power of the Holy Spirit. So it is important to know that only a priest can hear our confession and forgive our sins. The priest can never, for any reason whatsoever, tell anyone what we have confessed. He has promised to keep the seal of confession.

When the priest is giving us absolution, what does he do as a sign that we are being forgiven?

83

## 2 We celebrate the Sacrament of Penance and Reconciliation.

*God, thank you for your forgiveness and your love.*

Begin by reminding the students that God has given each of us the gift of free will. We are free to choose either to do good or evil. Explain that God has given us our conscience. Read and ask the students to highlight or underline the definition of *conscience* in the first sentence of the first paragraph.

Stress that God's love for each of us is immeasurable. He is always ready to forgive us if we are sorry. Remind the students of the forgiving father in the story of the prodigal son or Jesus' words and actions in the story of Zacchaeus. Then read aloud the first and second paragraphs. You may want to refer to Unit 4: *More for You to Know*, page 98 for the paragraphs about the formation of conscience, social sin, and eternal life.

On the board or on a large sheet of paper, write the words *contrition*, *confession*, *penance*, and *absolution*. Explain that these are the four main parts of the celebration of the sacrament. Have a volunteer read the explanation of each part.

**Note:** Sometimes when giving a penance, a priest asks someone to perform a Work of Mercy. The Works of Mercy are presented in Chapter 12.

Have the students look at the photographs on pages 82–83 as you read aloud the last two paragraphs. Explain that the priest extends his right hand over a person's head when he is giving absolution.

For the celebration of the sacrament, read with the students the Sacrament of Penance on *The Seven Sacraments* chart on pages 104–105 and the *Rites of Penance* on page 108.

## Liturgy Connection

Explain to the students that many parishes celebrate the Sacrament of Penance as a parish community during the seasons of Advent and/or Lent. Review the Rite for Reconciliation of Several Penitents with Individual Confession and Absolution on page 108. Encourage the students to look in the parish bulletin for the notice of a parish community celebration and if possible, to participate in the celebration.

## 3 In the Sacrament of Penance we receive Christ's peace.

*Jesus, help us to forgive others.*

Begin your presentation by asking: *What words or phrases do you think of when you hear the word* peace. List the students' responses on the board or on a large sheet of paper. Remind the students about the discussion of the story "Best Friends" at the beginning of the chapter. Ask: *Why do you think it was important that Adam forgive Carlos?*

Have volunteers read the paragraphs. Ask the students to highlight or underline Jesus' words in Scripture. Also remind the students of the words of the Lord's Prayer: "Forgive us our trespasses/ as we forgive those/who trespass against us."

Ask the students to look at the photographs on the page. For each photo, have volunteers role-play what the boys are saying to each other.

Read the concluding question. Pause for a few minutes of quiet reflection.

### 3 In the Sacrament of Penance we receive Christ's peace.

At the end of the celebration of the Sacrament of Penance, the priest tells us, "Go in peace." We are able to go in peace because our sins have been forgiven. We, in turn, are called to share Christ's peace with others.

One of the ways we share Christ's peace is by forgiving others. Sometimes this is difficult to do. Yet Jesus taught us that we must forgive others. One day when the Apostle Peter asked, "Lord, if my brother sins against me, how often must I forgive him? As many as seven times?" Jesus told him, "I say to you, not seven times but seventy-seven times" (Matthew 18:21, 22). Jesus was telling Peter that he should always be forgiving. And each of us must remember this teaching of Jesus, too!

When we forgive others, we are living out the Beatitude:

"Blessed are the peacemakers,
for they will be called children of God"
(Matthew 5:9).

By asking for forgiveness and forgiving others, we are following Jesus' teaching. We are showing our love for God and others. And we are spreading Christ's message of peace in our community and throughout the world.

How can you share Christ's peace with others this week?

84

## Optional Activity

Give each student a strip of light-colored construction paper. On the strip have the students write one way they can share Christ's peace with others during the coming week. Then tape or staple the strips together to make a paper chain. Display the chain in the prayer space as a reminder that Jesus calls each of us to be a peacemaker. Explain: *If we answer Jesus' call and work together, we can help spread peace in our community.*

## Review

Circle the correct answer.

1. A (penance/contrition/confession) is an action that shows we are sorry for our sins.
2. Our (confession/contrition/conscience) is our ability to know the difference between good and evil, right and wrong.
3. (Some/No/Every) sin weakens our friendship with God.
4. Telling our sins to the priest is (confession/conversion/conscience).

Discuss the following. (See side column.)

5. What do we mean by *conversion*?
6. Why is it important for us to forgive others?
7. What is the role of the priest in the celebration of the Sacrament of Penance?

conversion (page 82)
conscience (page 83)
sin (page 83)
contrition (page 83)
confession (page 83)
penance (page 83)
absolution (page 83)

## With My Family

### Sharing Our Faith

1. Jesus taught us about God's love and forgiveness.
2. We celebrate the Sacrament of Penance and Reconciliation.
3. In the Sacrament of Penance we receive Christ's peace.

### PRAYING TOGETHER

Here is an Act of Contrition that you can pray while celebrating the Sacrament of Penance or pray at any time.

My God,
I am sorry for my sins with all my heart.
In choosing to do wrong
and failing to do good,
I have sinned against you
whom I should love above all things.
I firmly intend, with your help,
to do penance,
to sin no more,
and to avoid whatever leads me
to sin.
Our Savior Jesus Christ
suffered and died for us.
In his name, my God, have mercy.

### Living Our Faith

The Church teaches that we must form, or educate, our conscience by studying Scripture and the teachings of the Church. As a family, identify one way that you will form your conscience this week.

85

## CATECHISM FOCUS

"The sacrament of Penance is a whole consisting in three actions of the penitent and the priest's absolution. The penitent's acts are repentance, confession or disclosure of sins to the priest, and the intention to make reparation and do works of reparation." (CCC, 1491)

For additional reference and reflection, see CCC, 1485–1490 and 1492–1498.

# Conclusion (__ min.)

## Review

Provide five to ten minutes for the students to work independently to complete the first part of the *Review*. Check the students' answers. Clarify any misconceptions. Then discuss the questions in the second part of the *Review*. Possible responses follow.

**5.** Conversion is turning back to God with all one's heart. Jesus makes our conversion possible by offering forgiveness for our sins.

**6.** Jesus calls us to forgive others, even if it is sometimes difficult to do this. When we are willing to forgive, we are showing our love for God and others.

**7.** See the last paragraph on page 83.

### *Faith Words*

Ask the students to read the definitions of the Chapter 12 Faith Words from the *Glossary* on pages 124–125.

## With My Family

### *Sharing Our Faith*

Encourage the students to share with their families what they have learned about God's forgiveness and how we celebrate his forgiveness in the Sacrament of Penance and Reconciliation.

### *Praying Together*

Read the Act of Contrition. Discuss the meaning of the words. Then have the students bring their books and gather in the prayer space. Pray this Act of Contrition together. Encourage the students to share the prayer with their families and pray it with them this week.

### *Living Our Faith*

Read the paragraph about forming our conscience. Explain that this a lifelong endeavor. Encourage the students to discuss with their families ways that they can educate their conscience.

# Chapter 13

## GOALS

*to understand that Jesus wants us to show mercy and compassion to those who are in need; to learn and practice the Works of Mercy*

## GETTING READY

**Opening Prayer:** *On the prayer table, place the Bible, a cross or crucifix, and a battery-operated candle.*

**Materials Needed:** *for a group social-action project for* ***Optional Activity*** *(page 89), Invite a member of the parish social-action committee to speak to the group. (See page 89.)*

## Catechist Background

What do you consider to be meaningful work? As disciples of Jesus, we may consider our most meaningful work to be that of serving others. In the parable of the sheep and the goats, Jesus told us that whatever we do to the least of our brothers and sisters we do to him (Matthew 25:31–46).

The Church has applied Jesus' teachings about serving others by listing specific ways of helping—the Works of Mercy. We learn to do these "works," or actions of service, through practice and effort.

There are two types of Works of Mercy: Corporal and Spiritual. The Corporal Works of Mercy are ways we take care of others' physical needs by feed-

## Opening Prayer

Invite the students to gather in the prayer space. Read the following opening prayer and petitions. Ask the students to respond "Lord, have mercy" to each one.

*Let us pray together today for all who need the help and comfort of God and others.*

- *For those who are sick*
- *For those who are victims of natural disasters*
- *For those who are victims of violence*
- *For those who have lost their homes*
- *For those who are poor and hungry*
- *For those who are lonely*
- *For those who need counseling*
- *For those who have a family member or friend who has died*
- *For those who are able to help people in need, we pray that they may respond with generous hearts.*

Pause to allow students to add their own intentions.

# 13 We Serve in Jesus' Name

## What to Do?

**Complete the following stories.**

Last night Cara's little brother was sick. Throughout the night, her parents had taken turns caring for him. This morning Cara noticed that both her mother and father were very tired. Cara decided that

______________________________

______________________________

Last week our pastor made a special announcement. He said, "Next week the parish community will have a collection for the families who lost their homes in the downtown fire. Anyone who wishes to help these families may donate clothing, food, or money."

On the way home Matthew Cheng talked with his parents about what the Cheng family would contribute. Matthew and his parents decided that

______________________________

______________________________

Family Fund

ing the hungry, giving drink to the thirsty, clothing the naked, visiting the imprisoned, sheltering the homeless, visiting the sick, and burying the dead.

The Spiritual Works of Mercy are ways we can care for people's spiritual needs by admonishing the sinner, instructing the ignorant, counseling the doubtful, comforting the sorrowful, bearing wrongs patiently, forgiving all injuries, and praying for the living and the dead. Through the discipline of doing these Works of Mercy, we are building up the Kingdom of God. We are following Jesus and preparing ourselves for eternal life.

## Reflection

"We cannot be sure if we are loving God, although we may have good reasons for believing that we are, but we can know quite well if we are loving our neighbor."

*Saint Teresa of Avila*

At Tuesday's meeting of the Protect the Environment Club, Mrs. De Grassi asked the members to participate in a beach sweep. She explained that the club had been asked to clean up Sunset Beach. The sweep would take a few hours. Marissa's best friend, Joanne, said she did not want to participate. Marissa decided that

______________________________

______________________________

### We Will Learn...

1 Jesus is our greatest example of service to others.

2 We are called to care for the physical needs of others.

3 We are called to care for the spiritual needs of others.

87

## Introduction ( ___ min.)

Have the students work in pairs. Ask the partners to read each story and write about the decision the young person made.

When the students have finished writing, ask each pair to choose one of the three situations and take turns presenting a role-play for the situation and what the young person did to help.

If time permits, have the partners role-play other situations in which someone is in need of help and what can be done to help.

### We Will Learn...

Read the three statements. Explain that in this chapter the students will learn ways Jesus' disciples are called to serve others.

# Presentation ( _ min.)

## 1 Jesus is our greatest example of service to others.

*Jesus, show us the way to life forever with God.*

Explain to the students that throughout the Gospels we read about ways Jesus wants us to love God and others. Ask a volunteer to read the first paragraph. You may want to share the following Gospel accounts to point out specific examples of Jesus serving others:

- Jesus cures Peter's mother-in-law (Matthew 8:14–15)
- Jesus shows mercy to many (Mark 3:7–12)
- the cleansing of the ten lepers (Luke 17:11–19)
- the multiplication of the loaves (John 6:1–15)

Point out that Jesus challenged his disciples to not only care for friends and family members but all people.

Explain that at the end of time, Jesus will return in glory. He will judge us on the way we have followed his example of service. Ask a volunteer to read the second, third and fourth paragraphs. Have the students highlight or underline Jesus' words in Scripture.

**Note:** You may want to read the paragraph "Eternal Life" that is presented on page 98, Unit 4: *More for You to Know.*

Read the concluding question. Pause briefly to allow the students time to reflect quietly about their responses.

### 1 Jesus is our greatest example of service to others.

Jesus told his disciples that they should love others as he loved them. And he gave them an example of this love by the way he lived. He cared for those who were in need. He helped those who were sick, visited those who needed his care, and provided food for the hungry.

Jesus told his disciples that at the end of time all of us would be judged by the way we have treated others.

At the Last Judgment at the end of time, Jesus Christ will come again in glory. He will say to those who have led lives of service to others, "For I was hungry and you gave me food, I was thirsty and you gave me drink, a stranger and you welcomed me, naked and you clothed me, ill and you cared for me, in prison and you visited me" (Matthew 25:35–36).

For Jesus tells us, "Amen, I say to you, whatever you did for one of these least brothers of mine, you did for me" (Matthew 25:40).

What can you do this week to show that you are living a life of service to others?

### Do You Know?

As disciples of Jesus Christ, we are called to work for justice and peace for all people. We can do this by being a friend to others, especially those who feel lonely or left out. We can treat everyone fairly and help those who are treated unfairly. We can welcome neighbors who are new to our country. We can learn about and care for people who need our help in our own country and throughout the world. We can write to our local and national leaders to ask them to protect the rights and safety of children and all people, especially those in need.

88

### Do You Know?

Have a volunteer read the paragraph. At this time you may want to present the seven themes of *Catholic Social Teaching* on page 114 of the student text.

## 2 We are called to care for the physical needs of others.

Responding to the needs of others is an important part of our Catholic faith. When we respond to others' needs, we are following Jesus' example of showing mercy. The loving acts that we do to care for the needs of others are called the Works of Mercy.

The Corporal Works of Mercy are acts of love that help us care for the physical and material needs of others.

**Corporal Works of Mercy**

- Feed the hungry.
- Give drink to the thirsty.
- Clothe the naked.
- Visit the imprisoned.
- Shelter the homeless.
- Visit the sick.
- Bury the dead.

The Church encourages all members to care for those who are not able to care for themselves. You can check to find out ways your parish community practices the Corporal Works of Mercy.

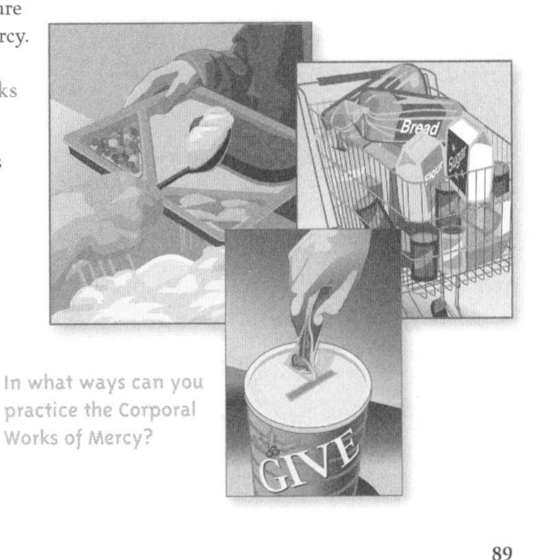


In what ways can you practice the Corporal Works of Mercy?

89

## 2 We are called to care for the physical needs of others.

*Holy Spirit, help us to use the gifts that God has given us to help others.*

Before presenting this page, you may want to check with one of your parish coordinators about outreach programs with which your parish is involved. Also, you may want to invite someone on the parish social-action committee to speak to the students.

Ask a volunteer to read the first paragraph. Explain that there are two types of Works of Mercy: Corporal and Spiritual. Write the word *corporal* on the board or a large sheet of paper. Explain that it comes from the Latin word *corpus* which means "body." Then read the second paragraph.

Have a volunteer read the list of the Corporal Works of Mercy. Then discuss the ways the people in the photographs on pages 90 and 91 are performing the Corporal Works. If time permits, you may want the students to write captions for the photos.

Read the concluding question. Discuss with the students ways that they can practice the Corporal Works of Mercy.

**Note:** Please stress with the students that they should always check with a parent, teacher, or other known and responsible adult before helping people whom they do not know.

## Optional Activity

Have the students decide on a charitable project in which they can all take part: a food and/or clothing drive, making and sending get-well cards for children in a local hospital. Then provide time and materials necessary for the project.

## We are called to care for the spiritual needs of others.

*Jesus, we pray for all people in need.*

Remind the students that Jesus helped people through his teachings and his words of comfort and forgiveness. Jesus prayed and he taught his disciples to pray. He listened to people as they told him of their problems. He stated that it was important to take time to listen and pray.

Explain that people have spiritual needs that Jesus expects us to respond to in whatever ways we are able. Read the first paragraph and the Spiritual Works of Mercy. For the first Spiritual Work listed, explain that we have to be careful not to judge others harshly or falsely. See Jesus' teaching in Matthew 7:1–5.

Emphasize the importance of praying for others and forgiving those who hurt us.

Read the concluding question. Have the students work in pairs. Assign one of the Spiritual Works to each set of partners. Have each pair list ways that young people their age might do the particular assigned work. Then appoint a TV talk-show host for a program feature "How Catholic Young People Show They Care." The host should invite the pairs to come "on stage" to talk about the ways of care that they have listed. Remind the students that people their age can share knowledge and advice about Jesus' teachings and how following these teachings helps us to live in harmony with God and others.

### We are called to care for the spiritual needs of others.

Another way that we can care for the needs of others is through the **Spiritual Works of Mercy**. These are acts of love that help us care for the needs of people's hearts, minds, and souls.

**Spiritual Works of Mercy**

- Admonish the sinner. (Give correction to those who need it.)
- Instruct the ignorant. (Share our knowledge with others.)
- Counsel the doubtful. (Give advice to those who need it.)
- Comfort the sorrowful. (Comfort those who suffer.)
- Bear wrongs patiently. (Be patient with others.)
- Forgive all injuries. (Forgive those who hurt us.)
- Pray for the living and the dead.

Both the Corporal and Spiritual Works of Mercy are important practices of our Catholic faith. We can ask the Holy Spirit to guide us in carrying out these acts of love in our daily lives. When we carry out these Works of Mercy, we are giving witness to Jesus Christ.

**Which of the Spiritual Works of Mercy can people your age do? How?**

90

## Liturgy Connection

Explain that the Sacrament of the Anointing of the Sick is a celebration of the whole Church community. In this sacrament the community asks God to save those who are seriously ill or suffering because of their old age. The priest who administers the sacrament and those gathered represent the whole Church, offering those who are sick their comfort, support, and encouragement. See the Anointing of the Sick section of the chart on pages 104–105 of the text.

## Review

**Complete the following.**

1–2. Write two Corporal Works of Mercy.

See page 89.

3–4. Write two Spiritual Works of Mercy.

See page 90.

**Discuss the following.** (See side column.)

5. In what ways did Jesus care for others?
6. Why is it important for us to follow Jesus' example?
7. What will happen at the Last Judgment?

Works of Mercy (page 89)
Corporal Works of Mercy (page 89)
Spiritual Works of Mercy (page 90)

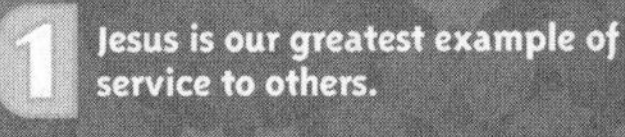


### Sharing Our Faith

1. Jesus is our greatest example of service to others.
2. We are called to care for the physical needs of others.
3. We are called to care for the spiritual needs of others.

### PRAYING TOGETHER

The following prayer is one the Church prays for those who have died.

**Eternal rest grant unto them, O Lord,**
**And let perpetual light shine upon them.**
**May they rest in peace.**
**Amen.**
**May their souls and the souls of all the faithful departed,**
**through the mercy of God, rest in peace.**
**Amen.**

### Living Our Faith

Think of possible slogans to encourage people to do the Works of Mercy. List them below. Then choose one and on poster board design an ad for a magazine or Web site using your slogan. Share the ad with family and friends.

91

# Conclusion (__ min.)

## Review

Provide five to ten minutes for the students to work independently to complete the first part of the *Review*. Check the students' answers. Then discuss the questions in the second part of the *Review*. Possible responses follow.

**5.** Jesus cared for others by helping, comforting, and healing people who were sick; he visited with people who were in need, and he provided food for people who were hungry.

**6.** It is important for us to follow Jesus' example because he told us to love others as he loved them. Jesus told his disciples that at the end of time we will be judged by the way we have treated others.

**7.** The Last Judgment will be at the end of time when Jesus returns in glory. At this time he will judge all people by the way they have treated others.

***Faith Words***

Review the Corporal and Spiritual Works of Mercy with the students.

## With My Family

***Sharing Our Faith***

Encourage the students to share with their families what they have learned about following Jesus' example.

***Praying Together***

Explain that the words *eternal* and *perpetual* mean "everlasting." Invite the students to bring their books and gather in the prayer space. Pray the prayer together. Encourage the students to share this prayer with their families this week.

***Living Our Faith***

Read aloud the activity directions. Ask the students to identify familiar ads that encourage people to do the Works of Mercy. Encourage the students to complete the activity with their families this week.

## CATECHISM FOCUS

"The *works of mercy* are charitable actions by which we come to the aid of our neighbor in his spiritual and bodily necessities." (*CCC*, 2447)

# Chapter 14

## GOALS

*to understand that the saints give us examples of ways to love God, others, and ourselves; to recognize and appreciate that Mary, the Mother of God, is the greatest saint*

## GETTING READY

**Opening Prayer:** *On the prayer table, place the Bible opened to the story of the Annunciation (Luke 1:26–38).*

**Materials Needed:** *paper, markers for* ***Optional Activity*** *(page 96), poster board, index cards, markers for Faith Words activity (page 97)*

## Catechist Background

Just as we learn a trade or a skill, such as teaching, by being apprentices with the guidance of mentors, so we learn how to live our faith by following the example of others. By our Baptism we are part of the Church, the Communion of Saints, those baptized members living on earth, those in Purgatory, and those in Heaven (*CCC*, 946). In addition to turning to our mentors of discipleship on earth, we also turn to the saints in Heaven.

We acknowledge all the members of the Church who have died and now live in everlasting life as saints. We formally acknowledge particular people as saints through the process of canonization. Canonization is the solemn proclamation that a

## Opening Prayer

In the prayer space, place a statue of Mary or fine-art prints that are available. Ask the students to look at the statue and/or pictures as you read the story of the angel's announcement to Mary (Luke 1:26–38). Pause briefly and ask the students to reflect quietly about the event.

Then invite the students to gather in the prayer space. Ask them to respond "pray for us" as you read each of the following titles of Mary that are included in the Litany of the Blessed Mother:

- *Holy Mary*
- *Holy Mother of God*
- *Mother of Christ*
- *Mother of the Church*
- *Comfort of the troubled*
- *Help of Christians*
- *Queen of families*
- *Queen of peace*

## 14 We Belong to the Communion of Saints

# A Patron Saint

Last Sunday when Juan's family was on the way to Aunt Iris's house, Juan noticed that they were not taking the roads they usually did. He asked, "Where are we going?"

His father explained, "We're going to look at the new church my company has been building."

When the car stopped at the construction site, Juan and his parents got out of the car. Juan's dad said, "The pastor of this new parish is going to be Father Donnelly.

When Father came to the site, he told our team that the bishop announced that the name of the new parish will be Saint John the Baptist."



92

person has practiced heroic virtue and lived in fidelity to God's grace (*CCC*, 828). These saints have become models and intercessors for us, guiding us on our journey of faith. Our greatest model is Mary, the Mother of God.

The Church acknowledges Mary as the greatest saint. She is Jesus' first disciple. After Jesus' Death and Resurrection, Mary stayed with the disciples to continue Jesus' work. In Mary we find the perfect disciple; the "model and source" of holiness for our lives (*CCC*, 2030).

The Church has a rich history of devotion to Mary. We honor Mary through prayers, feast-day celebrations, and processions. We emulate her faithfulness and her obedience to God.

## Reflection

The angel said to Mary, "The holy Spirit will come upon you, and the power of the Most High will overshadow you. Therefore the child to be born will be called holy, the Son of God. . . . Mary said, ' Behold, I am the handmaid of the Lord. May it be done to me according to your word.' Then the angel departed from her."

*(Luke 1:35, 38)*

Juan's mother said, "Saint John the Baptist is your patron saint, Juan. You were born on Saint John's feast day, so your dad and I decided to give you the name Juan, the Spanish name for John."

Juan was surprised. He said, "I know that Saint John was Jesus' cousin, but now I really want to learn more about him."

Then Juan's father said, "When I told Father Donnelly that Saint John was my son's patron saint, he told me that his first name is Sean. Sean is the Irish name for John. And Saint John the Baptist is his patron saint, too."

Later that week, Father Donnelly visited Juan's father's office to see the model of the new parish. Juan and his mother went there to meet him. "Hi Juan," said Father, "let me tell you about our patron saint, John the Baptist!"

• • •

**Who is your patron saint? your favorite saint?**

**What do you know about him or her?**

St. John the Baptist Catholic Church

### We Will Learn...

1 The Church honors the saints.
2 Mary is Jesus' first disciple and the greatest saint.
3 The Church honors Mary, the Mother of God and the Mother of the Church.



## Introduction ( ___ min.)

Begin by having volunteers read aloud the story "A Patron Saint." Then pose the following questions for discussion: *Why did Juan's parents name him for Saint John? Why do you think Juan wants to learn more about Saint John? How can Juan learn more about his patron saint?*

Read the questions that follow the story. Then ask volunteers to share their responses.

Talk with the students about the patron saint of your parish. You may want to invite a member of the parish leadership team to talk to the students about this saint.

### We Will Learn...

Have a volunteer read the three statements. Ask the students to think for a few moments about what they have previously learned about Mary and the saints. Have a few volunteers share their responses.

# Presentation ( __ min.)

## 1 The Church honors the saints.

*God, may we look to the saints for good example.*

You may want to begin the presentation about saints by asking: *Do you know that you are a saint in the making?* Have a volunteer read the first sentence of the first paragraph which defines what a saint is. Ask the students to highlight or underline the sentence.

Have a volunteer read the first paragraph. You may want to tell the students that the Gospel for All Saints' Day is the account of Jesus' teaching of the Beatitudes. Ask the students why this teaching is most appropriate for this celebration. Help them conclude that the saints have lived the Beatitudes and now are living in eternal happiness as promised by Jesus in this teaching.

Point out that, by our Baptism, we are all called to be saints. Explain that when we are baptized, we become a part of the Communion of Saints. Then read aloud the second and third paragraphs. You may want to explain that those who die in "God's grace and friendship," but are still "imperfectly purified" go through a final purification, Purgatory. (See *CCC*, 1030).

Read aloud the feature *Do You Know?* before discussing the concluding question. Then have the students name saints about whom they would like to learn. List the saints' names on the board or a large sheet of paper.

### 1 The Church honors the saints.

Saints are followers of Christ who lived lives of holiness on earth and now share in eternal life with God in Heaven. From the example of the saints' lives, we can learn ways to love God, ourselves, and others. We can learn how to be disciples of Jesus, as they were. Each November 1 the Church honors all the saints in Heaven on the Feast of All Saints. On this day we recall the saints' lives of service and prayer. We remember that their love and prayers for the Church are constant. On this day and throughout the year, we ask the saints to pray to God for us.

As members of the Church, the Body of Christ, we are united to all who have been baptized.

The Communion of Saints is the union of the baptized members of the Church.

- Members on earth respond to God's grace by living a good life and becoming role models for one another.
- Members in Heaven led lives of holiness on earth and now share in the joy of eternal life with God.
- Members in Purgatory are preparing for Heaven, by growing in the holiness necessary to enjoy the happiness of Heaven. The faithful on earth can help them by prayer, especially the Mass, and by offering good works for them.

What saints would you like to learn more about?

#### Do You Know?

A canonized saint is a person who has been officially named a saint by the Church. The life of this person has been examined by Church leaders. They have decided that this person's life has been an example of faith and holiness. When a person is canonized a saint, his or her name is entered into the worldwide list of saints recognized by the Catholic Church. The following are some of the many canonized saints of the Church:

- Saints Maria and Isidore were married. They worked on a farm in Spain. They cared for God's gifts of Creation and shared the earth's resources with the poor.
- Saint Frances of Rome worked among the poor people of Rome, Italy. She nursed those who suffered from a terrible disease that killed thousands of people.



### Do You Know?

You may want to explain that there are different stages involved in the canonization process, which usually takes place over several years. The process is explained on certain Church sites on the Internet. You may want to refer the students to the *Lives of the Saints* feature on the Web site www.webelieveweb.com.

## 2 Mary is Jesus' first disciple and the greatest saint.

Mary, the Mother of Jesus, is his first and most faithful disciple. She shares in God's holiness in a very special way because God chose her to be the Mother of his Son. Mary believed in Jesus from the moment that the angel Gabriel told her that God wanted her to be Jesus' Mother. The event at which the announcement was made that Mary would be the Mother of the Son of God is called the **Annunciation**.

Because Mary was to be the Mother of the Son of God, God blessed her in a special way. This special blessing was only given to Mary. God created her free from Original Sin and from all sin since the very first moment of her life, her conception.

This truth about Mary's sinlessness is called the **Immaculate Conception**.

Mary loved Jesus all through his life. She cared for him as he grew. She supported him throughout his ministry. She remained by his side as he died on the cross. She stayed with the Apostles after Jesus' Ascension as they waited for the coming of the Holy Spirit.

Throughout her life Mary trusted in God's will. She had a pure heart and lived a life of holiness. When Mary's work on earth was done, God brought her body and soul to live forever with the risen Christ. This event is known as Mary's **Assumption**.

Why do we consider Mary to be Jesus' first disciple?

*Annunciation*, Maurice Denis, 1870–1943

95

## 2 Mary is Jesus' first disciple and the greatest saint.

*Jesus, thank you for giving us Mary as our mother, too.*

Ask the students to look at the art of Mary at the Annunciation on page 95. You may also want to show the students other fine-art prints of Mary found in art books or on different Web sites.

Ask the students: *How did Mary know that she was going to be the Mother of God's Son?* Refer the students to page 14 in Chapter 2. Then have a volunteer read the first paragraph.

At this time, you may want to present the Hail Mary prayer on page 97. Read the prayer aloud. Then have the students highlight or underline the first part of the prayer, starting with the word *Hail* and ending at the name *Jesus*. Explain that these prayer verses are based on the angel's message to Mary at the Annunciation and the greeting of Elizabeth when Mary visited her. Read aloud Luke 1:28 and 42.

Before reading the second paragraph, ask a volunteer to explain what Original Sin is. Then read aloud the second paragraph.

Point out to the students that Mary loved Jesus very much. Then have volunteers read the last three paragraphs.

Read the concluding question. Pause to allow students to reflect quietly on their responses.

### Scripture Connection

Share one or more of the following Scripture accounts of Mary: Mary visits her cousin Elizabeth (Luke 1:39–45); presenting Jesus in the Temple (Luke 2:22–38); the finding of Jesus in the Temple (Luke 2:41–52); the wedding at Cana (John 2:1–12); Mary standing by Jesus as he died on the cross (John 19:25–27); the Apostles and Mary in Jerusalem (Acts 1:13–14).

## 3 The Church honors Mary, the Mother of God and the Mother of the Church.

*Mary, Mother of God, pray for us.*

Ask the students to recall some of the titles with which they addressed Mary in the *Opening Prayer.* Then have volunteers read the explanatory paragraphs about the titles of Mary.

If possible, have volunteers look in parish missalettes or hymnals to find hymns to Mary. Have them share the titles for Mary used in the hymns.

Read the list of Mary's feast days. Have a volunteer identify the next feast day of Mary that the Church will celebrate. Explain that in the United States the feasts of Mary, Mother of God, the Assumption of the Blessed Virgin Mary, and the Immaculate Conception are Holy Days of Obligation. On these days the parish community gathers for Mass.

**Note:** You may want to present praying the Rosary on pages 118–119 of the text.

Our Lady of Angels, Los Angeles, CA

### 3 The Church honors Mary, the Mother of God and the Mother of the Church.

Mary is special example for all of us. The Church has many titles for Mary. These titles help us to understand Mary's role in our lives and in the life of the Church.

- Blessed Virgin Mary—Mary was not married when the angel told her that she was to be Jesus' Mother. The angel told her that Jesus was to be conceived by the power of the Holy Spirit. And Mary remained a virgin throughout her married life with Joseph. Thus, Mary is known as the Blessed Virgin, the Blessed Virgin Mary, and the Blessed Mother.
- Mother of God—Jesus Christ, the Son of God and Mary's son, is truly human and truly divine. He is the second Person of the Blessed Trinity who became man. Thus, Mary is known as the Mother of God.
- Mother of the Church—As Jesus was dying on the cross, he saw Mary and the Apostle John at his feet. Jesus said to Mary, "Woman, behold, your son." He said to John, "Behold, your mother" (John 19:26, 27). In this way Jesus showed that Mary is the mother of all those who believe and follow him. Thus, Mary is known as the Mother of the Church.

**Here are some of the feast days on which the Church honors Mary.**

Mary, Mother of God—*January 1*

The Annunciation of Our Lord —*March 25*

The Visitation of the Blessed Virgin Mary—*May 31*

The Assumption of the Blessed Virgin Mary—*August 15*

The Birth of Mary—*September 8*

Immaculate Conception of the Blessed Virgin Mary—*December 8*

Our Lady of Guadalupe—*December 12*

The Church shows love for Mary through devotions and prayer. You will find some of these devotions and prayers in the prayer section of your book (pages 118–123).

Why is Mary so important to the Church?



Discuss the concluding question. Possible responses include: Mary is the mother of all who believe and follow Jesus Christ; she gave us example in trusting in God's will and living a life of holiness; as Jesus was dying on the cross, he told his disciples that Mary is our mother.

## Optional Activity

**Have the students work in pairs. Ask each pair to write a poem or song verse about Mary. Ask the partners to illustrate the verse. Provide time for the students to share their verses with the group. Consider binding the pages in a booklet and keeping the book in the prayer space.**

## Review

**Write *True* or *False* for the following sentences. On a separate piece of paper, change the false sentences to make them true.**

1. ___True___ The truth that Mary was free from Original Sin from the moment she was conceived is the Immaculate Conception.
2. ___False___ When Mary's work on earth was done, God brought her body and soul to live with the risen Christ. This is the ~~Annunciation~~ Assumption.
3. ___False___ ~~Joseph~~ announced to Mary that she was to be the Mother of God's Son. The angel Gabriel
4. ___True___ Saints are followers of Christ who now share in eternal life with God in Heaven.

**Discuss the following.** (See side column.)

5. What do you most admire about Mary?
6. Why do we honor the saints?
7. What can you do to learn more about Mary and about the other saints?

**Faith Words**

saints (page 94)
Communion of Saints (page 94)
Annunciation (page 95)
Immaculate Conception (page 95)
Assumption (page 95)

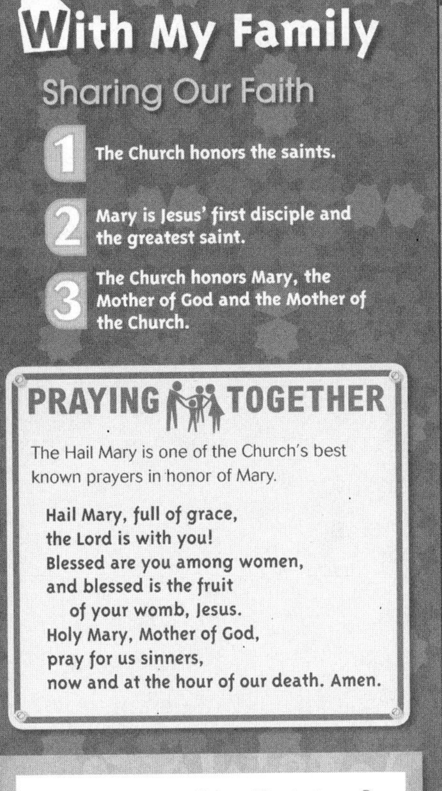

## With My Family

### Sharing Our Faith

1. The Church honors the saints.
2. Mary is Jesus' first disciple and the greatest saint.
3. The Church honors Mary, the Mother of God and the Mother of the Church.

### PRAYING TOGETHER

The Hail Mary is one of the Church's best known prayers in honor of Mary.

**Hail Mary, full of grace,**
**the Lord is with you!**
**Blessed are you among women,**
**and blessed is the fruit**
**of your womb, Jesus.**
**Holy Mary, Mother of God,**
**pray for us sinners,**
**now and at the hour of our death. Amen.**

### Living Our Faith

In this chapter you have learned that Mary and the saints are models of holiness and discipleship. List below your family's favorite saints and/or patron saints. Discuss how these saints show us ways to love God, ourselves, and others and ways we can follow their example.

97

## Conclusion (__ min.)

### Review

Provide five to ten minutes for the students to work independently to complete the first part of the *Review*. Discuss the questions in the second part of the *Review*. Possible responses follow.

**5.** Accept reasonable responses.

**6.** We honor the saints because they are examples of faith and holiness who now share in eternal life with God in Heaven. Their love and prayers for the Church are constant.

**7.** Possible responses include: reading the New Testament, reading a book about the lives of the saints, doing research on the Internet.

***Faith Words***

Have the students work in small groups to design a game based on the Faith Words of this unit. Ask the groups to design the game board, write the game rules, and then write clues for the words. Have the groups take turns presenting their games.

***More for You to Know***

On page 98 you will find *More for You to Know* for Unit 4. The topics of the articles on this page are: formation of conscience, cardinal virtues, chastity and modesty, social sin, and eternal life.

### With My Family

***Sharing Our Faith***

Encourage the students to share with their families what they have learned about Mary and the saints.

***Praying Together***

Ask the students to stand and pray the Hail Mary. Encourage them to pray these words often with their families this week.

***Living Our Faith***

Encourage the students to work with their families to complete the activity.

## CATECHISM FOCUS

"By her complete adherence to the Father's will, to his Son's redemptive work, and to every prompting of the Holy Spirit, the Virgin Mary is the Church's model of faith and charity." (*CCC*, 967)

For additional reference and reflection, see *CCC*, 957–975.

# MORE for You to Know

**FORMATION OF CONSCIENCE** Failure to form our consciences can result in wrong choices that may be sinful. Certain acts are always wrong and we may never choose to do wrong even if we think good will come from it. We must continue forming our consciences throughout our lives. We can do this by learning all that we can about our faith, and the teachings of the Church; by praying, asking the Holy Spirit to strengthen and guide us; by reading and reflecting on Scripture; by seeking advice from wise, responsible, and faith-filled people; and by examining our consciences often. We must always follow our well-formed consciences.

**VIRTUES** The theological virtues of faith, hope, and charity are the foundation of the human virtues—habits that come about by our own efforts, with the help of God's grace. Two of the human virtues are chastity and modesty. When we practice the virtue of chastity, we use our human sexuality in a responsible and faithful way. Jesus Christ is the model of chastity for all of us. Every baptized person is called to lead a chaste life. The virtue of modesty helps us to think, speak, act, and dress in ways that show respect for ourselves and others.

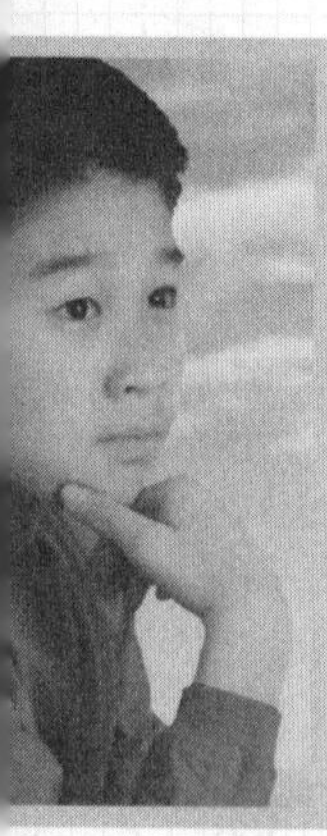

All the human virtues are grouped around the four cardinal virtues. **Prudence** helps us to make good judgments and direct our actions toward what is good. **Justice** helps us to respect the rights of others and give them what is rightfully theirs. **Fortitude** helps us to act bravely in the face of troubles or fears. **Temperance** helps us to keep our desires under control and to balance our use of material goods.

**SOCIAL SIN** Personal sin can lead to unjust situations and conditions in society that are contrary to God's goodness. This is social sin. Some results of social sin in society are: prejudice, poverty, homelessness, crime, violence, and the destruction of our environment. The Church speaks strongly against social sin.

God wants all of his children to respond to his grace. He calls those who have turned away from him to return to his love and receive his forgiveness, especially in the Sacrament of Penance. When we are sorry for our sins because we believe in God and love him, our sorrow is known as *perfect contrition*. When we are sorry for our sins for other reasons, it is *imperfect contrition*.

**ETERNAL LIFE** At the moment of death, we are judged by Christ as to how well we loved and served God and others. This is called our *particular judgment*. Those who have lived lives of holiness on earth will immediately share in the joy of Heaven and eternal life. Others whose hearts need to be made perfectly pure will prepare for Heaven in Purgatory. There they will grow in the holiness necessary to enjoy the happiness of Heaven.

Unfortunately, some people have chosen to completely break their friendship with God. They have continually turned away from God's mercy, and have refused his forgiveness. They remain separated from God and do not share in eternal life. This eternal separation from God is called *Hell*. There are those who through no fault of their own do not know Christ or the Church. The Church teaches that such people, who through grace try to seek God and do his will, also have the hope of eternal life.

# UNIT 4 Assessment

**Write the letter that best defines each term.**

1. ___d___ covenant
2. ___c___ contrition
3. ___e___ conscience
4. ___b___ charity
5. ___a___ Communion of Saints

**a.** the union of all baptized members of the Church

**b.** the theological virtue that allows us to love God and others

**c.** heartfelt sorrow for our sins

**d.** a special agreement between God and his people

**e.** our ability to know the difference between right and wrong

**Circle the correct answer.**

6. The theological virtue that enables us to trust in God's promise to share his life with us forever is (**faith**/**hope**/**charity**). [circled: hope]
7. God bringing Mary body and soul to live forever with the risen Christ is known as Mary's (**Annunciation**/**Immaculate Conception**/**Assumption**). [circled: Assumption]
8. The (**First**/**Fourth**/**Fifth**) Commandment is "Honor your father and your mother." [circled: Fourth]
9. Jesus wants us to (**always**/**sometimes**/**never**) forgive others. [circled: always]
10. When we do an action or say a prayer that shows we are sorry for sins, we are doing (**a confession**/**a penance**/**an absolution**). [circled: a penance]

**Write your responses on a separate piece of paper.**

11. Write one title of Mary that you have learned about in this unit. Explain its meaning. **See pages 95-96 of Chapter 14.**
12. Explain ways in which we keep the Third Commandment. **See page 71 of Chapter 10.**
13. Name two of the Corporal Works of Mercy. Identify ways you can practice these works during the coming weeks. **See page 89 of Chapter 13.**
14. Write the definition of the Beatitudes. **The Beatitudes are Jesus' teachings that describe the way to live as his disciples.**
15. Why is it important for the members of the Church to celebrate the Sacrament of Penance and Reconciliation? **See page 82-83 of Chapter 12.**

# Semester 2 Assessment

**Circle the letter of the correct answer.**

1. The sacrament that is the foundation of the Christian life is _____.
   a. Matrimony
   b. Holy Orders
   c. Penance
   (d.) Baptism

2. After we hear the readings at Mass, the priest or deacon then _____.
   a. tells us to leave
   b. asks us questions
   c. prays the Our Father
   (d.) explains their meaning for our lives

3. The first three commandments tell us _____.
   a. how good we are
   b. how to make friends
   (c.) how to love God
   d. when to sing during Mass

4. The Fourth through the Tenth Commandments tell us _____.
   a. to read the Bible daily
   (b.) how to love others
   c. how to pray the rosary
   d. how to live a long life

5. The Spiritual Works of Mercy are _____.
   a. what the priest says at the end of Mass
   b. things our parents make us do at home
   c. actions such as visiting the sick
   (d.) ways we can care for the needs of people's hearts, minds, and souls

**Complete the following.**

6. The Beatitudes are Jesus' teachings that describe the way to live as his disciples.

7. As members of the Church, we respond to the needs of others because Jesus asked us to do this. When we respond to others' needs, we are following Jesus' example of loving others.

8. From the example of Mary and the saints we can learn ways to love God, ourselves, and others. We can learn how to be Jesus' disciples.

9. We forgive others because Jesus taught us that we must forgive others.

10. In Holy Communion we receive the Body and Blood of Christ under the appearances of bread and wine.

**Write the letter to complete each sentence.**

11. e The Eucharist
12. a The Gift of the Holy Spirit
13. d The Assumption
14. b Conversion
15. c The Communion of Saints

a. is strengthened within us at Confirmation.
b. is turning back to God.
c. is the union of all baptized members of the Church.
d. is the event when God brought Mary body and soul to live forever with the risen Christ.
e. is a memorial, a meal, and a sacrifice.

**Write your responses on a separate piece of paper.**

16. Name two ways we can follow the Third Commandment. We gather with the parish community for Mass. We rest from work or other activities.

17. What is the Great Commandment?

18. Why did God give us the Ten Commandments? to help us to live in his love.

19. Name the four main parts of the Sacrament of Penance and Reconciliation. contrition, confession, a penance, absolution.

20. Jesus said, "Come, follow me." As a member of the Church, how can you do this? Accept reasonable responses.

17. "You shall love the lord, your God, with all your heart, with all your soul, and with all your mind. You shall love your neighbor as yourself."

**GOAL**

*to understand and appreciate that the liturgical year is the celebration of the mystery of Christ in the liturgy*

**Catechist Reflection**

"All things are of your making, all times and seasons obey your laws." Preface for Sunday in Ordinary Time

## Introduction (__ min.)

Have the students work in pairs. Ask the partners to identify their favorite season of the year and the colors, symbols, and activities that they associate with these seasons. Also ask the partners to identify major holidays that fall within the favorite seasons.

## Presentation (__ min.)

Explain to the students that the Church has certain seasons that we celebrate each year. Ask a volunteer to read the first three paragraphs on page 102. Emphasize that, during each liturgical year, we remember and celebrate the whole life of Jesus Christ.

Draw the students' attention to the liturgical year chart. As a volunteer reads the explanatory paragraph of each season, have the students point to that particular season's section on the chart on page 103. Ask the students to identify the current liturgical season.

Explain that for each season the Church has chosen an appropriate theme for the Sunday readings and Gospels. The Church also has certain customs and prayer practices for the season: for example, each week of Advent, we light a candle or candles of the Advent wreath as we prepare to celebrate

# The Liturgical Year

The liturgy is the official public prayer of the Church. In the liturgy we gather as a community joined to Christ to celebrate what we believe. The Church year is based on the life of Christ and the celebration of his life in the liturgy. So, the Church's year is called the *liturgical year.*

In one liturgical year we recall and celebrate the whole life of Jesus Christ. We celebrate his birth, younger years, his years of teaching and ministry, and most especially his suffering, Death, Resurrection, and Ascension into Heaven.

The readings we hear, the colors we see, and the songs we sing help us to know what season we are celebrating. The liturgical year begins in late November or early December with the season of Advent.

**Advent**

The season of Advent is a time of joyful preparation. We await the celebration of the Christmas season during which we remember the first coming of the Son of God. We celebrate that God comes into our lives every day. We look forward to Christ's second coming at the end of time. The color for Advent is purple, a sign of expectation.

**Christmas**

The season of Christmas begins on Christmas Day with the celebration of the birth of the Son of God. During this season we celebrate that God is with us. The color for Christmas is white, a sign of joy.

**Lent**

Lent is the season in which we strive to grow closer to Jesus through prayer, fasting, and penance. During Lent we pray for and support all who are preparing to receive the Sacraments of Christian Initiation. During Lent we prepare for the Church's greatest celebration. The color for Lent is purple, for penance.

**Triduum**

The Easter Triduum is the Church's greatest and most important celebration. The word *triduum* means "three days." During these three days, from Holy Thursday evening until Easter Sunday night, we remember Jesus' gift of the Eucharist, his Death, and his Resurrection. The color for Good Friday is red, for Jesus' suffering. The color for the other days of Triduum is white.

102

## Optional Activity

Have the students work in small groups. Assign a liturgical season to each group. Ask the group to design and make a poster that includes a brief prayer that would be appropriate for the assigned season. Display the posters in the prayer space.

**Easter**
The season of Easter begins on Easter Sunday evening and continues until Pentecost Sunday. During this season we rejoice in the Resurrection of Jesus Christ and the new life he shares with us. We also celebrate Christ's Ascension into Heaven. The color for the Easter season is white, while the color for Pentecost is red and signifies the descent of the Holy Spirit upon the Apostles.

**Ordinary Time**
The season of Ordinary Time is celebrated in two parts: the first part is between Christmas and Lent, and the second part is between Easter and Advent. During this time we celebrate the whole life of Christ and learn the meaning of living as his disciples. The color for Ordinary Time is green, a sign of life and hope.



## CATECHISM FOCUS

**"Beginning with the Easter Triduum as its source of light, the new age of the Resurrection fills the whole liturgical year with its brilliance. Gradually, on either side of this source, the year is transfigured by the liturgy. It really is a 'year of the Lord's favor."**
**(CCC, 1168)**

that Jesus, the Light of the World, came to save us from sin.

Ask the students to identify ways that they and the members of their families can participate in the parish's liturgical celebrations throughout the year. Emphasize with the students that their participation in the Church's liturgy nourishes and supports them as they continue their journey of faith.

# Conclusion (__ min.)

### Responding in Prayer

Before you begin to pray, ask three volunteers to carry the following items and lead a procession to the prayer space: a statue or picture of Jesus, an open Bible, and a cross or crucifix.

Invite the students to process respectfully to the prayer space. Then lead them in the following prayer. For each seasonal prayer, ask the students to repeat the verse.

*Jesus, help us to remember your constant presence:*

- *In Advent, we pray, "Come, Lord Jesus."*
- *At Christmas, we pray, "Jesus, our Savior, we rejoice in your birth."*
- *During the Triduum, we pray to Jesus:*
  *"Dying you destroyed our death, rising you restored our life. Lord Jesus, come in glory."*
- *At Easter we pray, "Alleluia. Alleluia. Jesus, we believe that you are the risen Lord."*
- *In Ordinary Time we pray, "Jesus, help us to live as your disciples."*

*God, our loving Father, we thank you for this day. We ask you to bless all our days, in the name of Jesus Christ, your Son, who lives and reigns with you and the Holy Spirit, one God forever and ever. Amen.*

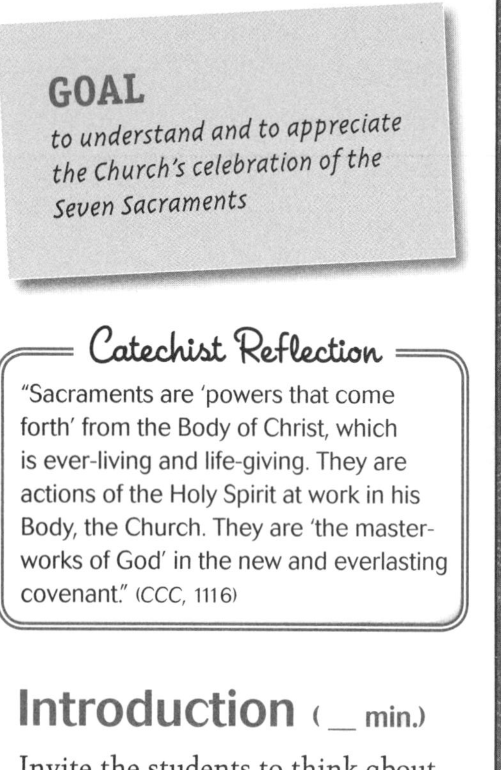

## GOAL

*to understand and to appreciate the Church's celebration of the Seven Sacraments*

### Catechist Reflection

"Sacraments are 'powers that come forth' from the Body of Christ, which is ever-living and life-giving. They are actions of the Holy Spirit at work in his Body, the Church. They are 'the master-works of God' in the new and everlasting covenant." (CCC, 1116)

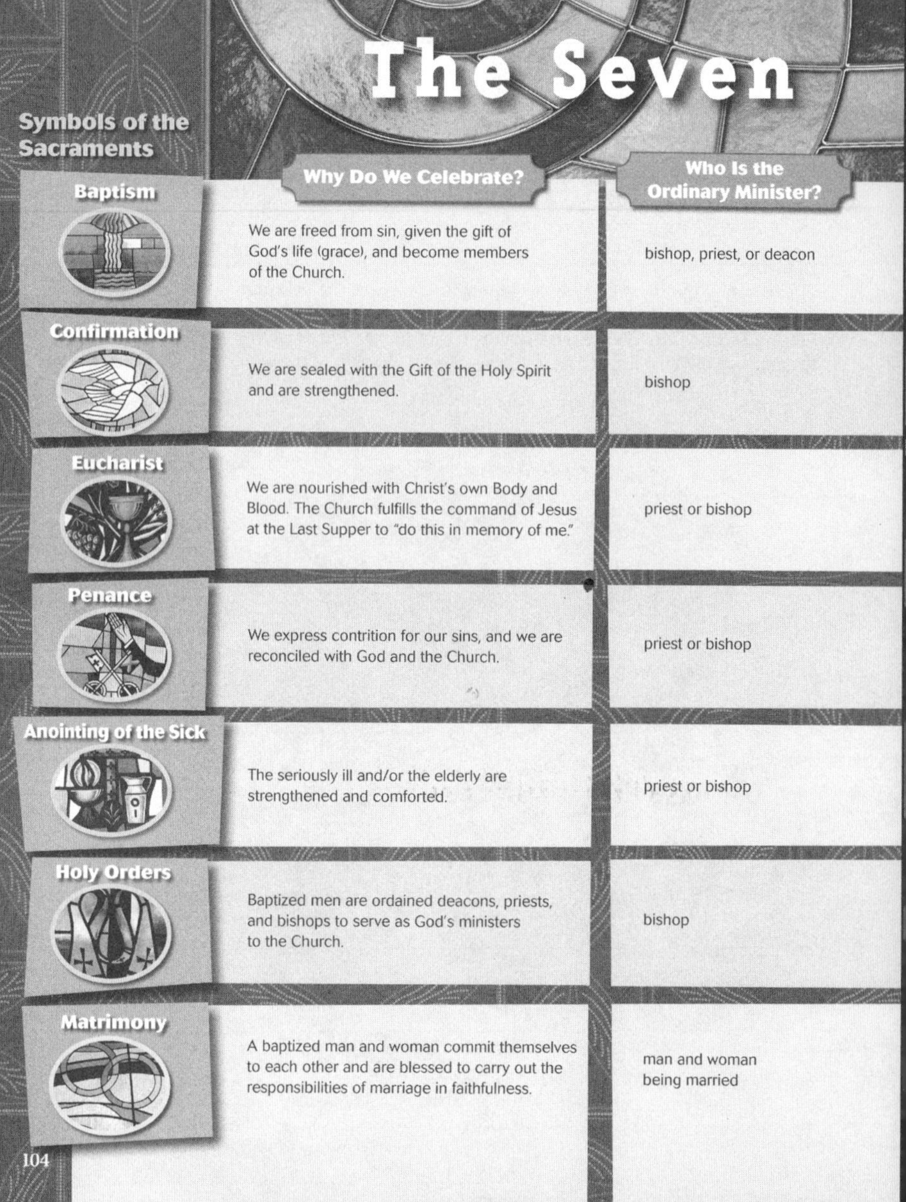

# The Seven

| Symbols of the Sacraments | Why Do We Celebrate? | Who Is the Ordinary Minister? |
|---|---|---|
| Baptism | We are freed from sin, given the gift of God's life (grace), and become members of the Church. | bishop, priest, or deacon |
| Confirmation | We are sealed with the Gift of the Holy Spirit and are strengthened. | bishop |
| Eucharist | We are nourished with Christ's own Body and Blood. The Church fulfills the command of Jesus at the Last Supper to "do this in memory of me." | priest or bishop |
| Penance | We express contrition for our sins, and we are reconciled with God and the Church. | priest or bishop |
| Anointing of the Sick | The seriously ill and/or the elderly are strengthened and comforted. | priest or bishop |
| Holy Orders | Baptized men are ordained deacons, priests, and bishops to serve as God's ministers to the Church. | bishop |
| Matrimony | A baptized man and woman commit themselves to each other and are blessed to carry out the responsibilities of marriage in faithfulness. | man and woman being married |

104

## Introduction ( __ min.)

Invite the students to think about the last celebration in which they took part. Ask: *What were you celebrating? Who took part in the celebration?* Have a few volunteers share their responses. Then ask the students to describe the sights and sounds of the celebration.

## Presentation ( __ min.)

*Please note that this chart extends the lesson presented in Chapter 6: *The Church Celebrates Seven Sacraments.*

Ask the students: *What is a sacrament?* (A sacrament is an effective sign given to us by Jesus Christ through which we share in God's life.) Then ask the students to name the Seven Sacraments.

Invite the students to reflect quietly about the celebrations of the sacraments in which they have participated. Then have volunteers share their reflections with the group.

For each sacrament, help the students read across both pages to present and review the meaning, the ordinary minister, and the actions and words of the sacrament. Refer to Chapter 6 as needed.

## Guest Speaker

Invite one of the priests of the parish to speak to the students about his role in parish sacramental celebrations. If possible, ask the priest to show the students the Chrism and oils used in the Sacraments of Baptism, Confirmation, and Anointing of the Sick. Also ask the priest to show the students the sacred vessels (chalice, paten, and ciborium) used for the Sacrament of the Eucharist. If acceptable to the guest, provide a few minutes in which the students can ask him questions.

# Sacraments

| What Do We See? | What Do We Hear? |
|---|---|
| Pouring of water over forehead or immersion in baptismal pool | "(Name), I baptize you in the name of the Father, and of the Son, and of the Holy Spirit." |
| Laying on of hand while anointing with Chrism on forehead | "(Name), be sealed with the Gift of the Holy Spirit." |
| The priest, who through the power of the Holy Spirit, consecrates the bread and wine which become the Body and Blood of Christ. Communicants receiving the Body and Blood of Christ | The priest saying the words of Consecration, "This is my Body. . . ." "This is the cup of my Blood. . . ." The communicants responding "Amen" to "The Body of Christ" and "The Blood of Christ." |
| Priest extends right hand or both hands over head of penitent and says words of absolution. | ". . . I absolve you from your sins in the name of the Father, and of the Son, and of the Holy Spirit." |
| Anointing of the sick on their foreheads and hands; laying on of hands on heads of those who are ill | "Through this holy anointing may the Lord in his love and mercy help you with the grace of the Holy Spirit. May the Lord who frees you from sin save you and raise you up." |
| Laying on of hands; anointing of the hands of newly-ordained priests | (For priests): "Almighty Father, grant this servant of yours the dignity of the priesthood. Renew within him the Spirit of holiness. . . ." |
| Joining of right hands by the man and woman | "I, (name), take you, [name], to be my wife [husband]. I promise to be true to you in good times and in bad, in sickness and in health. I will love you and honor you all the days of my life." |

105

## CATECHISM FOCUS

**"The seven sacraments touch all the stages and all the important moments of the Christian life: they give birth and increase, healing and mission to the Christian's life of faith. There is thus a certain resemblance between the stages of natural life and the stages of the spiritual life."** (*CCC*, 1210)

Remind the students that Baptism, Confirmation, and Eucharist are Sacraments of Christian Initiation; Penance and Anointing of the Sick are Sacraments of Healing; and Holy Orders and Matrimony (Marriage) are Sacraments at the Service of Communion. (For the Sacrament of Holy Orders, more information is provided on pages 110 and 111. For the Sacrament of Matrimony, more information is provided on page 112.)

If possible, you may want to show the students the parish's copy of *The Rites* book. Explain that the words and actions used in the celebrations of the sacraments are in this book.

## Conclusion ( __ min.)

### Responding in Prayer

Lead the students in the following prayer. Invite them to gather in the prayer space. Then assign volunteers to be readers. Ask the students to respond to each reader's prayer with the words: *Jesus, you are the vine. We are the branches.*

Reader 1: *Let us reflect on the following words of Jesus, spoken on the night before he died: " I am the vine, you are the branches"* (John 15:5).

Reader 2: *Jesus, we believe that the sacraments unite Catholics all over the world with you and with one another.*

Reader 3: *Jesus, thank you for giving us the sacraments. You have given us a way to share in God's life, the gift of grace.*

Reader 4: *Through the grace we receive in the sacraments, may we continue to grow in holiness. Jesus, may we continue to live as your disciples.*

**GOALS**

*to learn about the prayers and responses of the four parts of the Mass; to appreciate the richness of the celebration of the Mass*

## Catechist Reflection

In the homily of the concluding Mass of World Youth Day in Cologne, Germany on August 21, 2005, Pope Benedict XVI told the assembly: "Do not be deterred from taking part in Sunday Mass, and help others discover it too. . . . Let us discover the intimate riches of the Church's liturgy and its true greatness: it is not we who are celebrating for ourselves, but it is the living God himself who is preparing a banquet for us."

# The Mass

### Introductory Rites

**Entrance** Altar servers, readers, the deacon, and the priest celebrant process forward to the altar. The assembly sings as this takes place. The priest and deacon kiss the altar and bow out of reverence.

**Greeting** The priest and the assembly make the Sign of the Cross, and the priest reminds us that we are in the presence of Jesus.

**Act of Penitence** Gathered in God's presence the assembly sees its sinfulness and proclaims the mystery of God's love. We ask for God's mercy in our lives.

**Gloria** On some Sundays we sing or say this hymn of praise. (page 123)

**Collect or Opening Prayer** This prayer expresses the theme of the celebration and the hopes and needs of the assembly.

### Liturgy of the Word

**First Reading** This reading is usually from the Old Testament. We hear of God's love and mercy for his people before the time of Christ. We learn of God's covenant with his people and of the ways they lived his law.

**Responsorial Psalm** We reflect in silence as God's Word enters our hearts. Then we thank God for the Word we just heard.

**Second Reading** This reading is usually from the New Testament letters, the Acts of the Apostles, or the Book of Revelation. We hear about the first disciples, the teachings of the Apostles, and the beginning of the Church.

**Alleluia or Gospel Acclamation** We stand to sing the Alleluia or other words of praise. This shows we are ready to share the Good News of Jesus Christ.

**Gospel** This reading is always from the Gospel of Matthew, Mark, Luke, or John. Proclaimed by the deacon or priest, this reading is about the mission and ministry of Jesus Christ. Jesus' words and actions speak to us today and help us know how to live as his disciples.

**Homily** The bishop, priest, or deacon talks to us about the readings. His words help us understand what God's Word means to us today. We learn what it means to believe and be members of the Church. We grow closer to God and one another.

**Profession of Faith** The whole assembly prays together the Nicene Creed (page 121) or the Apostles' Creed (page 121). We are stating aloud what we believe as members of the Church.

**Prayer of the Faithful** We pray for the needs of all God's people.

106

## Introduction (__ min.)

Have the students work in pairs. Ask the partners to think about a family or local community celebration and to describe the parts of the celebration. Ask the students to think about what the people did as they gathered, what stories were exchanged, what people did for the main part of the celebration, and what people did as they prepared to leave. Have the students reflect on how participating in family and community celebrations enriches their lives.

## Presentation (__ min.)

Invite the students to think about what they have learned about the Mass. You may want them to refer to Chapter 9, pages 60–65.

If possible, show the students the books used at Mass. Explain that the *Sacramentary* contains the prayers of the priest and the assembly's responses. Also point out the two books used during the Liturgy of the Word: the Lectionary contains the readings of the

## Optional Activity

Have the students work in small groups. Give each group four index cards. Ask the students in each group to write an action of the Mass on the front of each card and on the reverse side have them write the part of the Mass in which the action takes place. (For example, on front: the deacon and altar servers prepare the altar; on back: Liturgy of the Eucharist/Preparation of the Gifts). Then have the groups take turns presenting their clues and having the students in the other groups identify the correct part of the Mass.

## Liturgy of the Eucharist

**Preparation of the Gifts** The altar is prepared by the deacon and the altar servers. We offer gifts. These gifts include the bread and wine and the collection for the Church and for those in need. As members of the assembly carry the bread and wine in a procession to the altar, we sing. The bread and wine are placed on the altar.

**Prayer over the Offering** The priest asks God to bless and accept our gifts. We respond, "Blessed be God for ever."

**Eucharistic Prayer** This is the most important prayer of the Church. It is our greatest prayer of praise and thanksgiving. It joins us to Christ and to one another. The beginning of this prayer, the Preface, consists of offering God thanksgiving and praise. We sing together "Holy, Holy, Holy." The rest of the prayer consists of: calling on the Holy Spirit to bless the gifts of bread and wine; the Consecration of the bread and wine, recalling Jesus' words and actions at the Last Supper; recalling Jesus' Passion, Death, Resurrection, and Ascension; remembering that the Eucharist is offered by the Church in Heaven and on earth; praising God and praying a great "Amen" in love of God: Father, Son, and Holy Spirit.

**Communion Rite** We prepare to receive the Body and Blood of Jesus Christ as spiritual food in Holy Communion.

**Lord's Prayer** Jesus gave us this prayer that we pray aloud or sing to the Father.

**Rite of Peace** We pray that Christ's peace be with us always. We offer one another a Sign of Peace to show that we are united in Christ.

**Breaking of the Bread** We say aloud or sing the Lamb of God, asking Jesus for his mercy, forgiveness, and peace. The priest breaks apart the Host, and we are invited to share in the Eucharist.

**Holy Communion** Each person receiving Communion is shown the Host and hears "The Body of Christ." Each person is shown the cup and hears "The Blood of Christ." Each person responds "Amen" and receives Holy Communion. While people are receiving Holy Communion, we sing as one. After this we silently reflect on the gift of Jesus that we have just received and of God's presence with us. The priest then prays that the gift of Jesus will help us live as Jesus' disciples.

## Concluding Rites

**Greeting** The priest offers the final prayer. His words serve as a farewell promise that Jesus will be with us all.

**Blessing** The priest blesses us in the name of the Father, Son, and Holy Spirit. We make the Sign of the Cross as he blesses us.

**Dismissal** The deacon or priest sends us out to love and serve God and one another. The priest and deacon kiss the altar. They, along with other ministers at the Mass, bow to the altar, and process out as we sing the closing song.

107

Mass; the *Book of the Gospels* contains the Gospels.

Have a volunteer read *The Introductory Rites* section on page 106. You may want to pray together the *Confiteor* and the *Gloria* on page 123 of the text.

Have a volunteer read the *Liturgy of the Word* section on page 106. At this time you may want to read the previous Sunday's or the upcoming Sunday's readings, Responsorial Psalm, and Gospel (found in a missalette). Also you may want the students to pray together the Nicene Creed on page 121.

Emphasize that, during the Liturgy of the Eucharist, the bread and wine become Christ's Body and Blood. Ask a volunteer to read the *Liturgy of the Eucharist* section on page 107. You may want the students to pray the Lord's Prayer and Lamb of God on page 123.

Ask a volunteer to read the *Concluding Rites* section on page 107. Stress that we show we are thankful for the gift of the Eucharist when we serve God and help others all during the week.

## Catechism Focus

"The command of Jesus to repeat his actions and words 'until he comes' does not only ask us to remember Jesus and what he did. It is directed at the liturgical celebration, by the apostles and their successors, of the memorial of Christ, of his life, of his death, of his Resurrection, and of his intercession in the presence of the Father." (*CCC*, 1341)

# Conclusion (__ min.)

### Responding in Prayer

Invite the students to reflect quietly about their participation during the celebration of Mass. Ask: *Do you join in singing? Do you listen closely to the readings and the Gospel? Do you pray the responses?* Then invite the students to make a resolution to try to participate fully in every celebration of the Mass.

Ask the students to gather in the prayer space. Pray together the Lord's Prayer. You may also want the group to pray the Prayer After Communion on page 123. Substitute the pronoun *me* with the pronoun *us*. Close by praying: *Let us serve the Lord in joy and peace.*

# GOALS

*to learn about the two usual ways the Church celebrates the Sacrament of Penance and Reconciliation; to make an examination of conscience*

## Catechist Reflection

"What man among you having a hundred sheep and losing one of them would not leave the ninety-nine in the desert and go after the the lost one until he finds it? And when he does find it, he sets it on his shoulders with great joy and, upon his arrival home, he calls together his friends and neighbors and says to them, 'Rejoice with me because I have found my lost sheep.' I tell you, in just the same way there will be more joy in heaven over one sinner who repents than over ninety- nine righteous people who have no need of repentance." (Luke 15:4–7)

## Rites of Penance

The Church has two usual ways to celebrate the Sacrament of Penance and Reconciliation. One way, or rite, is used when an individual meets with the priest for the celebration of the sacrament. The other rite is used when a group gathers to celebrate the sacrament with one or more priests.

### Rite for Reconciliation of Individual Penitents

I examine my conscience before meeting with the priest.

**Welcoming** The priest greets me and I make the Sign of the Cross. The priest asks me to trust in God's mercy.

**Reading of the Word of God** The priest or I may read something from the Bible.

**Confession and Penance** I confess my sins. The priest talks to me about loving God and others. He gives me a penance.

**Prayer of Penitent and Absolution** I pray an Act of Contrition. The priest extends his hand and gives me absolution.

**Proclamation of Praise and Dismissal** The priest says, "Give thanks to the Lord, for he is good." I respond, "His mercy endures for ever." The priest sends me out saying, "The Lord has freed you from your sins. Go in peace."

### Rite, for Reconciliation of Several Penitents with Individual Confession and Absolution

**Introductory Rites** We gather as an assembly and sing an opening hymn. The priest greets us and prays an opening prayer.

**Celebration of the Word of God** The assembly listens to the Word of God. This is followed by a homily and then by our examination of conscience.

**Rite of Reconciliation** The assembly prays together an Act of Contrition. We may say another prayer or sing a song, and then pray the Our Father.

I meet individually with the priest and confess my sins. The priest talks to me about loving God and others. He gives me a penance.

The priest extends his hand and gives me absolution.

After everyone has met with the priest, we join together and praise God for his mercy. The priest then offers a prayer of thanksgiving.

**Concluding Rite** The priest blesses us, and dismisses the assembly saying, "The Lord has freed you from your sins. Go in peace." We respond, "Thanks be to God."

108

## Introduction ( _ min.)

Ask the students to think of ways people show their forgiveness. Have volunteers share their responses. Possible responses include: shaking hands or exchanging other gestures of friendship.

Talk about the importance of asking for forgiveness and forgiving others.

## Presentation ( _ min.)

Please note that pages 108 and 109 extend the lesson for Chapter 12: *God Gives Us Forgiveness and Peace.*

Remind the students that the Church celebrates God's forgiveness in the Sacrament of Penance and Reconciliation. Emphasize that the sacrament is a celebration.

## Optional Activity

Have the students turn to page 85 and read together the Act of Contrition. Then ask the students to use a different color crayon to underline the following parts of the prayer: Part 1—words we use to tell God we are sorry for our sins (from "My God" to "above all things"); Part 2—words we use to promise God that we will try not to sin again (from "I firmly intend" to "leads me to sin"); Part 3—words we use to ask God to forgive us (from "Our Savior" to "have mercy").

## An Examination of Conscience

When we examine our consciences, we can thank God for giving us the strength to make good choices. Reflecting on the choices we have made helps us to make choices that bring us closer to God. Take a few minutes to think quietly and prayerfully about ways you follow each of the commandments. The Ten Commandments state serious obligations to God and our neighbor. The list of commandments is on page 70.

**The First Commandment**
- Do I try to love God above all things?
- Do I really believe in, trust, and love God?
- Do I pray to God sometime each day?
- How do I take an active part in the worship of God, especially in the Mass and the other sacraments?

**The Second Commandment**
- Do I respect God's name and the name of Jesus?
- How have I used God's name?
- Have I called on God and asked him to be with me?
- How do I act when I am in church?

**The Third Commandment**
- How have I kept the Lord's Day holy?
- What do I do to participate in Mass every Sunday?
- On Sundays in what ways have I rested and relaxed? shared time with my family? praised and thanked God?

**The Fourth Commandment**
- Do I obey my parents, grandparents, or guardians in all that they ask me?
- Do I help them?
- Do I respect my brothers and sisters?
- How have I shown respect for older people?
- Do I obey my teachers and others in authority?
- Have I followed the laws of my city, state, and country?

**The Fifth Commandment**
- Have I respected the dignity of all people?
- Have I shown by my actions that all people have the right to life?
- Have I done anything that could harm myself or others?
- Have I spoken out against violence and injustice?
- Have I lived in peace with my family and neighbors?

**The Sixth Commandment**
- Do I honor myself as special and created by God?
- Do my actions show love and respect for myself and others?
- Do I use my body in responsible and faithful ways?

**The Seventh Commandment**
- Have I cared for the gifts of Creation?
- Have I taken care of my belongings?
- Have I taken things that do not belong to me?
- Have I been honest in taking tests and playing games?
- Have I respected the property of others?
- Have I shared what I have with those in need?

**The Eighth Commandment**
- Have I taken responsibility for my words and been truthful?
- Have I respected the privacy of others?
- Have I made promises that I did not keep?

**The Ninth Commandment**
- Do I stay away from things and people who do not live by the virtue of chastity and do not value human sexuality?
- Do I try to show my feelings in a respectful way?
- In what ways do I practice modesty, the virtue by which we think, speak, act, and dress in ways that show respect for ourselves and others?

**The Tenth Commandment**
- Do I wish that I had things that belong to others?
- Am I sad when others have things that I would like?
- Am I willing to share with others, especially people who are poor and needy?
- Do I give money to the poor and needy?
- Am I happy with what I have or am I always asking for more things?

109

Ask a volunteer to read the introductory paragraph on page 108. Stress that confession, contrition, penance, and absolution are all parts of both rites.

Have a volunteer read the *Rite for Reconciliation of Individual Penitents.* Check the parish bulletin to find out when this Rite is celebrated. In many parishes people can celebrate in this way on Saturday afternoons.

Ask a volunteer to read *Rite for Reconciliation of Several Penitents with Individual Confession and Absolution.* Explain that many times the Sacrament of Penance and Reconciliation is celebrated this way during the liturgical seasons of Advent and Lent.

If possible, show the students the reconciliation room or confessional in your parish church. Stress that in both Rites a person always confesses his or her sins to the priest in private. Remind the students that the priest is obliged not to tell others what sins a person has told him when confessing.

Ask the students: *What is an examination of conscience?* Have volunteers share their responses. Ask the students to read *Do You Know?* on page 82. Then read together the introductory paragraph on page 109.

## CATECHISM FOCUS

"The reception of this sacrament ought to be prepared for by an *examination of conscience* made in the light of the Word of God. The passages best suited to this can be found in the Ten Commandments, the moral catechesis of the Gospels and the apostolic Letters, such as the Sermon on the Mount and the apostolic teachings." *(CCC, 1454)*

# Conclusion (_ min.)

### Responding in Prayer

Help the students to make an examination of conscience. After reading each question on page 109, pause for a brief moment of silence to allow the students to reflect quietly about their responses.

Then ask the students to stand and pray together the Act of Contrition on page 85.

**GOAL**
*to understand that those who receive Holy Orders are called to love and serve Christ and the Church in a particular way*

## Catechist Reflection

"Every morning prepare your soul for a tranquil day."

Saint Francis de Sales (1567–1622), Bishop of Geneva, Switzerland and patron saint of educators, writers, and journalists

## Introduction ( __ min.)

Ask the students to name the pope, the bishop of your diocese, and the pastor and priests of your parish. Help the students to recall what they have learned about the roles of the pope, bishops, and priests. (See Chapter 5 of the text.)

## Presentation ( __ min.)

Have a volunteer read the introductory paragraph about the Sacrament of Holy Orders on page 110. Point out that the men who receive Holy Orders are forever sealed with a sacramental character that marks them as forever in the service of Christ and the Church.

Ask a volunteer to read the two paragraphs about deacons. If there is a permanent deacon in your parish, invite him to speak with the students about his ministry. Point out that a deacon serves under the leadership of the bishop. The deacon assists the parish priests by administering the Sacrament of Baptism, by reading the Gospel during Mass, by visiting the sick people of the parish, and by bringing Holy Communion to the people who are sick or homebound.

# The Sacrament of Holy Orders

Holy Orders is the sacrament in which baptized men are ordained to serve the Church as deacons, priests, and bishops. It is a Sacrament at the Service of Communion—a sacrament of service to others. While there are many ministries in the Church, deacons, priests, and bishops are the only ordained ministers. Those who receive Holy Orders take on a special mission in leading and serving the People of God.

### In the Sacrament of Holy Orders:

Those who receive Holy Orders are forever sealed with a sacramental character. This joins them to Christ and marks them as forever in the service of Christ and the Church. Thus, the Sacrament of Holy Orders cannot be repeated.

**Deacons** Through Holy Orders, a deacon shares in Christ's mission by assisting bishops and priests in the mission of the Church. Some men, single or married, become permanent deacons, remaining deacons for life.

Other men remain unmarried and become deacons as a step toward the priesthood. Having been ordained as deacons, they continue on to be ordained into the priesthood.

**Priests** A priest is ordained to preach the Gospel and serve the faithful, especially celebrating the Eucharist and other sacraments.

**Bishops** To become a bishop, a priest must be chosen by the pope, with the advice of other bishops and Church members. A bishop receives the fullness of the Sacrament of Holy Orders and continues the Apostles' mission of leadership and service.

**Ordination** In the sacramental act called *ordination*, bishops, priests, and deacons receive one or more of the three degrees of orders: episcopate, (bishops) presbyterate (priests), and diaconate (deacons). A bishop always ordains a newly chosen bishop, as well as candidates for the priesthood and diaconate.

The celebration of Holy Orders always takes place during the Mass. After the bishop celebrant gives a homily, he talks to the men to be ordained, questioning them about their responsibilities to lead and serve in Jesus' name. Then the whole assembly prays for these men.

110

## Preparing for the Priesthood

**Explain to the students that men prepare for the priesthood by studying for several years. If a man has been accepted as a candidate for the priesthood, he enters a seminary. While in the seminary, the men, who are called seminarians, study Scripture, the history of the Church, and the sacraments. They also are given the opportunity to pray about the lives of ministry for which they are preparing.**

After the assembly's prayer, the laying on of hands takes place. During the laying on of hands, the bishop celebrant prays in silence. When a priest is ordained, the other priests who are present also lay their hands upon the candidate. This is a sign of their unity in priesthood and service to the diocese. When a bishop is ordained, other bishops lay their hands upon the bishop-elect as a sign of their unity in service to the Church.

After the laying on of hands, the bishop celebrant prays the prayer of consecration, which is different for each degree of orders. The bishop celebrant extends his hands, and by the power of the Holy Spirit ordains each man to continue Jesus' ministry in a particular service in the Church. The laying on of hands and the prayer of consecration are the main parts of the Sacrament of Holy Orders.

The newly ordained men are presented with signs of their service and ministry in the Church. At ordination:

- Deacons receive a stole, which is to be worn across the left shoulder and fastened at the right, a sign of ministry, and the Book of the Gospels, a sign of preaching the Good News of Christ.
- Priests have their stoles placed around the neck and down over the chest; they have the palms of their hands anointed so that they can make the People of God holy through the sacraments. They receive a chalice and a paten, signs that they may celebrate the Eucharist to offer the sacrifice of the Lord.
- Bishops' heads are anointed, and they receive a miter or pointed hat, a sign of the office of bishop; a ring, a sign of faithfulness to Christ and the Church; and a pastor staff, a sign of a bishop's role as shepherd of Christ's flock.

111

Ask a volunteer to read the paragraphs about priests and bishops. Emphasize that priests and bishops live a life of service to the Church.

Then read the first two paragraphs about ordination. Emphasize that it is always a bishop who ordains a newly appointed bishop and candidates for the priesthood and diaconate. Ask the students to look at the photographs at the top of page 110. Explain that the photo on the right shows the men, who are being ordained, lying prostrate as the Litany of Saints is prayed. The photo on the left shows a candidate kneeling before the bishop as the bishop extends his hands over the candidate and prays the Prayer of Consecration. Emphasize that the laying on of hands and the Prayer of Consecration are the main parts of the Sacrament of Holy Orders. Then read the remaining paragraphs about ordination.

Read together the descriptions of the ordained mens' signs of service and ministry in the Church.

## CATECHISM FOCUS

**"The ministerial priesthood has the task not only of representing Christ—Head of the Church—before the assembly of the faithful, but also of acting in the name of the whole Church when presenting to God the prayer of the Church, and above all when offering the Eucharistic sacrifice."**
**(CCC, 1552)**

# Conclusion (__ min.)

### Responding in Prayer

Invite the students to gather in the prayer space. Read the following prayer. Pause briefly at each stop mark (/) to allow the students time to repeat the words.

*O Father, thank you for the bishops and priests of the Church./ Guide these ordained ministers as they guard/ the blessed memory of your Son Jesus/ through the preaching of his word/ and the celebration of the sacraments./*

*Be with and nourish the bishops, priests, and deacons of our Church/ so that they may faithfully fulfill their mission/ at the service of the Gospel./*

*We also pray for seminarians who are preparing to serve the Church./ This we pray through Christ our Lord. Amen.*

## GOALS

*to learn about and respect the sacredness of the sacramental commitment involved in marriage; to understand the particular call to service lived out by those in the laity, the consecrated life, and the ordained ministry*

### Catechist Reflection

"Give me the happiness, Lord, to place myself completely in your hands."

Mother Celine Chludzinska Borzecka (1833–1913) Mother Celine dedicated herself to serving God and others—first, as a wife and mother and then, after her husband's death as a religious sister. See *Lives of the Saints*, www.webelieveweb.com.

## Introduction ( __ min.)

Begin by asking: *What words do you associate with the word* commitment? List the students' responses on the board or on a large sheet of paper. Possible responses include: vows, promises, relationship, oaths, agreement.

Also ask: *What commitments do men and women make to each other and to their families?* Pause briefly to allow the students to reflect on the question. Then invite volunteers to share their responses.

## Presentation ( __ min.)

Ask a volunteer to read the first four paragraphs of *The Sacrament of Matrimony*. Emphasize that the marriage covenant is a life-long commitment. Have the students highlight or underline the second sentence of the second paragraph.

Have a volunteer read the fifth and sixth paragraphs on page 112. Point out to the students that men and women preparing for marriage should

# The Sacrament of Matrimony

The Sacrament of Matrimony is the sacrament in which a man and woman become husband and wife, and promise to be faithful to each other for the rest of their lives. It is a Sacrament at the Service of Communion.

The Church sees marriage as a covenant. The marriage covenant is the life-long commitment between a man and a woman to live as faithful and loving partners. It is modeled on Christ's love for the Church, sometimes called the Bride of Christ.

The love that a husband and a wife share with each other is a sign of God's love for all his people. It is a sign of Christ's love for his Church. The love between a husband and wife is meant to be generous, faithful, and complete.

Once Jesus was teaching about marriage, and he said "what God has joined together, no human being must separate" (Matthew 19:6). Thus, Christ and the Church teach us that the marriage covenant is not to be broken. In the Sacrament of Matrimony, the husband and wife promise to be loyal and true to each other for the rest of their lives. If a married couple does have problems in their relationship, they can turn to their family and the parish community for prayer and support. And God's grace continues to help husbands and wives, especially in the Sacraments of the Eucharist and Penance.

The married couple's expression of their love includes the procreation of children, and the education of the children in the faith. With the help of God's grace, married couples are called to create and nurture a loving family, a community of faith, hope, and love.

Every family is called to be a domestic Church, "a Church in the home." It is in the family that we learn to pray and worship God together, to forgive and be forgiven, and to be disciples of Jesus, helping and comforting others, especially those in need.

The celebration of the Sacrament of Matrimony often takes place within the Mass. The Rite of Marriage takes place after the Gospel is proclaimed. The Rite of Marriage begins as the priest or deacon asks the couple three questions. Are they free to give themselves in marriage? Will they love and honor each other as husband and wife throughout their lives? Will they lovingly accept children from God and raise them in the faith?

Then the bride and groom exchange their vows. The deacon or priest asks God to fill the couple's lives with many blessings. Then the deacon or priest blesses the rings, and the couple exchanges them as a sign of their love and faithfulness. After the assembly prays the Prayer of the Faithful, the Mass continues with the Liturgy of the Eucharist. After the Lord's Prayer, the priest prays a special prayer for the couple. The bride and groom, if they are Catholic, receive Holy Communion as a sign of their union with Christ.

112

### Optional Activity

**If there is a religious brother or sister working in your parish, invite him or her to speak to the group about community life and the work of the community.**

**You may also want the students to find information about some religious communities: Franciscans, Jesuits, Salesians, Sisters of Charity, Sisters of Mercy, Sisters of the Blessed Sacrament.**

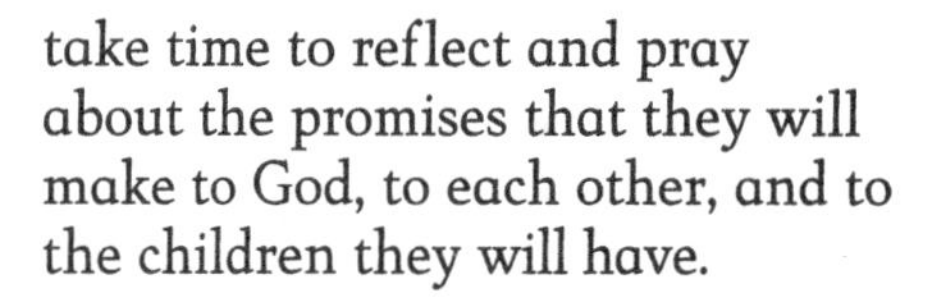

## Vocations

In Baptism God calls all of us to serve him. A *vocation* is God's call to serve him in a particular way. Each baptized person has a vocation to love and serve God. There are specific ways to follow our vocation: the married or single life, the religious life, or the life of an ordained priest or permanent deacon.

Many Catholics live out their vocation as laypeople in the married life or the single life. Through marriage a husband and wife share God's love in a special way with each other and form a new Christian family. They spend much of their time and energy in loving, caring, and sharing their faith with their families, but can also serve others in their parishes, neighborhoods, and communities. Single people often devote themselves to sharing their gifts and talents with others through their work. They may have more time to dedicate to their parents, families, parishes, and local communities.

Some men and women follow Jesus Christ in the religious life. They are priests, brothers, or sisters who belong to religious communities and make vows, or promises to God. They promise: *poverty*—to live simply as Jesus did, owning no property or personal goods; *chastity*—to live a life of celibacy, remaining single and devoting themselves to the work of God and the Church; *obedience*—to listen carefully to God's direction in their lives by obeying the leaders of the Church and their religious communities.

Some religious live apart from the world spending their days in prayer. Others combine prayer and service in teaching, social work, or the medical field.

God calls some baptized men to be priests and permanent deacons. Priests promise to live a life of celibacy, remaining single. This allows them to serve all of God's people. Diocesan priests serve a diocese, usually in a parish. They serve in the work assigned to them by the bishop. Priests in religious communities serve wherever their communities need them.

Permanent deacons are often married and have an occupation or a career to support themselves and their families. They are ordained to assist the bishops and priests and to serve the whole Church. They preach, baptize, witness marriages, preside at burials, and at Mass they read the Gospel, prepare the altar, and distribute Holy Communion.

Each person can prepare to serve in a particular vocation by praying and reflecting on ways God might be calling him or her to live. See "Prayer for My Vocation" on page 122.

113

take time to reflect and pray about the promises that they will make to God, to each other, and to the children they will have.

Ask the students to read the section about Matrimony on *The Seven Sacraments* chart on pages 104 and 105. Then have a volunteer read the last two paragraphs about the celebration of the Sacrament of Matrimony.

Direct the students' attention to page 113. Have a volunteer read the first three paragraphs. You may want to refer the students to the explanation of our common vocation on page 66, Unit 3: *More for You to Know*.

Have a volunteer read the paragraphs about life in religious communities. You may want to point out that many saints of the Church were religious brothers, sisters, or priests. Ask the students to identify those about whom they have learned.

Have a volunteer read the last three paragraphs. Emphasize to the students that they can start preparing to serve in a particular vocation now.

### CATECHISM FOCUS

"It is in the Church, in communion with all the baptized, that the Christian fulfills his vocation." (CCC, 2030)

For additional reference and reflection, see CCC, 934–945, and 1659–1666.

## Conclusion (__ min.)

### Responding in Prayer

Provide a few minutes for the students to reflect silently about the vocation that God may be calling them to in the future. Point out that they have several years in which to prepare.

Ask the students then to bring their texts and gather in the prayer space. Pray together *Prayer for My Vocation* on page 122.

## GOALS

*to understand and live out Catholic social teaching; to learn about the Gifts and the fruits of the Holy Spirit;*

## Catechist Reflection

"It was not you who chose me, but I who chose you and appointed you to go and bear fruit that will remain, so that whatever you ask the Father in my name he may give you. This I command you: love one another." (John 15:16–17)

"But when he comes, the Spirit of truth, he will guide you to all truth."(John 16:13)

# Catholic Social Teaching

Jesus' life and teaching are the foundation of Catholic social teaching. This teaching calls us to work for justice and peace as Jesus did. Catholic social teaching is based on the belief that every person has human dignity. Human dignity is the value and worth that come from being created in God's image and likeness.

There are seven themes of Catholic social teaching.

**Life and Dignity of the Human Person** Human life is sacred because it is a gift from God. Because we are all God's children, we all share the same human dignity. As Christians we respect all people, even those we do not know.

**Call to Family, Community, and Participation** We are all social. We need to be with others to grow. The family is the basic community. In the family we grow and learn the values of our faith. As Christians we live those values in our family and community.

**Rights and Responsibilities of the Human Person** Every person has a fundamental right to life. This includes the things we need to have a decent life: faith and family, work and education, health care and housing. We also have a responsibility to others and to society. We work to make sure the rights of all people are being protected.

**Option for the Poor and Vulnerable** We have a special obligation to help those who are poor and in need. This includes those who cannot protect themselves because of their age or their health.

**Dignity of Work and the Rights of Workers** Our work is a sign of our participation in God's work. People have the right to decent work, just wages, safe working conditions, and to participate in decisions about work.

**Solidarity of the Human Family** Solidarity is a feeling of unity. It binds members of a group together. Each of us is a member of the one human family. The human family includes people of all racial and cultural backgrounds. We all suffer when one part of the human family suffers whether they live near or far away.

**Care for God's Creation** God created us to be stewards, or caretakers, of his Creation. We must care for and respect the environment. We have to protect it for future generations. When we care for Creation, we show respect for God the Creator.

Note: The **Corporal Works of Mercy** are found on page 89.
The **Spiritual Works of Mercy** are found on page 90.

114

# Introduction (__ min.)

Invite the students to think about the qualities, talents, or other characteristics that God has given to them. Ask the students to reflect about ways they use their gifts or talents to help themselves, their families, friends, and other people.

Pause briefly and ask the students to pray quietly to thank God for their gifts and talents and to ask God for help in developing these gifts and talents.

# Presentation (__ min.)

*Catholic Social Teaching*

Emphasize that Jesus taught us how we are to care for others. Have volunteers read the introductory paragraphs and the explanation for each Catholic social teaching theme. Lead a brief discussion about ways young people can carry out the Church's teaching.

## Optional Activity

Have the students research the saints who made evident the fruits of the Holy Spirit in their lives. Consider having the students look at the *Lives of the Saints* feature at www.webelieveweb.com.

# Responding to the Holy Spirit

**The Gifts of the Holy Spirit** When we are baptized, the Holy Spirit shares seven spiritual gifts with us. These gifts help us to be faithful followers of Jesus Christ. The Gifts of the Holy Spirit are:

- wisdom—helps us to know and be able to follow God's will in our lives
- understanding—helps us to love others as Jesus calls us to do
- counsel (right judgment)—helps us to make good choices
- fortitude (courage)—helps us to be strong in giving witness to our faith in Jesus Christ
- knowledge—helps us to learn more about God and his plan
- piety (reverence)—helps us to have a love and respect for all that God has created
- fear of the Lord (wonder and awe)—helps us to recognize that God's presence and love fills all creation

**The Fruits of the Holy Spirit** When we respond to the Holy Spirit and use the gifts we have received, the Fruits of the Holy Spirit are evident in our lives. The Fruits of the Holy Spirit are charity, joy, peace, patience, kindness, goodness, generosity, gentleness, faithfulness, modesty, self-control, chastity.

**The Precepts of the Church**
(from *Catechism of the Catholic Church,* 2041–2043)

1. You shall attend Mass on Sundays and Holy Days of Obligation and rest from servile labor.
2. You shall confess your sins at least once a year.
3. You shall receive the Sacrament of the Eucharist at least during the Easter season.
4. You shall observe the days of fasting and abstinence by the Church.
5. You shall help to provide for the needs of the Church.

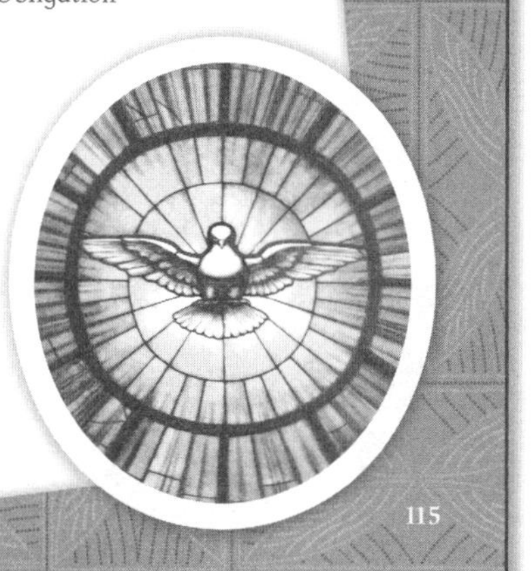

115

## CATECHISM FOCUS

"The *fruits* of the Spirit are perfections that the Holy Spirit forms in us as the first fruits of eternal glory." (CCC, 1832)

*Responding to the Holy Spirit*

Remind the students that at Baptism the Holy Spirit shares seven spiritual gifts with us. Emphasize that at Confirmation the Holy Spirit strengthens these gifts within us. Have a few volunteers read the *Gifts of the Holy Spirit* on page 115.

You may want to begin your explanation of the fruits of the Holy Spirit by drawing a grape vine on the board or on a large sheet of paper. Draw branches, leaves, and a few grape clusters. Point out that when growers tend the vines by watering and feeding the vine, the fruit grows. Then ask a volunteer to read *The Fruits of the Holy Spirit.* You will find an explanation of modesty and chastity on page 98, Unit 4: *More for You to Know.*

Explain to the students that a precept is a law or rule. The Church's precepts help us to obey the Ten Commandments and the Great Commandment. Have a volunteer read the precepts.

## Conclusion (__ min.)

### Responding in Prayer

Give an index card to each student. Ask the students to write on the cards a few ways that they can use their gifts or talents in helping others and carrying out the Church's social teaching. Have them fold the cards and bring the cards as they gather in the prayer space. Ask the students to place the cards in a basket or container on the prayer table.

Then pray Come, Holy Spirit. The prayer is on page 31 in Chapter 4 of the student text.

## GOALS

*to learn about and appreciate Jesus' teaching about prayer; to recognize the different forms of prayer; to respond to God's love through prayer*

## Catechist Reflection

"We begin to pray, believing that it is our own initiative that compels us to do so. Instead, we learn that it is always God's initiative within us, just as Saint Paul has written. *This initiative restores in us our true humanity; it restores in us our unique dignity*. Yes, we are brought into the higher dignity of the children of God, the children of God who are the hope of all creation."

Pope John Paul II, *Crossing the Threshold of Hope*

## Introduction (__ min.)

Pose the following questions to help the students reflect on a recent conversation that they had with a family member or friend.

- *Was the conversation a long one or short one?*
- *Who spent the most time talking?*
- *Who spent the most time listening?*

Then lead the students in a discussion about the importance of communication with family members and friends.

## Presentation (__ min.)

Have a volunteer read the first two paragraphs on page 116. Then ask the students to think about the ways in which they pray most often.

# About Prayer

Prayer is the raising of our hearts and minds to God. Throughout history—from Creation to the present day—God has called his people to prayer. Prayer is like a conversation: God calls to us, and we respond. Our prayer is a response to God's constant love for us.

We can pray in the silence of our hearts, or we can pray aloud. We can pray alone or with others. Sometimes we do not use words to pray, but sit quietly trying to focus only on God. But however we pray, we turn to God with hope and faith in his love for us.

Jesus taught us to pray by showing us how he prayed. Jesus prayed by quietly focusing on God, studying Scriptures, praying the psalms, giving thanks to his Father, healing people, forgiving people, and talking to God about his feelings. From the example and words of Jesus we learn to pray above all to God the Father. Jesus taught us to do this most especially in the Lord's Prayer.

### The Lord's Prayer

The Lord's Prayer, also called the Our Father, "is truly the summary of the whole gospel" (*Catechism of the Catholic Church*, 2761). It sums up Jesus' message of trust in and love for the Father.

When we pray the Lord's Prayer, we are asking our Father to act in our lives and in our world so that we do what he wills. We ask the Holy Spirit to help us to make the Kingdom of God come alive in people's hearts and lives. And we hope for the Lord's return at the end of time.

### Praying Always

The Holy Spirit guides the Church to pray. Saint Paul wrote to the early Christian communities, "Pray without ceasing" (1 Thessalonians 5:17). We do this, too, calling on God throughout the day, remembering his presence among us.

The habit of daily prayer grows by making special times for personal prayer:

- in the morning, offering our entire day to God
- before and after meals, giving God thanks for our food
- at night, reflecting on ways we have or have not shown love for God and others.

The habit of daily prayer also grows by joining in prayer with other members of the Church. We do this when we gather with our parish for the celebration of the Mass. Another way is through the Liturgy of the Hours. The Liturgy of the Hours is made up of psalms, readings from Scripture and Church teaching, prayers and hymns. It is celebrated at various times during the day, and helps us to praise God throughout the entire day. Praying the Liturgy of the Hours reminds us that God is always active and present in our lives.

116

## Optional Activity

Have the students work in pairs. Ask each set of partners to write a one-or two- sentence prayer that they can pray throughout the day to help them remember that God is with them. You may want the partners to illustrate their verses. Collate the verses and make a prayer booklet. Keep the booklet in the prayer space so it is available for the students to read often.

## Forms of Prayer

Urged by the Holy Spirit, we pray these basic forms of prayer.

**Prayers of blessing**

"The grace of the Lord Jesus Christ and the love of God and the fellowship of the holy Spirit be with all of you." (2 Corinthians 13:13)

To bless is to dedicate someone or something to God or to make something holy in God's name. God continually blesses us with many gifts. Because God first blessed us, we, too, can pray for his blessings on people and things.

**Prayers of petition**

"O God, be merciful to me a sinner." (Luke 18:13)

In prayers of petition we ask something of God. Asking for forgiveness is the most important type of petition.

**Prayers of intercession**

"And this is my prayer: that your love may increase ever more and more in knowledge." (Philippians 1:9)

Intercession is a type of petition. When we pray a prayer of intercession, we are asking for something on behalf of another person or a group of people.

**Prayers of thanksgiving**

"Father, I thank you for hearing me." (John 11:41)

In prayers of thanksgiving, we show our gratitude to God for all he has given to us, most especially for the life, Death, and Resurrection of Jesus. The greatest prayer of thanksgiving is the greatest prayer of the Church, the Eucharist.

**Prayers of praise**

"I shall praise the LORD all my life, sing praise to my God while I live." (Psalm 146:2)

In prayers of praise we give glory to God for being God. We praise God simply because he is God.

117

Emphasize that Jesus prayed to his Father often and showed us different ways to pray. Have a volunteer read the third paragraph.

Point out that Jesus taught us the Lord's Prayer, the Our Father. Have a volunteer read the paragraphs for The Lord's Prayer. Ask the students to read the words of the prayer on page 17. Also, you may want to refer to The Lord's Prayer section of Unit 2: *More for You to Know* on page 44.

Point out that it is important to set aside time for daily prayer. Have volunteers read *Praying Always.*

Talk with the students about the reasons people pray. Point out that there are different prayer forms. Have volunteers read the explanatory paragraphs about the prayer forms on page 117. Emphasize that the Church's greatest prayer of thanksgiving is the Mass.

# Conclusion ( __ min.)

### Responding in Prayer

Explain to the students that many times when Jesus prayed, he prayed the words of the psalms. Point out that today the psalms are an important part of the prayer life of the Church. We pray the psalms when we gather to worship God in celebrating the sacraments and when we pray the Liturgy of the Hours.

Invite the students to gather in the prayer space. Read the following verses of Psalm113. Pause at the end of each line. Ask the students to repeat the verse.

*"Praise you servants of the LORD,*
*praise the name of the LORD.*
*Blessed be the name of the LORD*
*both now and forever.*
*From the rising of the sun to its setting*
*let the name of the LORD be praised."* (Psalm 113:1–3)

## CATECHISM FOCUS

"The Spirit who teaches the Church and recalls for her everything that Jesus said was also to form her in the life of prayer." (CCC, 2623)

For additional reference and reflection, see *CCC*, 2624–2724.

## GOALS

*to understand that sacramentals help us to respond to God's grace; to appreciate that praying the rosary helps us to reflect on special events in the lives of Jesus and Mary*

### Catechist Reflection

"Standing by the cross of Jesus were his mother, and his mother's sister, Mary the wife of Clopas, and Mary of Magdala. When Jesus saw his mother and the disciple there whom he loved, he said to his mother, 'Woman, behold, your son.' Then he said to the disciple, 'Behold, your mother.' And from that hour the disciple took her into his home." (John 19:25–27)

## Introduction (__ min.)

Discuss with the students how looking at photographs of family members and friends or retelling family stories help you to be closer to them.

Then ask volunteers to describe their favorite photographs or share favorite stories of family or friends.

## Presentation (__ min.)

*Do you know about sacramentals?*

Have a volunteer read the paragraph about sacramentals. Point out that palms and ashes are blessed by the priest. On Ash Wednesday, the day Lent begins, the priest puts ashes on our foreheads as a sign that we are to do penance during Lent. We carry blessed palms in a procession on Passion Sunday, Palm Sunday, which is the Sunday before Easter Sunday. We recall Jesus' triumphant entry into Jerusalem before his Death and Resurrection.

## Prayers and Practices

### Do you know about sacramentals?

Blessings, actions, and objects that help us respond to God's grace received in the sacraments are *sacramentals*. Sacramentals are used in the liturgy and in personal prayer. Here are some examples of sacramentals:

- blessings of people, places, foods, and objects
- objects such as rosaries, medals, crucifixes, blessed ashes, and blessed palms
- actions such as making the Sign of the Cross and sprinkling holy water.

### The Rosary

The rosary is a sacramental. Praying the rosary is a popular devotion to Mary. We can pray the rosary alone or with others. We can pray the rosary at any time of the day.

The rosary is usually prayed using a set of beads with a crucifix attached. We repeatedly pray the Our Father, Hail Mary, and Glory to the Father on these beads. This creates a peaceful rhythm of prayer during which we can reflect on special events in the lives of Jesus and Mary. The mysteries of the rosary recall these special events. We remember a different mystery at the beginning of each set of prayers, or decade of the rosary.

### Mysteries of the Rosary

**The Joyful Mysteries**
(by custom prayed on Monday and Saturday)
- The Annunciation
- The Visitation
- The Birth of Jesus
- The Presentation of Jesus in the Temple
- The Finding of Jesus in the Temple

**The Sorrowful Mysteries**
(by custom prayed on Tuesday and Friday)
- The Agony in the Garden
- The Scourging at the Pillar
- The Crowning with Thorns
- The Carrying of the Cross
- The Crucifixion and Death of Jesus

**The Glorious Mysteries**
(by custom prayed on Wednesday and Sunday)
- The Resurrection
- The Ascension
- The Descent of the Holy Spirit upon the Apostles
- The Assumption of Mary into Heaven
- The Coronation of Mary as Queen of Heaven

**The Mysteries of Light**
(by custom prayed on Thursday)
- Jesus' Baptism in the Jordan
- The Miracle at the Wedding at Cana
- Jesus Announces the Kingdom of God
- The Transfiguration
- The Institution of the Eucharist

118

## Optional Activity

Have the students look through their *Our Catholic Faith* texts to find illustrations of some of the mysteries of the rosary. (See Jesus Announces the Kingdom of God, pages 14–15; the Institution of the Eucharist pages 20 and 56; the Crucifixion and Death of Jesus, page 21; the Annunciation, page 95.)

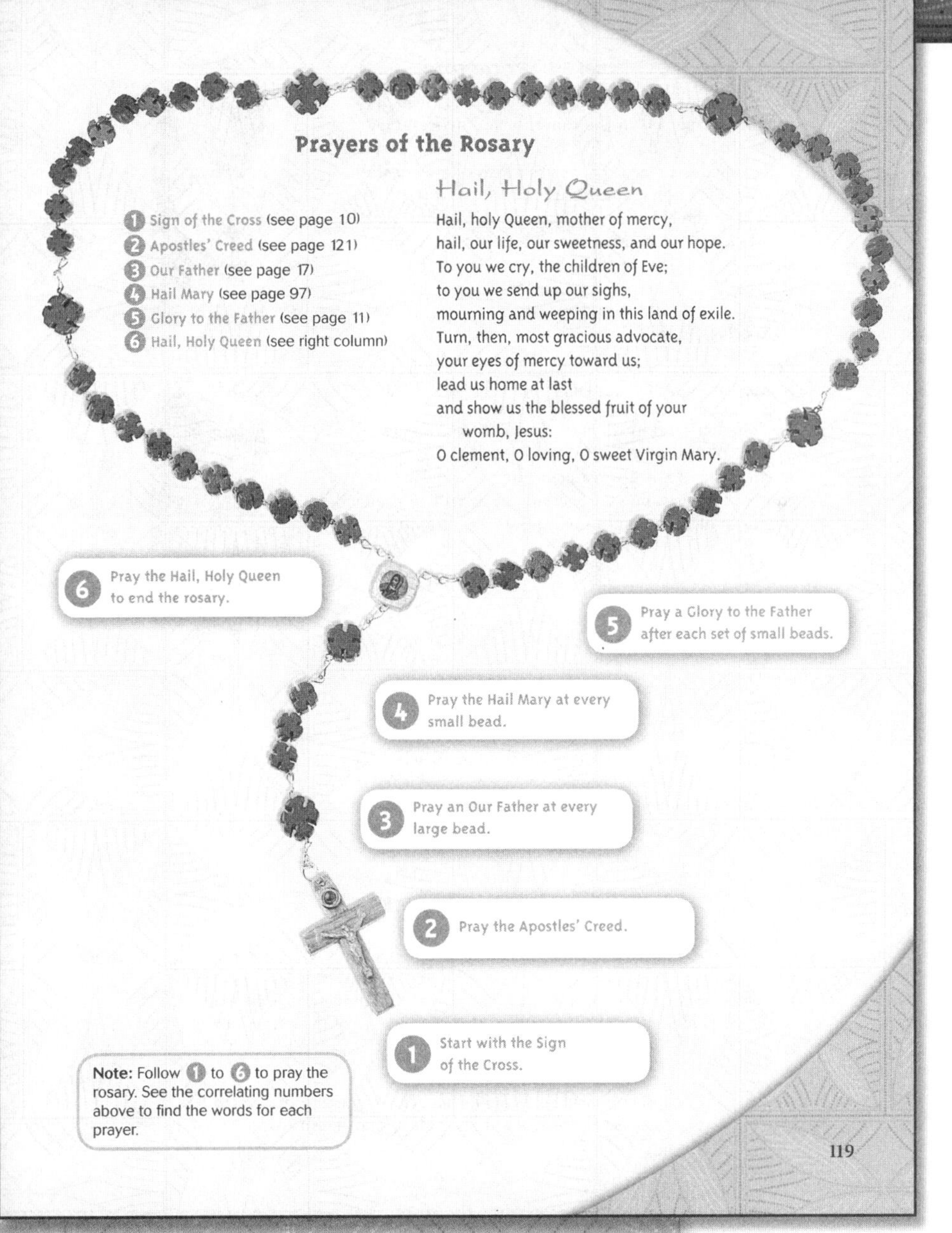


*The Rosary*

Ask the students to look at the rosary diagram as a volunteer reads the paragraphs about the rosary on page 118. Point out that the word *mystery* in this explanation refers to an event in Jesus' and Mary's life.

Read the list of mysteries. If time permits, talk about each event. Ask which set of mysteries should be prayed on the day you present the lesson.

Then direct the students' attention to the rosary diagram on page 119. As you read the text, have the students point to the appropriate bead. Before reading the prayer Hail, Holy Queen, explain that an advocate is a helper or sponsor. Also point out that the word *clement* means "merciful."

You may want to tell the students that the Feast of Our Lady of the Rosary is October 7. Also, the Church honors Mary by praying the rosary in the month of October and throughout the year.

## Conclusion ( __ min.)

### Responding in Prayer

Invite the students to gather in the prayer space. Ask the students to identify the set of mysteries prayed on this day of the week.

Choose one of the mysteries of the set. If there is a Scripture account of the event, read it aloud. Then pray with the students a decade of the rosary: the Our Father, ten Hail Marys, and Glory to the Father.

Encourage the students to ask their families for a rosary or to make one of their own. Also encourage the students to pray the rosary with their families or by themselves.

**CATECHISM FOCUS**

"The Christian prayer tries above all to meditate on the mysteries of Christ, as in *lectio divina* or the rosary. This form of prayerful reflection is of great value, but Christian prayer should go further: to the knowledge of the love of the Lord Jesus, to union with him."
(CCC, 2708)

## GOALS

*to learn about and appreciate devotions to Jesus in the Blessed Sacrament; to understand the Nicene Creed and the Apostles' Creed*

### Catechist Reflection

"When we go before the Blessed Sacrament, let us open our heart; our good God will open His. We shall go to Him; He will come to us; the one to ask, the other to receive. It will be like a breath like one to the other."

Saint John Vianney (1786–1859)

## Introduction (__ min.)

Write the words *benediction*, *monstrance*, and *creed* on the board or on a large sheet of paper. Explain that these words derive from Latin words. Point out that the word *bene* means "well" or "good," and *dicere* means "to say." So the English word *benediction* literally means "to speak well of" and has come to mean "to give or pray for a blessing."

Explain that the word *monstrance* comes from the Latin word *monstrare* which means "to show." Also point out that the word *creed* comes from the Latin word *credere* which means "to believe."

## Presentation (__ min.)

Direct the students' attention to the photograph of the tabernacle at the top of page 120. Ask a volunteer to read *Visit to the Blessed Sacrament*. Explain that we can make a visit before Mass or after Mass. When we make a visit, we can pray by saying traditional prayers or sitting quietly as we talk to Jesus about our lives, our families

### Visit the Most Blessed Sacrament

After Communion at Mass, the consecrated Hosts that remain are placed in the tabernacle. This reserved Eucharist is called the Most Blessed Sacrament. A special light, called the *sanctuary lamp*, is always kept burning nearby. This light reminds us that Jesus Christ is truly present in the Most Blessed Sacrament. We can "make a visit to Jesus" in the Most Blessed Sacrament. Our prayer shows Jesus our love for him. It continues the thanksgiving that was begun at Mass.

### Benediction

Benediction is a very old practice in the Church. The word *benediction* comes from a Latin word for "blessing."

At Benediction a large Host that was consecrated during Mass is placed in a special holder called a *monstrance*, (comes from a Latin word meaning "to show") so that all can see the Most Blessed Sacrament. Benediction includes hymns, a blessing, and praying the "Divine Praises."

#### Divine Praises

Blessed be God.
Blessed be his holy name.
Blessed be Jesus Christ, true God and true man.
Blessed be the name of Jesus.
Blessed be his most sacred heart.
Blessed be his most precious blood.
Blessed be Jesus in the most holy sacrament of the altar.
Blessed be the Holy Spirit, the Paraclete.
Blessed be the great mother of God, Mary most holy.
Blessed be her holy and immaculate conception.
Blessed be her glorious assumption.
Blessed be the name of Mary, virgin and mother.
Blessed be Saint Joseph, her most chaste spouse.
Blessed be God in his angels and in his saints.

### Processions

Many parishes have processions on special feast days. Often the priest leads the procession carrying the Blessed Sacrament in a monstrance. Benediction of the Blessed Sacrament often takes place at the end of the procession.

### Pilgrimages

Some people make pilgrimages, or prayer journeys, to holy places or shrines to honor Mary and the saints.

120

## About Perpetual Adoration

Some parishes have established the practice of perpetual adoration. They have set aside special chapels that are open twenty-four hours a day, seven days a week. This has been done with the permission of the bishops of the dioceses. People come to pray before Jesus in the Blessed Sacrament. The consecrated Host is placed in a monstrance which is placed on the altar. People who visit pray for themselves and others in their own words or in traditional prayers of the Church.

## Nicene Creed

We believe in one God,
the Father, the Almighty,
maker of heaven and earth,
of all that is seen and unseen.

We believe in one Lord, Jesus Christ,
the only Son of God,
eternally begotten of the Father,
God from God, Light from Light,
true God from true God,
begotten, not made, one in Being
with the Father.
Through him all things were made.
For us men and for our salvation
he came down from heaven:
by the power of the Holy Spirit
he was born of the Virgin Mary,
and became man.

For our sake he was crucified
under Pontius Pilate;
he suffered, died, and was buried.
On the third day he rose again
in fulfillment of the Scriptures;
he ascended into heaven
and is seated at the right hand
of the Father.
He will come again in glory to judge
the living and the dead,
and his kingdom will have no end.

We believe in the Holy Spirit, the Lord,
the giver of life,
who proceeds from the Father
and the Son.
With the Father and the Son he is
worshiped and glorified.
He has spoken through the Prophets.
We believe in one holy catholic
and apostolic Church.
We acknowledge one baptism
for the forgiveness of sins.
We look for the resurrection of the dead,
and the life of the world to come.
Amen.

## Apostles' Creed

I believe in God, the Father almighty,
creator of heaven and earth.
I believe in Jesus Christ,
his only Son, our Lord.
He was conceived by the power
of the Holy Spirit
and born of the Virgin Mary.
He suffered under Pontius Pilate,
was crucified, died, and was buried.
He descended to the dead.
On the third day he rose again.
He ascended into heaven,
and is seated at the right hand
of the Father.
He will come again to judge
the living and the dead.

I believe in the Holy Spirit,
the holy catholic Church,
the communion of saints,
the forgiveness of sins,
the resurrection of the body,
and the life everlasting. Amen.

**Note:** The Sign of the Cross is on page 10.
Glory to the Father is on page 11.
The Lord's Prayer, is on page 17.
Come, Holy Spirit is on page 31.
Act of Contrition is on page 85.
Hail Mary is on page 97.
Hail, Holy Queen is on page 119.

121

and friends, our worries, and our hopes and dreams. We can read stories from Scripture and think about how we can help spread the Good News of God's love.

Read *Processions.* Explain that on the Solemnity of the Most Holy Body and Blood of Jesus, many parishes have a solemn procession and Benediction. This feast is celebrated on the second Sunday after Pentecost.

Then read *Pilgrimages.* You may want to mention that many people make pilgrimages to the Holy Land to see the places where Jesus lived and prayed. You may also want to help the students do research on the Internet to find out other places to which people make prayer journeys.

Explain that Catholics state their beliefs in the two creeds on page 121. The Apostles' Creed is a summary of the faith of the Apostles. The Nicene Creed expands upon the Apostles' Creed and was drawn up at the two first ecumenical councils of the Church in the fourteenth century. We profess the Nicene Creed each Sunday at Mass.

## CATECHISM FOCUS

"The Catholic Church has always offered and still offers to the sacrament of the Eucharist the cult of adoration, not only during Mass, but also outside it, reserving the consecrated hosts with the utmost care, exposing them to the solemn veneration of the faithful, and carrying them in procession."
(*CCC*, 1378)

For additional reference and reflection see *CCC*, 1379–1380.

# Conclusion (_ min.)

### Responding in Prayer

Together with your students make a visit to the Blessed Sacrament. Point out the tabernacle. Remind the group that Jesus is truly present in the Blessed Sacrament.

Provide a few minutes for the students to pray quietly to Jesus. Then lead the students in praying the Divine Praises.

## Morning and Evening Prayer

Too many of us get caught up in schedules that are rushed and hectic. That is why the Church has long advocated the use of time set aside for prayer at particular hours of the day.

Ask the students to think about how they can pause for prayer throughout the day. Encourage them to pray the Morning Offering and Evening Prayer on page 122 as a starting point.

## Table Prayer

Grace before meals may very well be the mostly commonly used prayer of households around the world. The ones on this page utilize two other forms of prayer, *blessing* and *thanksgiving*. Encourage the students to invite their families to pray these prayers at family meals.

### Morning Offering

O Jesus, I offer you all my prayers,
works and suffering of this day
for all the intentions of your most
Sacred Heart.
Amen.

### Evening Prayer

Dear God, before I sleep
I want to thank you for this day,
so full of your kindness and your joy.
I close my eyes to rest
safe in your loving care.

### Grace Before Meals

Bless us, O Lord, and these your gifts
which we are about to receive from
your goodness.
Through Christ our Lord.
Amen.

### Prayer After Meals

We give you thanks for all your gifts,
almighty God,
living and reigning now and for ever.
Amen.

### Prayer for My Vocation

Dear God,
you have a great and loving plan
for our world and for me.
I wish to share in that plan fully,
faithfully, and joyfully.

Help me to understand what it is
you wish me to do in my life.
Help me to be attentive to the signs
that you give me about preparing
for the future.

Help me to learn to be a sign of the Kingdom
of God, whether I am called to the priesthood
or religious life, the single or married life.

And once I have heard and understood
your call, give me the strength
and the grace to follow it
with generosity and love. Amen.

### Prayer for My Discipleship

Jesus, you invite me to be your disciple.
You showed me how to love God the Father
with all my heart, with all my soul, and with
all my mind.
You showed me how to love my neighbors
and the importance of loving myself.

It is not always easy to be a disciple.
I am grateful for the example you have
given to me.
Jesus, continue to guide me
and strengthen me on my journey
to be your disciple. Amen.

122

**Prayers from the Celebration of the Eucharist**

### Confiteor

I confess to almighty God,
and to you, my brothers and sisters,
that I have sinned through my own fault
in my thoughts and in my words,
in what I have done,
and in what I have failed to do;
and I ask blessed Mary, ever virgin,
all the angels and saints,
and you, my brothers and sisters,
to pray for me to the Lord our God.

### Gloria

Glory to God in the highest,
and peace to his people on earth.

Lord God, heavenly King,
almighty God and Father,
we worship you, we give you thanks,
we praise you for your glory.

Lord Jesus Christ, only Son of the Father
Lord God, Lamb of God,
you take away the sin of the world:
have mercy on us;
you are seated at the right hand of the Father:
receive our prayer.

For you alone are the Holy One,
you alone are the Lord,
you alone are the Most High,
Jesus Christ,
with the Holy Spirit,
in the glory of God the Father. Amen.

### Lamb of God

Lamb of God, you take away the sins of the world:
have mercy on us.
Lamb of God, you take away the sins of the world:
have mercy on us.
Lamb of God, you take away the sins of the world:
grant us peace.

### Prayer After Communion

(These words may be prayed quietly after you receive Holy Communion.)

Jesus,
thank you for coming to me in Communion.
Thank you for strengthening me
to be your disciple and to serve others.
Help me to be grateful for each day
and to stay close to you always.
Amen.

**Note:** The Nicene Creed is on on page 121.
Holy, Holy, Holy is on page 65.
Memorial Acclamations are on page 23.



## Prayer from the Mass

Encourage the students to participate at Mass by praying the prayers on page 123 and the other prayers and responses that the assembly prays together.

# Glossary

**absolution** (page 83) forgiveness of our sins by the priest in the name of Christ and the Church and through the power of the Holy Spirit in the Sacrament of Penance and Reconciliation

**Annunciation** (page 95) the announcement to Mary that she would be the Mother of the Son of God

**Apostles** (page 15) the twelve men whom Jesus chose to share in his mission in a special way

**Ascension** (page 28) Jesus' return in all his glory to his Father in Heaven

**assembly** (page 62) the community of people who gather for the celebration of the Mass

**Assumption** (page 95) the truth that when Mary's work on earth was done, God brought Mary body and soul to live forever with the risen Christ

**Baptism** (page 50) the sacrament in which we are freed from sin, become children of God, and are welcomed into the Church

**Beatitudes** (page 77) Jesus' teachings that describe the way to live as his disciples

**Bible** (page 8) the book about God's love for us and about our call to live as God's people: the Bible is the Word of God.

**bishops** (page 34) men who have received the fullness of the Sacrament of Holy Orders, and as the successors of the Apostles continue to lead the Church

**Blessed Trinity** (page 10) the three Persons in one God: God the Father, God the Son, and God the Holy Spirit

**celebrant** (page 51) the bishop, priest, or deacon who celebrates a sacrament for and with the community

**charity** (page 78) or love, the greatest of all virtues that enables us to love God and to love our neighbor

**Chrism** (page 51) perfumed oil blessed by the bishop

**Church** (page 29) the community of people who are baptized and follow Jesus Christ

**Communion of Saints** (page 94) the union of the baptized members of the Church on earth with those who are in Heaven and in Purgatory

**Concluding Rites** (page 64) the last part of the Mass in which we are sent to love and serve the Lord each day by bringing the peace and love of Jesus to everyone we meet

**confession** (page 83) telling our sins to the priest in the Sacrament of Penance and Reconciliation

**Confirmation** (page 52) the sacrament in which we receive the Gift of the Holy Spirit in a special way

**conscience** (page 83) our ability to know the difference between good and evil, right and wrong

**contrition** (page 83) being sorry for our sins and promising not to sin again

**conversion** (page 82) turning back to God with all one's heart

**Corporal Works of Mercy** (page 89) acts of love that help us care for the physical and material needs of others

**covenant** (page 70) a special agreement between God and his people

**deacon** (page 36) a baptized man who in the Sacrament of Holy Orders, has been ordained to serve the Church by preaching, baptizing, performing marriages, and doing acts of charity

**diocese** (page 34) local areas of the Church, each led by a bishop

**disciples** (page 15) those who follow Jesus

**divine** (page 14) a word we use to describe God

**Eucharist** (page 56) the sacrament of the Body and Blood of Christ, Jesus is truly present to us under the appearances of bread and wine

**faith** (page 78) the virtue that enables us to believe in God and all that the Church teaches us

**grace** (page 41) the gift of God's life in us

**hope** (page 78) the virtue that enables us to trust in God's promise to share his life with us forever

**Immaculate Conception** (page 95) the truth that God created Mary free from Original Sin and from all sin from the very first moment of her life, her conception

**Incarnation** (page 14) the truth that God the Son, the second Person of the Blessed Trinity, became man

**Introductory Rites** (page 62) the part of the Mass that unites us as a community, prepares us to hear God's Word, and to celebrate the Eucharist

**Kingdom of God** (page 16) the power of God's love active in our lives and in our world

**Last Supper** (page 20) the last meal Jesus shared with his disciples before he died

**Liturgy of the Eucharist** (page 63) the part of the Mass when the bread and wine become the Body and Blood of Christ

**Liturgy of the Word** (page 62) the part of the Mass when we listen and respond to God's Word

**Marks of the Church** (page 35) the four characteristics of the Church: one, holy, catholic, and apostolic

**Original Sin** (page 9) the first sin committed by the first human beings

**parish** (page 36) a community of believers who gather together to worship God and work together

**pastor** (page 36) the priest who leads the parish in worship, prayer, teaching, and service

**penance** (page 83) a prayer or an act of service that we do to show we are sorry for our sins

**Pentecost** (page 29) the day the Holy Spirit came upon Jesus' disciples

**pope** (page 34) the Bishop of Rome who leads and guides the Catholic Church

**priests** (page 36) baptized men who are ordained to preach the Gospel and serve the faithful, especially by celebrating the Eucharist and the other sacraments

**Real Presence** (page 20) the true presence of Jesus Christ in the Eucharist

**Resurrection** (page 22) the mystery of Jesus Christ rising from the dead

**sacrament** (page 41) an effective sign given to us by Jesus Christ through which we share in God's life

**sacrifice** (page 57) a gift offered to God by a priest in the name of all the people

**saints** (page 94) followers of Christ who lived lives of holiness on earth and now share in eternal life with God in Heaven

**Savior** (page 22) a title given to Jesus because he died and rose from the dead to save us

**sin** (page 83) a thought, word, deed, or omission against God's law

**Spiritual Works of Mercy** (page 90) acts of love that help us care for the needs of people's hearts, minds, and souls

**Ten Commandments** (page 70) the laws of God's covenant given to Moses for all the people

**virtue** (page 78) a good habit that helps us to act according to God's love for us

**Works of Mercy** (page 89) the loving acts that we do to care for the needs of others

# Index



 Italicized numbers refer to definitions.

## Photo Credits

**Cover:** Alamy/ 14images-travel-1: *top right background*; Alamy/Paul Gisby Photography: *center right*; Alamy/Jim Lundgren: *center left*; Alamy/Oleksiy Maksymenko: *top right inset*; The Crosiers/Gene Plaisted, OSC: *top left background*; Getty Images/Photographer's Choice RR/Murat Taner: *top left inset*; Jupiter Images/amanaimages/Orion Press: *bottom center*; Greg Lord: *bottom right*; W.P. Wittman Ltd: *bottom left inset*.

**Interior Photos:** Alamy/Corbis Super RF: 68 *bottom*; JL Images: 44; Alan Oliver: 7 *center top inset*; Gary Roebuck: 112 *bottom*; Neil Setchfield: 96. AP Images/Mel Evans: 72 *top right*. Jane Bernard: 41 *bottom*, 58, 82 *top*, 83 *bottom*. Karen Callaway: 41 *center*, 42 *bottom center*, 107 *bottom*, 120. Corbis/ Rick Barrentine: 109; BelOmbra/Jeam Pierre Arnet: 111 *left*; Godong/Philippe Lissac: 111 *right*; Osservatore Romano/Arturo Mari: 34–35. The Crosiers/Gene Plaisted, OSC: 9 *bottom*, 56, 70, 104, 107 *top*, 108, 116 *right*, 123. Culture and Sport Glasgow (Museums), Salvador Dali/Christ of St. John of the Cross: 21. Digital Stock Corporation: 116 *left*, 121. The Diocese of Pittsburg: 34. Neal Farris: 26–27, 32–33, 36, 62 *left*, 63, 84, 98, 106, 117 *left*, 122. Lucas Foglia, 112, *top*. Getty Images/Blend Images/Hill Street Studio: 49; Digital Vision: 48 *top*; The Image Bank/Larry Dale Gordon: 60 *bottom*; National Geographic/James L. Stanfield: 22; Stock 48: 72 *bottom left*; Taxi/Arthur Tilley: 88 *left*. The Image Works/Assunta Del Buono/John Birdsall Archive: 90 *top right*; Bob Daemmrich: 90 *top left*; Jeff Greenberg: 114, Syracuse Newspapers/David Lassman: 89 *top right*. Jupiter Images/amana images/Orion Press: 6–7; Bananastock: 78; Brand X Pictures: 88 *right*; Comstock: *112* center; Corbis: 48 *bottom*, 90 *bottom*; Creatas: 87 *top*; IT Stock International: 82 *bottom*; liquidlibrary: 89 *bottom*; Pixland: 6 *bottom center inset*. Ken Karp: 10, 41 *top*, 50, 66, 71, 86 *bottom*, 103, 117 *right*. Greg Lord: 119. Evelyn O'Connor/Manager of the Public Relations of Resurrection Medical Center in Chicago, IL: 113. Photodisc/C Squared Studios: 72 *bottom right*, 95 *frame*; Siede Preis: 72 *top left*. Photo Edit Inc./Myrleen Ferguson Cate: 69 *bottom*. Punchstock/Blend Images: 61 *center left*; Creatas: 61 *top*; Design Pics: 9 *top*; Digital Vision: 69 *top*; Image Source: 68 *top*; Photodisc: 60 *top*, 84 *background*. Used under license from Shutterstock.com/Karl R. Martin: 24 *top*; Noah Strycker: 87 *bottom background*; Jiri Vaclavek: 68–69 *background*; Ulnar: 48 *background*; Petr Vaclavek: 122 *background*. ©Robert Silvers 2001, Photomosaics™ is the trademark of Runaway Technology, Inc., www.photomosaic.com US Patent No. 6, 137, 498: 8. Sisters of the Resurrection: 89 *top left*. Stockbyte: 115 *top*. Superstock/ Diane Ong: 94; Peter Willi/Maurice Denis/©Artists Rights Society, New York/ADAGP, Paris: 95. ©Ubisoft: 26 *digital chess game inset*. Veer/Corbis: 72 *bottom right inset*; Fancy Photography: 86 *top*; Stockbyte: 87 *bottom*. W.P. Wittman Ltd: 42 *top*, 42 *top center*, 42 *bottom*, 51, 52, 57, 62 *right*, 115 *bottom*.

## Illustration Credits

Matt Archambault: 92–93. David Barnett: 14–15, 28–29, 40. Tom Barrett: 64. Kenneth Batelman: 16. Eric Fortune: 54–55. John Haysom: 20–21, 71, 76–77. Jacey: 60–61. W.B. Johnston: 104, 105. John Lavin: 18–19. Dave LaFleur: 50–51. Darryl Ligason: 12–13. Angela Martini: 80–81. Neil Slave: 30. Lin Wang: 74–75. Brian White: 38–39.